D1604230

Hewett and Friends

Edgar Lee Hewett, San Diego, California, 1932. Photograph by Jack Adams.
Courtesy of the Museum of New Mexico.

Hewett and Friends

A BIOGRAPHY OF
SANTA FE'S VIBRANT ERA

By Beatrice Chauvenet

MUSEUM OF NEW MEXICO PRESS
SANTA FE

LP

The following negatives from the Museum of New Mexico were used in HEWETT AND FRIENDS: p. 19, Neg. no. 9112; p. 27, Neg. no. 7336; p. 29, Neg. no. 13333; p. 54, Neg. no. 60501; p. 55, Neg. no. 60525; p. 73, Neg. no. 42070; p. 74, Neg. no. 10257; p. 78, Neg. no. 6719; p. 79, Neg. no. 13078; p. 81, Neg. no. 7331 and Neg. no. 10313; p. 86, Neg. no. 60952 and Neg. no. 7745; p. 91, Neg. no. 46552; p. 103, Neg. no. 13126 and Neg. no. 13312; p. 105, Neg. no. 42261 and Neg. no. 16991; p. 112, Neg. no. 7344 and Neg. no. 47796; p. 117, Neg. no. 36469; p. 125, Neg. no. 28111; p. 126, Neg. no. 12969; p. 130, Neg. no. 22973; p. 149, Neg. no. 59754, Neg. no. 59757 and Neg. no. 30737; p. 159, Neg. no. 11234; p. 165, Neg. no. 7341; p. 172, Neg. no. 7361; p. 179, Neg. no. 16754; p. 189, Neg. no. 55203; p. 191, Neg. no. 43506; p. 201, Neg. no. 7373; p. 219, Neg. no. 7388; p. 228, Neg. no. 10489.

This publication was made possible through the generosity of the Museum of New Mexico Foundation and the following individuals:
Mr. and Mrs. George H. Atherton, J. Burchenal Ault, Mary Grisso, Margaret R. Hinck, Marjorie F. Lambert, Loraine Lavender, Mrs. M. L. McCune, Mr. and Mrs. John Gaw Meem, T. M. Pearce, John E. Stodder, and John K. S. Walter

Copyright © 1983, Museum of New Mexico Press

Printed in the United States of America.

Library of Congress Cataloging in Publication Data:
Chauvenet, Beatrice.
Hewett and friends.

Bibliography: p.
Includes index.
1. Hewett, Edgar Lee, 1865-1946.   2. Archaeology — United States — History.   3. Museum of New Mexico — History.   4. Indianists — United States — History.   5. Archaeologists — United States — Biography.   6. Historians — United States — Biography.   I. Title.
E76.45.H48C5   973.9'092'4 [B]   82-2186
ISBN 0-89013-136-8   AACR2

Museum of New Mexico Press
P. O. Box 2087
Santa Fe, New Mexico 87503

01/14/91

CONTENTS

Illustrations   vii
Foreword   ix
Acknowledgements   xi
 1. Beginnings   3
 2. Lewis Henry Morgan and Adolph Bandelier   13
 3. Growing Up in Missouri   23
 4. The Teacher Becomes an Archaeologist   33
 5. Some Bridges Are Burned   43
 6. The Doctoral Degree and the Fellowship Year   51
 7. The Cliff Dwellings of Manitou Springs   59
 8. The Old Palace   63
 9. The School of American Archaeology is Established   71
10. The School Broadens Its Activities   85
11. Hewett Takes on the San Diego Exposition   97
12. Hewett Takes on the Santa Fe Chamber of Commerce   109
13. Santa Fe's Art Museum   121
14. Art, Archaeology and Politics   135
15. Hewett and the Santa Fe Fiesta   147
16. Wrecked in the Desert   163
17. Santa Fe Fights the Cultural Colony   175
18. Opening Up the Indian Country   187
19. Shifting Loyalties   195
20. Emphasis on Writing   205
21. Looking Back for the Record   213
22. Aftermath   223
Notes   229
Works Cited   239
Index   243

ILLUSTRATIONS

Page

Staff and students, El Rito de los Frijoles, 1919   *Frontispiece*

Harvey Hanson Hewett   7

Tabitha Stice Hewett   7

Lewis Henry Morgan   15

Adolph Alphonse Bandelier   19

Edgar Lee Hewett, high-school student   24

Edgar Lee Hewett, college student   27

Cora Whitford Hewett   29

Edgar Lee Hewett, high-school principal   36

Alice Cunningham Fletcher   44

Balcony House, Mesa Verde, 1907   54

Balcony House, Mesa Verde, 1910   55

Staff and managing board, School of American
    Archaeology, on ladder   73

Justice John R. McFie   74

Palace of the Governors, ca. 1900-1910   78

Palace of the Governors during renovation, 1913   79

Edgar Lee Hewett in Guatemala   81

Sylvanus G. Morley   81

Quimu and Charles F. Lummis in Guatemala   86

Jesse L. Nusbaum and Charles F. Lummis in Guatemala   86

Donizetta Jones Wood Hewett   88

Frederick W. Hodge   88

Julian Martinez at El Rito de los Frijoles   91

Tyuonyi, El Rito de los Frijoles, ca. 1908   91

Paul A. F. Walter   103

Kenneth M. Chapman   103

New Mexico Building, Panama-California Exposition   105

Carlos Vierra   105

Edgar Lee Hewett in Palace of the Governors   112

Bronson M. Cutting   112

Charles F. Lummis   117

Frank Springer   125

Interior of St. Francis Auditorium, Museum of Fine Arts,
    during construction, ca. 1917   126

Museum of Fine Arts, ca. 1920   130

Ina Sizer Cassidy and Gerald Cassidy   149

Alice Corbin Henderson and William Penhallow Henderson   149

Sheldon Parsons   149

Tsianina Blackstone   159

Donizetta and Edgar Lee Hewett, travelers   165

Oriental School party in Syria   167

Wreck in Arabian Desert waddy   169

John D. Rockefeller, Jr., and Edgar Lee Hewett   172

"J.D.R." and Edgar Lee Hewett   172

Mary Austin   179

Harvey-cars on Indian Detour   188

Maria and Julian Martinez at work   189

Santiago Naranjo   191

Edgar Lee Hewett, 1932   201

Donizetta and Edgar Lee Hewett at Xochimicalco, Mexico   207

The Old Man in his study, 1946   219

The Hewett garden   228

FOREWORD

New Mexico at the turn of the century was still a territory of these United States; Santa Fe, the capital, was a very small community, an oasis in the desert in the view of most; the Palace of the Governors, which had housed the regional governments of Spain and Mexico, was in a state of advanced decrepitude, despite which fact it was the home of the Territorial Governor and seat of the Legislature.

The tide of westward expansion which flowed across the continent had left the Southwest a backwater, within which the little town of Santa Fe was scarcely more than an eddy current. Even so, the community was already exercising a strange appeal, and to it, by chance or by choice, came a rich and fascinating assortment of highly individualistic — one is tempted to say passionate — personalities. Writers, painters, poets, anthropologists, businessmen, journalists, politicians, and many others found their niche here. It was a time, or so it seems in retrospect, when idealism and romanticism contested with hard realities...and often won.

In any time, in any place, Edgar Lee Hewett would have stood out from the crowd. But in Santa Fe in the early part of this century, it took some doing. Hewett had come to New Mexico to head the Normal School in Las Vegas; he seems to have found his natural milieu here, and he stayed to put his indelible mark on Santa Fe, on New Mexico, and on the whole of the Southwest. Judging by his accomplishments alone, he was a man of considerable vigor, of high ambition and great determination. Such a man could be expected to attract many devoted adherents...and an equal number of adversaries; Edgar Lee Hewett had his share of both. He did not shy from controversy, indeed he seems at times to have courted it, nor did he confine his attentions to Santa Fe and New Mexico; he extended his ventures from the nation's capitol to California with telling effect.

This book, however, is more than the personal history of one man; it is an important chapter in the continuing chronicle of Santa Fe, a town which has managed to retain a distinction of character among all the towns and cities of the United States. Edgar Hewett was one of those who cherished, perpetuated and even created that distinction, and throughout his life he was at the center of this community, sometimes in league with, sometimes in adversity to those responsible for the shaping of Santa Fe. To all those who know and care about Santa Fe, be they old-timers with cherished memories, newcomers who may have wondered how it came about, or visitors intrigued by the "City Different," this will prove a fascinating account.

On a more personal level, I am indebted to Beatrice Chauvenet for breathing life into a legend. As one of the handful of individuals who have succeeded to the position which Edgar Lee Hewett created, I have crossed his path innumerable times. Late of night, reading the letters and memoranda by which he conducted the business of the Museum of New Mexico, and struggling with the complexities of its history, I have pondered the man whose strong will and efforts brought this institution — and so many other things — into being. Beatrice Chauvenet, from personal knowledge — and extensive research — let me, and all of us, come to know him. And for that I am grateful.

George Ewing
Cultural Affairs Officer

ACKNOWLEDGEMENTS

For more than fifty years I have been following the trails of the characters in this book. Some were known to me only as the respected elders who pioneered in promoting the American Southwest and its prehistoric past. Other archaeologists and anthropologists were familiar figures in Santa Fe and gave generously of their knowledge to eager listeners: Edgar L. Hewett, Frederick W. Hodge, Lansing Bloom, Paul A. F. Walter, Kenneth Chapman, Charles F. Lummis, and Sylvanus Morley among others.

My husband, William Chauvenet, was a devoted student of Dr. Hewett, earning his master's degree in archaeology at the University of New Mexico. Santa Fe was a sociable small town, and in the years between 1929 and 1934 a host of men and women whose names appear in this narrative were guests in our home on Buena Vista Street. Artists and writers were our friends: the Cassidys, the Hendersons, the Ellises, the Vierras, the Shusters, and the Sloans. Witter Bynner and Mary Austin we knew on a casual basis, and we had at least a speaking acquaintance with Santa Fe's political figures, business leaders and the editorial staff of the local newspaper. Now it is sometimes hard for me to remember whether I knew of an event from my own observation or from happy conversations about it.

Jennie Marie Avery knew the Hewetts from the time she came to Santa Fe in 1916. She and her close associate, Grace Bowman, once rented a little house from Doni Hewett's mother, Mrs. Louise Jones. Grace worked briefly as Hewett's secretary, but left the Museum when she and Jennie bought the business that became Avery-Bowman, Real Estate, Abstracts and Insurance. Through the years Hewett took Jennie's advice, and entrusted her with many of his confidential transactions. She became a fixture on the board of the School of American Research, and was considered an emeritus member when she died in 1976 at the age of ninety-two. Among the papers she bequeathed to me were the beginnings of a biography of Edgar Lee Hewett, and because of her insistence I felt I had to tell his story.

In the research and writing many have helped me. At the Museum of New Mexico George H. Ewing, Cultural Affairs Officer for New Mexico, Arthur Olivas and Richard Rudisill of the Photo Archives, and Stephany Eger of the History Division have been patiently helpful. Editors Richard Polese and Sarah Nestor and publisher James Mafchir of the Museum of New Mexico Press have guided the manuscript into a book. Dr. Douglas Schwartz, director, Jane Kepp, editor and Elizabeth Kingman, librarian of the School of American Research made valuable manuscripts and photographs available. Dr. John S. Johnson, professor of education emeritus, New Mexico Highlands University, provided data on Hewett's tenure at Las Vegas Normal University. Carlota Warfield Daves, long a co-worker with Dr. Hewett, who typed the first draft, and Marjorie Ferguson Lambert, George Fitzpatrick, Alice H. Rossin, and Helen Blumenschein, who read all or portions of the story, contributed needed suggestions. Special thanks are due to the School of American Research as well as to the following individuals for their kind permission to quote from various documents: Tsianina Blackstone, Gene M. Hodge, Rosemary Nusbaum, Marchesa Iris Origo, Alice H. Rossin, and John K.S. Walter.

In San Diego I had the help of my hostess and guide, Kathryn Frazer and of Dr. Spencer S. Rogers, scientific director and Ken Hedges, associate curator of the Museum of Man. Dr. Arthur B.J.O. Anderson of California State University at San Diego and Sylvia Arden, librarian of the San Diego Historical Society, gave gracious assistance. Olive Haun, retired librarian living in Colorado Springs, provided the research on the Cliff Dwellings of Manitou Springs.

Among the many former associates with whom I discussed Dr. Hewett's life were Ina S. Cassidy, Dr. Bertha Dutton, Ruth Elvin, Grace Fisher, Hester Jones, Paul Masters, Wayne Mauzy, Ruth Seligman, Genevieve Shenk, and Charles Steen. Very important to me has been the supportive encouragement of my daughter, Mary C. Guthrie. I thank them all, and I hope they will find the results rewarding.

Beatrice Chauvenet
Santa Fe, New Mexico

Hewett and Friends

1

BEGINNINGS

What is Man? Possibly a little more thought to the question What is Boy would help with the larger problem. — ELH

This is the story of a man whose genius left monuments in half a dozen Western states and whose prophetic planning is only now justified, eighty years after he began his campaign to preserve the heritage of the Old Ones. It is also a partial account of his associates — three generations of men and women who made the story of mankind on the American continents a respectable science. They were the pioneers who shovelled aside the drifted desert and hacked down the choked jungle covering ancient ruins of vanished civilizations, and thus salvaged much that would have been lost forever beneath the crushing wheels of twentieth-century progress. These are the early American archaeologists and ethnologists who were happy to trade security for the adventures found in exploration, excavation and — altercation. They pioneered in many parts of the Western Hemisphere, but sooner or later those who became Hewett's associates found their way to Santa Fe, the small mountain-hemmed capital of New Mexico.

When Edgar Hewett was born on November 23, 1865 in Warren County, Illinois, not far from the Mississippi River, the entire country was beginning to awaken from the nightmare of the Civil War. After General Robert E. Lee surrendered at Appomattox Court House and Abraham Lincoln was assassinated in April of that year, the disbanding Union troops that came from the Midwest straggled back to their farm homes, some arriving in time to help with the summer crops.

Compared to the massive confrontations east of the Mississippi the battles

3

fought in New Mexico had been scarcely more than skirmishes, but they had a bearing on the outcome of the war. In New Mexico as elsewhere, loyalties were divided and sides chosen with bitter partisanship.

In the years between 1846 and 1860 the United States had built across the Territory a thin line of military forts and outposts, designed to house the troops protecting settlers and travellers from Indian attack. Regular Army officers and men were expected to spend some part of their careers in such service. The governing civil authorities were chosen largely for their politics back East, and they found more turmoil than security in their offices.

At the outbreak of the Civil War many ranking Army officers in New Mexico resigned their commissions, and some civil authorities also quit their jobs, to join the Confederacy. Because these Confederate officers were expert and knew the country, they were successful in the early skirmishes that brought them northward from El Paso in a drive to capture Fort Union and take control of the gold fields of Colorado and California. Meeting only token opposition they progressed to Santa Fe, and on March 23, 1862 they ran up the Stars and Bars over the old Palace of the Governors on the north side of the Plaza.

Governor Connelly, loyal to the Union, had moved to a temporary capital in Las Vegas, New Mexico. The loyal troops that had fought the delaying action were joined by some from Fort Union, and both were reinforced by Colorado volunteers. In a battle that has been called "the Gettysburg of the West" (because of its decisiveness, not because of the number of troops engaged), the Union troops drove the Confederates into a retreat from Santa Fe to Albuquerque, and thence southward once more. California troops arrived later to complete the rout. At the end of the war when the Confederate Army disbanded, many veterans seeking to rebuild their shattered lives found refuge in New Mexico, where they were accepted in a society more preoccupied with building a future than with nursing old wounds.

Back on their Illinois farm Edgar Hewett's parents probably read small, belated notices of these events in the newspapers. Edgar's father had gone to California in the '49 gold rush, but not by way of New Mexico. The Southwest, acquired under the doctrine of Manifest Destiny, seemed alien and of little value to Midwesterners whose ancestors came from New England.

Edgar Hewett would have said that his story began when the universe was created, and he didn't care whether one subscribed to the literal interpretation of the book of Genesis or believed in Darwinian evolution. Either was a wonder, and he studied both diligently in the days when the controversy was thundered from the pulpit and debated in the classroom. However *homo sapiens* got started, Edgar soon decided that man had come a long way, still had a great distance to go for perfection, and must always earn his bread by the sweat of his brow. Security? "The Garden of Eden was a fiasco," he once said. "Too much security."[1]

He was the youngest of six children born to Harvey Hanson Hewett and Tabitha Stice, who had married in 1851. The Hewett and Stice families were bone and sinew of the great migration that came into the prairie and timber country of the middle states in the years between the Louisiana Purchase and the Civil War. They took up the new land, wrested farms from rich soil, and sank their tap roots deep within it.

Edgar's early childhood was as secure as any boy growing up on a comfortable Illinois farm might expect. He was surrounded by devoted parents, older brother and a sister, as well as numerous uncles, aunts and cousins. As the clan gathered for holiday meals or helped one another in haying and harvest, Edgar learned, hardly knowing what he heard, of the past they had left behind. On winter evenings when the chores were done and the family circled the stove for warmth, his eldest brother Alvin showed him pictures in the books their mother bought from itinerant salesmen, and taught him to read before he was ready for the country school.

Edgar liked the tales about his grandfather, Harvey J. Hewett — the one who traced his ancestry to gentry stock from Yorkshire, England — as he heard them from his father and his aunts and uncles. Grandfather Hewett had left the stony pastures of New England in the 1820s and moved his family west, making several unsatisfactory stops before he reached Warren County. He was nearly forty years old in 1838 when he found his promised land on the rich Illinois prairie. Once or twice a year he wrote to his parents, who had remained on the farm in Camden, Maine, giving them news of his wife Miriam and their children and describing how a knowledgeable man tamed the virgin prairie. One treasured letter dated April 24, 1839, which lists his address as Greenfield Township 8 North, 1 West, Warren County, Illinois, gives an exuberant account of the land on which he had been living for the past year.

"We are settled on 160 acres of smooth, dry prairie, half a mile from timber," he wrote, and went on to tell of the house he had built — thirty-six by twenty-four feet, one and a half stories high, with three fireplaces and an oven.

The first spring on the new land he fenced twenty acres of sod, where he raised enough corn to pay for breaking the ground. "We now have 20 acres more fenced," he wrote, "and shall brake it in the spring if nothing in Providence prevents. We have 4 acres of winter wheat growing. You would be delighted to see how fine our prairie acres are for farming. Not a stone or gravel or rock to obstruct the plow, three feet or more depth of soil. It takes three or four yoke of oxen to brake the sod; last season we broke 60 acres, 40 away from home at 2½ dollars an acre."[2]

Harvey boasted that this was the greatest stock country he had ever seen. The first winter he was able to feed four yoke of oxen, two horses, three cows, four sheep, and twelve swine. This nucleus grew into a thriving livestock business. Harvey was pleased, too, with the privileges his new neighborhood afforded. The family could attend Sunday preaching once in two weeks within half a mile of the homestead, and his sons were learning readily in the country school of thirty scholars.

For the next dozen years Harvey prospered. His children took as much schooling as the county offered, grew to maturity, and set out for themselves. He was respected and perhaps somewhat envied in his community. Then, when he was fifty-three, tragedy struck. With the assistance of a drover whom he considered his friend, he had driven stock to market in Peoria, Illinois. After some difficulty in securing payment, Harvey received a substantial sum in cash and started home alone. Two ruffians who followed him from town caught up with him on Kickapoo Hill and demanded his money. In the fight that ensued, he was beaten, robbed and left to die. His wife Miriam wrote a pitiful letter to Harvey's parents back in Maine, telling of his death.[3] Then she put on the widow's black dress and lace cap and withdrew from the social world, to be cared for on the homestead by a son and daughter. Young Edgar heard his family say that his grandmother never recovered from the shock of her husband's death, though she lived nearly half a century longer, to the age of ninety-one.

Edgar's father, Harvey Hansen, was a small boy when the family came west to Illinois. He had acquired considerable experience in farming and stock raising by the time he was twenty-one and was free to try his own fortune. In his turn he started west, working for three years in Mississippi before he was caught up in the gold rush to California. Instead of joining an overland caravan he chose the circuitous route by water, and finally arrived at the diggings after a strenuous journey. Years later he would sometimes tell his children of travelling with his luggage on his back across the Isthmus of Panama, up the Chagres River, over to Balboa on the Pacific side, then by sailboat up to San Francisco. There his dreams of instant wealth dissolved, and when news of his father's murder reached him he returned to Illinois. A year later he married his neighbor, Tabitha Stice, and settled down to establish a farm home of his own near the family homestead.

Tabitha's parents, Charles and Martha Stice, had come from Kentucky when she was old enough to share the adventure of the journey. Staunch Presbyterians of German and Scotch-Irish ancestry, they too were seeking better land when they packed their belongings on one horse and with their brood of eight children set out for western Illinois, living on the game and fruit of the wilderness as they came. They built their log cabin in the forest, closing its doors and windows with the skins of animals killed for food.

Among their neighbors were Black Hawk and his Sauk Indian band, whose friendship was respected and valued. Black Hawk's band planted their crops in the rich Illinois soil, but they were eventually driven off by the incoming wave of white settlers. Black Hawk tried desperately to recover some of his people's ancestral land, but with only temporary success. Tabitha Stice Hewett, who had known him as a trusted neighbor in her childhood, was outraged by the treatment the Sauk band received from the undisciplined Illinois militia, and by the failure of the Great White Father in Washington to protect them. It may have been the stories he heard of her friendship for Black Hawk that first interested young Edgar in the Indians need for defenders. In later years he said his mother had made him promise to do what he could for them.

Tabitha's mother bore her last two children on the Stice cabin floor before she died, leaving the eldest daughter to mother the little ones. At sixteen Tabitha was too busy caring for her brothers and sisters to think of marrying like most of her friends. Later, when the children no longer needed her so much, she managed to get away for some schooling at Cherry Grove Seminary, located a few miles south of Galesburg. She must have been an uncommon student because she soon qualified for a brief teaching career, including elementary astronomy among her subjects.

Tabitha Stice Hewett (1822-1914), mother of Edgar Lee Hewett. Courtesy of the School of American Research.

Harvey Hanson Hewett (1825-1904), father of Edgar Lee Hewett. Courtesy of the School of American Research.

Tabitha was twenty-nine — an old maid by the standards of the day — when she married Hanson Hewett, three years her junior. Hanson had brought back nothing from his California venture except a fund of anecdotes to tell at the family dinner table, but with the help of their many relatives in the neighborhood the couple was soon prospering. In the next fourteen years Tabitha bore her six children. Four boys — Alvin, Lawrence, Noy, and Edgar, and one girl — Cassie, survived, which was a high percentage for the time. A second little girl, Nora, died in early childhood of typhoid fever.

The Hewett and Stice kinfolk helped one another with barn raising and harvest, birthing and burying, hard times of epidemics and bad weather, good times of holidays and festivals. They were a hardy people, living temperate lives with plenty of strenuous exercise to burn up the calories of the abundant meals provided by the rich farm country.

Like his brothers, Edgar built a strong body accustomed to hard work, and learned habits of thrift and moderation which were to last a long lifetime. Unlike his brothers, he had curiosity, intellectual hunger and ambition which drove him far beyond their modest expectations. Edgar never thought of himself as the brainy one of the family. Perhaps — though he never said so — his book-loving mother had more time and strength to favor him, her baby. Perhaps, too, his older brothers lifted the heavier responsibilities of farm work from him.

When he was an old man Edgar looked back on the life of those boyhood days, on his parents, siblings and numerous cousins, with nostalgia, screening out the worst hardships and magnifying the virtues of the family and the abundance of the life they led.

Although he had never known his Grandfather Hewett, he remembered his grandmother as a sweet, gentle lady. "It was grand when we were allowed to go over to the old homestead to visit her and sit in her presence for an hour," he recalled. And lest that seem unnatural he added, "Then, too, the 'shinplasters' (paper 10¢ and 25¢ pieces) that she always gave us on leaving, made a favorable impression."[4]

Of his home farm he wrote, "A dozen or so hired men and two or three hired girls had to be looked after all the time. The big front gate was never closed. Travelers just drove in, put up their horses, sat down at the long dining table, and gave us the news from the outside world. No wayfarer was ever allowed to pay a copper for hospitality in those days."[5] Lest this sound like too much affluence, it must be remembered that many teenage girls worked for little more than board and room until they married, and many youths were glad to be fed at a bountiful farm table and housed in a hayloft when there was no employment except farm labor. On the expanding frontier the agrarian economy cushioned the worst blows of boom-and-bust cycles in the days before farms were mechanized. No one called the extra hands "servants" in the Midwest. They ate at the family table and mingled on a basis of complete equality.

Edgar was to remember one hired man with particular gratitude. One day his father brought from town a young athlete named Anderson, together with a set of boxing gloves. The four Hewett sons were trained by Anderson in the fundamentals of self-defense.

Edgar remembered his mother (affectionately known as Aunt Tabitha far beyond the circle of her own kin) as ministering to the welfare of the entire countryside. She carried baskets of food from the Hewett larder to less fortunate settlers, helped neighbor women in childbirth, and nursed children stricken with croup, which was a terrible scourge in the damp, bitter winters on the prairies.

Edgar was born when Tabitha was forty-three, when the financial fortunes of his parents were at their height, and at a time when extended family connections provided cooperative security. He remembered happy days at the county fairs and trips to the circus which inspired the boys to put on their own show, with the ticket office in front of the homestead barns. The Hewett Brothers Greatest Show on Earth featured exhibitions of tumbling and horizontal bar tricks, boxing, wrestling, and exciting bareback riding in the pasture. The side shows featured a pillow-upholstered hired girl as the fattest lady on earth, and exotic animals like the three-legged bulldog named Howler (the fourth leg had been lost in a reaper accident) and the ring-tailed giasticutus which in private life was Edgar's tomcat, dubbed "Broke-tail."

Most of life's necessities were homegrown. Money was scarce for the things a family must buy, and the annual sale of the surplus harvest was hardly enough to pay the interest on debts and buy the textiles required for homemade clothing and the tools that could not be fashioned on a farmyard forge. The children went to school for three or four months out of the year when their farm labor was not desperately needed. Still, there was enough money in the Hewett household to purchase a shelf of books, and it was surprisingly heavy with volumes about faraway places. A full set of Bayard Taylor's *Travels* set Edgar dreaming of the Seven Wonders of the Ancient World. The works of John L. Stephens made the names of sites in the Mayan world of Guatemala and Yucatan a familiar sight long before they could be properly pronounced: Copán, Quirigua, Palenque, Chichen Itzá, Uxmal. Edgar studied the pictures and stored them in his memory. The dream of exploring around the world came easily in a family where the adventure stories found in such periodicals as *Saturday Night* and *Youth's Companion* were read aloud. Nothing was unobtainable for boys brought up on Horatio Alger success stories. All it took was ambition, steady hard work and a modicum of luck.

Edgar started to school when he was six. He could read and could recognize the portraits of the presidents of the United States, thanks to those long winter evenings on his brother Alvin's lap. His first teacher — a delightful redhead — became his first love. It seems probable that she, in her turn, never forgot the eager, precocious little boy whose mother had taught her children to read maps of the stars and on clear nights helped them identify the constellations. "The Pleiades are my favorites," the smallest boy told her gravely.[6]

At home the local and Chicago newspapers were delivered by mail and the elders talked politics. Their father had heard the Lincoln-Douglas debates and could quote them firsthand. The impeachment trial of President Johnson had left its scars, and the bitter days of reconstruction and carpetbag government were discussed in a family where the father was a mild-mannered man who believed in dealing fairly with all men and the mother knew that Indians like Black Hawk and his band were real people.

In more relaxed moods the father repeated his tales of the gold rush days and the wilderness country of the Far West, and Uncle Jim Charles pulled the long bow in recounting his experiences in riding the trail with Kit Carson — whose life he claimed to have saved when Carson fell headlong into a welcome desert pool after a long, dry journey. Edgar came early to his hero worship of the Western scout.

"The boy who has to go through life without horses is swindled," Edgar Hewett once wrote.[7] On the Illinois farm he learned to ride gentle old Lion when he was six, holding on behind two bigger brothers. Lion was predictable except in one respect.

A Confederate cavalry officer's horse trained and ridden through the Civil War, the slender bay responded to the sound of a shot as an order to "Charge!" The trio of Hewett lads was astride him one day when a hunter's gun roared in a nearby field. Lion's head went up, his muscles grew taut, and his amble changed to the old cavalry lope, with the tempo increasing while the three boys clutched anything that might help them keep their seats. Lion went through the big front gate, turned the corner around the pigpen smartly, and Edgar went sailing into the big straw pile with the back of his brother Noy's shirt in his clenched fists.

Another horse, Charley, was pure white, round and fat. The boys trained him in the smooth lope of the circus horse and practiced on him for their performances until they could jump on and off at a gallup.

Then there was Kit, the iron-grey trotting lady, for whom pulling a light roadster a mile in three minutes was easy going. In his book of boyhood reminiscences, *Two Score Years,* Edgar painted a picture of the delicious excitement Kit brought into his life:

She always had the honor of taking my father to the railway station four miles away. He never started until exactly 18 minutes before train time. I always went along to drive Kit back .... We jogged leisurely as though we had all day for it for 15 minutes. At the three mile cross roads, I knew something would happen. The train would whistle for the crossing one mile west. We had a mile straight-away for the station, a mile south. The train had the diagonal of that square mile to make, we one side of it. At the sound of that whistle, Kit's ears went forward, her muscles tensed, she struck the sweeping trot that was preliminary to real going. Father tightened the lines, lifted the whip from the socket, but never did more than flick it over Kit's back. I jerked off my cap, tucked it under me and took a firm hold on the seat with both hands. Kit was under way. The fence posts flew past us; a cottontail rabbit had to make a quick jump for it to get off the road. Occasionally a covey of quail scurried into the weeds .... The wind in my face was now a gale, but how I loved it! Three-fourths of that mile was done in something under a three minute gait, but I knew Kit was not putting all she had into it. Then came the whistle of the train for the station. I took an extra grip on the seat .... Kit rushed to the finish. That burst of energy was Homeric. No interval between hoof beats now, but the steady whir of triphammers. It was a tornado. Not the mechanical response of stepping on the gas, but the answer of nerve and muscle to the drive of a mighty spirit. That rush was to me the climax of living.

We slowed down for the curve at the end, and whirled to a stop at the rear end of the train. Father stepped out deliberately, lit his pipe, greeted a few acquaintances, took the paper handed to him by the news butcher, swung up on the rear platform as the train pulled out, waved me a "Goodbye, Ed, be a good boy," and disappeared into the coach. "H. H.

Hewett never missed a train," neighbors said, "and never had a half minute to spare." Just time enough to light his pipe.[8]

There came a year when Hanson Hewett decided he could do better by entering the commission business in Chicago, so the family moved to the vicinity of Thirty-Third Street, on the outskirts of the city. They took along their prize horse, Pompey, a pure white Arabian. It was a period of rapid expansion for the lakeside city, but a risky time for a farmer turned speculator. Chicago's wooden heart was reduced to ashes in the big fire of 1871, Boston burned a year later, and business took a heavy loss in those two holocausts. Congress was tinkering with the money system, demonetizing silver. Some said that this radical change was lobbied by the national banks to make their paper money more valuable; others insisted that the big financiers manipulated the money because when gold was the only "real money" it was easier to corner. In the panic of 1873 business slashed wages and drastically cut employment. The desperate city workmen began to experiment with unionization. Helpless under existing laws, they turned to violence. Members of the establishment — newspaper editors, lawyers, business leaders, bankers, and even some theologians — fearing for their lives as well as their property, supported ever harsher measures to control the frantic laborers.

In those troublous times the Hewett boys found life in the city dull and barren by comparison with the freedom and variety of the farm, but in one lively encounter Edgar had a chance to test his fighting ability. Compared to the ruthless cruelty of modern city gangs, the boyhood warfare of that neighborhood was a model of chivalry. The Thirty-Third Street gang issued a challenge to the new country boy, believing him to be easy game. Their leader formed a ring, appointed a referee, and named a champion, one Eddie Spellacy, to fight Edgar Hewett, whose brother Noy served as his second. While they waited for the opening gong to be sounded on a battered tin plate, Noy kept admonishing his younger brother, "Don't forget what Anderson told you."

Eddie Hewett took his stance, fists on guard. As the sparring began he recalled that the hired man had said to size up your opponent's weaknesses. It seemed doubtful that young Spellacy had ever been taught scientific defense. Edgar aimed for the solar plexis. The blow landed; the gang champion turned pale and folded. He was helped to his feet, and Edgar shook his limp hand as the referee announced his decision in favor of the underdog.

Even better than giving a good account of himself in the ring, Edgar enjoyed riding the white Arabian up Michigan Avenue. He reported that a wealthy sportsman had made offers for the horse, running the price up to an incredible bid of a thousand dollars. "I told him we wouldn't sell Pompey for any money," he boasted.[9]

It must have been a temptation for his father, whose finances did not prosper in the city. Some people said that the commission house venture failed because of a rascal associate, and it may be true. It is also possible that Harvey Hanson Hewett was not a shrewd businessman, and the times were out of joint. In any event, the

Chicago experience was short-lived and the Hewett family returned to the Warren County farm, taking the beautiful Pompey with them.[10]

Life in the city had widened horizons for the children, whose father found that it was too late to recoup his fortunes on the Illinois farm. The Garden of Eden his own father had homesteaded no longer guaranteed security for this family. There must be a better place. In 1880 the Hewett family moved to a Missouri farm somewhat west of Pumpkin Center. Everything had been sold to cover debts; they were broke.

The move put an end to Edgar's childhood. At fourteen he could decide for himself whether he would seek a job as his older brothers had done or work for more education. Life on the new farm was not as abundant as in Illinois; the large, helpful circle of uncles, aunts and cousins had been left behind. Edgar's parents could spare him during the school year, and encouraged him to enter high school. Luckily, in spite of his catch-as-catch-can schooling, he had sufficient training in the basics to be accepted.

He was a well built lad with steady grey-blue eyes and a jutting jaw that signaled determination. (Many years later his students nicknamed him *El Toro.*) His muscles were farm hardened and his health was good. He was sufficiently expert in baseball to bring him an offer of a semi-pro career from a visiting coach. Yet it seemed that in her youngest child all of Tabitha's ambition for learning was concentrated. Not many farm boys enjoyed the privilege of a high school education. To earn it that first year Edgar was willing to trudge through the Missouri mud a mile and a half to the town of Hopkins and back each night in time to help with the chores.

The high school principal, a big man named D. L. Cheney, encouraged Edgar. Though Cheney himself was not learned, he administered inspiration and the need for self-discipline to his scholars in equal proportions — inspiration to set high goals and discipline to achieve them.

It was during his studies at Hopkins High School between 1880 and 1883 that Edgar first came across the works of Lewis Henry Morgan, who was at the height of his career as a social scientist. For Morgan 1880 was also a milestone year, marking the publication of his Southwest studies, and for his protégé Adolph Francis Bandelier the year marked his transition from businessman to social scientist. Both men were pioneers in a period of awakened scientific interest in pre-Columbian man in New Mexico. Morgan had made a journey to the Southwest which so stirred his imagination that he encouraged Bandelier to take his first plunge into active field research there. Because these two men shaped much of Edgar Hewett's early career in similar research, it seems appropriate to pause here in Edgar's story to tell something of them.

2

LEWIS HENRY MORGAN AND ADOLPH BANDELIER

I am fully aware...that a history based exclusively on documents, whether printed or written, must necessarily be imperfect because it is not impartial, since it summarizes the views of those who saw and understood but one side of the question, and judged it only from their own viewpoint. — A. F. Bandelier

Lewis Henry Morgan was born near Aurora, New York on November 1, 1818, the son of affluent parents who owned an estate near Lake Cayuga. The lad roamed the fields and woods around his home, growing with the natural world and picking up scattered artifacts of the Iroquois, such as arrowheads and pipe stems. His early reading about the Iroquois, who still lived in considerable numbers near his home, was in the fanciful *Leatherstocking Tales* of James Fenimore Cooper.

Probably the boy skipped the wordy descriptive passages that prolonged the suspense and picked out the narrative portions. In later years Morgan would know that Cooper was sentimental and imaginative, but that his superficial research was not all inaccurate. The stories, which inspired his countrymen to know more about the wilderness and the life-style of the Indian, taught that the first Americans probably had an Asiatic origin and that they practiced laws of hospitality inviolable even on occasions when as hosts they were put to a great disadvantage.

As Lew Morgan grew up he read other books under discussion at the time, including Darwin's *Origin of the Species.* By the time he graduated from Cayuga Academy and entered Union College, Darwin's theories were the hottest topic of debate, warmly defended or indignantly rejected by scientists and theologians. These clashing ideas served as yeast for Morgan's growing curiosity about the *real* life of the Indians, whose artifacts lured him and whose notions of the creative myth were rumored to be very different from the white man's.

After earning his degree from Union College, young Morgan read for the law and was licensed to practice in New York State. He was soon sufficiently successful in his profession and the business ventures growing out of it to afford some free time for his scientific study. He moved comfortably in the intellectual circles of Rochester.

Every properly educated man of the day had to be something of a classical scholar. Morgan learned a seven-step classification for the various levels of human society — early, middle and later savagery, early, middle and later barbarism, and finally civilization itself, which came with written language, settled agriculture and other attributes. His wide reading led him to classify the people of the Mediterranean civilizations as they progressed through these steps. As he expanded his methodical study of the Iroquois, Morgan gradually developed a thesis that the natives found on the North and South American continents had reached levels of the barbaric stage of society, through which all mankind must pass on the way to true civilization.

In 1851, when he was thirty-three, Morgan published the first of his scientific treatises. By 1855 his interest in Indians led him beyond the Iroquois. He spent his summer holidays in Marquette, Michigan, where wild life as well as "wild" men absorbed his attention. There he gathered data on the America beaver, which led to publication of a paper about the animal on which much of frontier life had depended. Beaver were still plentiful in northern Michigan.

By the time he was forty-four (in 1862), Morgan's fascination with science had so far superseded his interest in law that he gave up the legal profession to devote all his time to the study of primitive societies. Out of his reading on classical social systems and the data he collected about American Indians, Morgan evolved a synthesis that he called *Systems of Consanguinity and Affinity of the Human Family,* which was published in Volume XVII of the Smithsonian *Contributions to Knowledge.*

Morgan's researches were done on his own, without the backing of university or museum. He never held a paid official position in his life, but he was early invited to join the American Academy for the Advancement of Science, a rallying place for original thinkers.

Morgan became the most powerful American figure in anthropology in his day, with a wide and enthusiastic following. The Germans Engels and Marx were influenced by his work, although the phenomenon that Morgan called *communism* among the peoples he studied came closer to what is now termed *communality* than to the social and governmental communism of Marx. Paul Bohanan wrote, "Morgan was one of the primary inspirations for Marx and Engels. Engels' book on the family *is* Morgan, with minor modifications. Marx took extensive notes for, but never wrote a book on Morgan's theories."[1]

Of course many of those theories were subsequently superseded, and some years after Morgan's death it became fashionable to sneer at his accomplishments, but more recent scholars have found much to study in his work. His biographer, Leslie

Lewis Henry Morgan (1818-1881), lawyer and pioneer ethnologist. Courtesy of the School of American Research.

White, says of him, "It was Morgan who, single-handed, discovered the fact that kinship terminologies reflect systems of consanguinity and affinity, types of social organization. This tremendous discovery which embraced all people and tribes of the world revolutionized the study of society and placed it on a more fruitful basis."[2]

The house in Rochester where Morgan lived with his wife and son became a gathering place for the scientific intellectuals of the day. Among Lewis Morgan's close friends was Dr. W.B. Anderson, president of the University of Rochester, who was instrumental in bringing about a meeting between Morgan and an aspiring student-linguist, Adolph Bandelier. From their first evening encounter Morgan had an eager disciple in Bandelier. The two men began a correspondence, and in June 1878, while on his way to New Mexico, Morgan stopped over in Highland, Illinois for a visit to Bandelier's home. Both men attended a meeting of the American Association for the Advancement of Science in St. Louis several months later, and the following year Bandelier went to see Morgan in Rochester.

In 1880 the first Annual Report of the Archaeological Institute of America included a paper by Lewis Henry Morgan entitled *Study of the Houses of American Aborigines,* which was in large part derived from his journey to the Southwest. In this study the father of American archaeology urged careful, scientific exploration of the ruins to be found in New Mexico and Arizona, as well as those in Yucatan and Central America. It was a challenge that would be eagerly taken up by Adolph Bandelier, and some years later by Edgar Lee Hewett.

Morgan introduced Bandelier to the editor of *The Nation* and recommended him as a book reviewer. Adolph wrote several reviews and articles for the periodical afterwards, and thus became known to a rather wide public.

The fateful year 1880 marked for Adolph Francis Alphonse Bandelier the beginning of his true career. He was forty years old when on the evening of August 23 he arrived in Santa Fe, New Mexico to begin a survey of the Indian cultures of the Southwest. His journey from St. Louis by way of the Missouri Pacific and Atchison, Topeka & Santa Fe Railroad had been so stimulating that he had slept little during the three days and two nights. In Santa Fe he registered at the Grand Hotel and fell exhausted into bed. His journal for the next day reports, "Slept until 9 A.M. with bedbugs."[3]

Adolph Bandelier was born August 6, 1840 in Bern, Switzerland. His father was trained as a lawyer, and there is speculation that some adverse adventure in politics led him to emigrate, first to Brazil and then to the United States where he found the Swiss settlement of Highland, Illinois, to his liking. He sent for his wife and eight-year-old son to join him. In Highland the elder Bandelier became a banker and civic leader. Adolph went to school, with his education richly supplemented at home where he and his parents spoke French together and were equally at ease in German. When he later undertook the reading of Spanish books and documents he acquired fluency in that language also, although recent scholars have questioned his mastery of the finer points of grammar and semantics.

His father encouraged Adolph in scientific inquiry. They owned a telescope through which to study the heavenly bodies. Adolph probably had private lessons in art, music and elocution as well, since these subjects were customarily taught to children of affluent families. When he was seventeen Adolph went abroad to study geology under Professor Studer in Bern. Back in the United States five years later he married Josephine Huegy, daughter of his father's banking partner in Highland. The couple returned to Switzerland, where it has been said that Adolph studied law at the University of Bern, though some scholars have recently challenged this statement.[4]

In 1867 the young Bandeliers returned to Highland and Adolph became active in civic affairs, as well as writing and lecturing on "scientific subjects." His father wanted him to enter business, and Adolph was encouraged to spend time at the family bank, though he seems not to have held an official position there. Dutifully he tried to live up to expectations, but neither law nor business really seemed attractive. He read widely, more at home with books than with his neighbors. Out of the reading grew correspondence with the authors he admired, and gradually his interest focused on the Indian cultures of Mexico and the American Southwest.

Whether Adolph ever actually met Alexander von Humboldt is not known, but he certainly was influenced by von Humboldt's accounts of exploration and research in Latin America, and the two men probably corresponded. The most profound influence on the young scholar began, however, when the Reverend Doctor Anderson introduced him to Lewis Morgan. Much impressed, Adolph followed up the initial meeting with letters; as the two men became warm friends they visited in each other's homes.

Up to this time Bandelier's studies were limited to armchair research. He haunted university and city libraries and bought for his own personal collection all the books he could afford. Out of his friendship for Morgan he developed twin ambitions: to make enough money so that he would be financially free to devote his time to his studies, and to expand those studies into independent field research.

Although their backgrounds were different in many ways, Bandelier and Morgan had much in common. Both had grown up in comfortable homes with many advantages; both had failed to find satisfaction in their early vocations; both enjoyed scientific speculation and were drawn to original research. When it came to financial independence, however, Morgan proved himself a far better businessman.

In his efforts to get-rich-quick Adolph Bandelier involved himself in two business ventures — the Confidence Coal Mining Company (which he was later to call an infernal hole) and the Highland Mechanical Works. Dutifully he divided his time between the two companies, but he spent his nights and any spare daytime moments he could steal in research and writing. The business details bored and irritated him; he had no taste and little aptitude for them, and of course they did not prosper. As a result of his strenuous schedule and the frustrations of business his health suffered, and his doctor ordered him to slow down. He began a frantic search for some opportunity that would allow him to withdraw from business altogether and support himself with research.

Lewis Morgan came to his rescue. Out of his reading Bandelier had drawn material for three monographs dealing with ancient Mexicans and the sources of aboriginal history of Spanish America. These were published between 1877 and 1879. Impressed by Bandelier's scholarship, his friend Morgan approached the executive committee of the newly formed Archaeological Institute of America with a proposal that they sponsor Bandelier in a field trip to the Southwest. The president of the Institute was Charles Eliot Norton, a classicist who had little use for American archaeology; he did not favor Morgan's proposal. Two other members of the committee, Frederick W. Putnam and Francis Parkman, had real interest in western America, however. Morgan won them over to the cause of his protégé. Bandelier was offered $1,200 a year to cover travel and living expenses as well as any purchase of specimens he might wish to make. Eagerly he accepted the offer, and his health immediately improved.

Bandelier spent the first month in eastern travel, first visiting Major J. W. Powell, director of the Bureau of Ethnology in Washington. Powell's expeditions in the Southwest, especially his exploration of the Grand Canyon, made him both knowledgeable and enthusiastic about Bandelier's proposed undertaking. A second call — on Professor Norton at Harvard — was a courtesy visit, but since neither man had a very clear idea of Bandelier's possible activities and Norton thought they would turn out to be money wasted anyway, Bandelier got little help from that interview.

Adolph must have been aware from the beginning that his stipend would scarcely suffice for his needs. Possibly he had always received some financial assistance from his father, and rather expected it to continue. When he left Highland and set off for unknown territory he must have arranged for his wife Josephine to be subsidized either by his family or her own. Throughout the rest of his life Adolph rarely had enough money to cover his modest needs, and the lack of funds hampered most of his undertakings, but from the moment he was free to turn his scholarly hobby into a profession he was sure of his true vocation. Duty took him back to Highland from time to time, but he could never again settle down there or give more than perfunctory attention to the demands of business.

Life in New Mexico in the 1880s was primitive enough to satisfy Bandelier's yearning for pioneering field work. He set out immediately to establish his credentials and track down archival and documentary material. During his first morning in Santa Fe he called on the civil executive, Governor Lew Wallace; the judiciary representative, Judge Waldo; and the military authority, General Atkinson. He found none of them at home. The underpaid Territorial librarian, Samuel Ellison, was unavailable, being confined at home with a broken leg.

Adolph had better luck with his first ecclesiastical call; the vicar-general at the cathedral was friendly and helpful. Padre Eguillon told him that the archbishop had no documents of interest to him, and that the neglect and actual destruction of old archives stored in the governor's palace amounted to a scandal.

Adolph began the afternoon of that first day by writing up the information gathered during the morning; then he went to the vicar's residence where he met several other clerics. They showed him the archbishop's lovely garden, the chapel of Guadalupe, and the cathedral. As a result of his inquiries he decided to make his first field trip to the ruined pueblo of Pecos, some thirty miles from Santa Fe, on the following day. Arrangements were more complicated than anticipated, however, and he had to spend several more days reconnoitering Santa Fe. One of his first

Adolph Alphonse Francis Bandelier (1840-1914), historian and pioneer archaeologist. Courtesy of the Museum of New Mexico.

acquaintances was the curio dealer, Jake Gold, whose establishment at the corner of Burro Alley and San Francisco Street offered a lot of fine pottery which Bandelier judged to be recent. They agreed on a price of four dollars per dozen objects, subject to ratification by Professor Norton.

Bandelier then set out for Pecos, having rented a horse and buggy and secured the services of a photographer to accompany him. There he began to establish the pattern of research which he followed throughout the Southwest, visiting the sites of ancient and modern pueblos, talking with white settlers, clerics and Indians, and verifying his information when possible with the old Spanish records. He lodged with kindly priests at the missions and with friendly Indians in their villages.

Although he was often lonely, cold and hungry, Adolph kept doggedly at the tasks he set for himself. If he was in funds, he hired a horse; if he was broke, he walked. When his one pair of boots needed patching he stayed in his Santa Fe room and worked on his notes until the cobbler returned the boots.

There were episodes of ecstacy to reward his persistence. One favorite place (called in the Queres dialect *Tyuonyi,* and by the Spanish *El Rito de los Frijoles*) was a lovely canyon in the Pajarito Plateau of the Jemez Mountains. He camped there, sometimes with an Indian guide and sometimes alone, and as he explored the tumbled talus slopes and crawled into caves long abandoned, as he scrambled over the mounded ruins of a large communal dwelling on the canyon floor, he dreamed of the way it must have been when it was inhabited by the cliff-dwellers. The description he wrote of the valley was lyrical:

> The Rito is a beautiful spot. Situated in a direct line not over twenty miles from Santa Fe, it can still be reached only after a long day's tedious travel. It is a narrow valley, nowhere broader than half a mile; and from where it begins in the west to where it closes in a dark and gloomy entrance, scarcely wide enough for two men to pass abreast, in the east, its length does not exceed six miles. Its southern rim is formed by the slope of a timbered mesa, and that slope is partly overgrown by shrubbery. The northern border constitutes a line of vertical cliffs of yellowish and white pumice, projecting and re-entering like decorations for a stage — now perpendicular and smooth for some distance, now sweeping back in the shape of an arched segment. These cliffs vary in height, although nowhere are they less than two hundred feet. Their tops rise in huge pillars, in crags and pinnacles. Brushwood and pine timber crown the mesa of which these fantastic projections are but the shaggy border.
> Through the vale itself rustles the clear and cool brook to which the name of Rito de los Frijoles is applied. It meanders on, hugging the southern slope, partly through open spaces, partly through groves of timber, and again past tall stately pine-trees standing isolated in the valley. Willows, cherry-trees, cottonwoods, and elders form small thickets along its banks. The Rito is a permanent streamlet notwithstanding its small size. Its water freezes in winter, but it never dries up completely during the summer months.

Bunches of tall grass, low shrubbery, and cactus grow in the open spaces between rocky debris fallen from above. They also cover in part low mounds of rubbish, and ruins of a large pentagonal building erected formerly at the foot of a slope leading to the cliffs. In the cliffs themselves, for a distance of about two miles, numerous caves dug out by the hand of men are visible. Some of these are yet perfect; others have wholely crumbled away except the rear wall. From a distance the port-holes and indentations appear like so many pigeon's nests in the naked rock. Together with the cavities formed by amygdaloid chambers and crevices caused by erosion, they give the cliffs the appearance of a huge, irregular honeycomb.[5]

This was Tyuonyi as Bandelier first saw it in the 1880s. It seems a formidable hike from Santa Fe to the hidden canyons of the Pajarito, but Bandelier and his companions followed the watercourses and the old trails, a shorter route than that of modern roads.

After eight years spent in ethnological and archaeological delving, Bandelier turned from sober scientific reports to write his novel that would reconstruct the life of the cliff dwellers. He wrote it first in German and titled it with the name of a society he had observed in Pueblo ceremonials — *Die Koshare.* The men in this group, costumed to represent the spirits of the dead, apparently served a mixed function as clowns and policemen. Bandelier was in cruel financial distress at the time; he hoped the work would be popular and help to restore his fortunes. When the German version was not particularly successful, he translated it into English and eventually found a publisher for it under the title *The Delight Makers.*

In his scientific writing Bandelier tried hard to verify the theories of his venerated friend Morgan, but he found little supporting evidence. His work turned to archival and documentary research, which he found far more satisfying.

Morgan, Bandelier and, in his turn, Hewett, represent three generations of scientific exploration, each building on his predecessor. In 1880 Morgan was at the height of his prestige; he was to die a year later. Bandelier was a middle-aged scholar traveling to Santa Fe to embark on a new career that would bring him lasting fame but no fortune. Hewett was an ambitious youth struggling for a high school education and beginning the studies that would bring him eventually to Santa Fe.

In 1881 Bandelier journeyed to Rochester, hoping to discuss his work with Morgan and report on his problems. Morgan was by that time too ill to see him, and Bandelier went away dejected. When Hewett entered the archaeological field in the Southwest some fifteen years later Bandelier had completed most of the original work he was to do in that area, but the two men became lifelong friends, Hewett deferring to Bandelier even as Bandelier had been influenced by Morgan.

3

GROWING UP IN MISSOURI

*I have never been strong for autobiography, but I believe
that if the story of your life is going to be told, the first
twenty-year period should not be slighted.* — ELH

Back in Hopkins, Missouri, Edgar Hewett set out in 1880 doggedly and happily to
secure an education. When his family moved after a year to a farm four miles from
town he found it a far piece to walk to school in time for the opening bell and home
again in time for the evening chores, so he arranged to ride horseback with Charley
Wallace, son of a neighboring farmer who was also the county judge. The two boys
admired high school principal Cheney immoderately. They wore their overcoats
slung across their shoulders a la Cheney, and strove mightily to meet his standards
of excellence. When the local school board failed to appreciate Cheney's teaching
ability and dismissed him, Edgar and Charley joined a group of students who held
protest meetings and passed resolutions condemning the school board. They
threatened to transfer to another school in a nearby town, but the board was not to
be intimidated.

Cheney's replacement was a young man named George D. Bowman, slight of
figure, balding, scholarly. Better educated than Cheney, his emphasis was on learning and the need for self-expression. At first the boys were scornful, but Bowman
gradually won them over. One of his most difficult demands was a weekly exercise
in elocution. Young people of that period had not been brought up to "show and
tell," but rather to maintain a respectful silence in the presence of their elders,
unless the conversation was directed to them. Edgar's farm life had been spent
largely in the family circle, and the country schools of Warren County were

Edgar Lee Hewett, high-school student, ca. 1881. Courtesy of the School of American Research.

one-room affairs with thirty or forty students, many of whom were the cousins he knew well. Now he found that standing and speaking in front of the whole class — or worse, the whole school in assembly — was an agony of embarrassment. Under Bowman's tutelage he was forced to overcome his shyness. Thinking back on it sixty years later he wrote that Bowman "started an awkward, self-conscious country lad on a long, long road of action in which endless public speaking was a vital factor, God rest his soul!"[1]

During Edgar's third year in high school he lived with a doctor's family in town, milking the cows and taking care of the doctor's horses in payment for his room and board. By the fourth year he had earned fifty dollars from the sale of some shoats and calves he raised on the home farm, and was ready to sustain himself. In town he occupied a large room above the Hopkins drugstore where he paid the rent by helping out on Saturdays. His hoarded cash went for meals provided by a nice old lady who ran a small hotel and charged him a dollar and a half a week.

The loft room over the drugstore was furnished with a bed and bedding brought from the home farm and a rough table and some chairs which Edgar fashioned from scrap lumber begged from the local lumberyard. The only warmth was provided by a stovepipe passing through the loft from a potbelly stove in the store below. It was so cold in winter that Edgar and the companions who gathered in his quarters wore their overcoats as they studied and debated.

Among their activities Edgar and Charley wrote poetry—they referred to themselves, only half humorously, as the Boy Bards. Rivals in many classroom achievements, they admired each other, and Edgar soon admitted that Charley's poetry was far superior to his own. It seems likely that these two boys, both destined to be listed in *Who's Who,* had no peers in the class. They were graduated at mid-year and parted after making a pact that they would both go on to higher degrees. For Charley this was not so momentous a decision as for Edgar. The Wallace family was sufficiently affluent to send their son immediately to Western Normal College at Shenandoah, Iowa, but Edgar must earn his living before he could continue his education.

With a letter of recommendation from Professor Bowman and $14.50 (left from the original fifty) in his pocket, Edgar set out to make his fortune in the new town of Fairfax, in the northwest corner of Missouri. His cash was spent for a railway ticket and for the first day's room and board at the local hotel ($2 a day). He arrived in the forenoon and by bedtime had made several acquaintances among the young men lounging about the town. The next morning he answered the school bell and met the superintendent, Dan Lewis, who introduced him to a group of school teachers taking the county examination. Lewis suggested that Hewett join them. After writing most of the day and far into the evening without stopping for meals, he qualified for a teacher's certificate.

The test covered twenty-five categories, with grades given on a scale of one to ten. Six was the passing grade; seven was tolerable; eight was good; nine, extra good; and ten denoted perfection. Edgar's perfect grades were in orthography, physiology, mental and written arithmetic, rhetoric, zoology, botany, theory and practice (whatever that was—pedagogy, perhaps?), penmanship, English grammar, physical geography, reading, and physics. He was a bit weak—earning a grade of eight—in chemistry, trigonometry, mental philosophy, and general history. Professor Lewis told him that his certificate, showing such superior grades, was the equivalent of the four-year Bachelor of Science degree as then administered by the colleges of the state. Edgar decided he had better read up on philosophy and history, as they were two subjects that truly interested him.

The next day one of his newfound friends invited him for a ride into the country to meet a brother who was a member of a rural school board. By the end of that third day young Hewett had a contract in his pocket to teach in the country school for the remaining three-month term, at a salary of $36 a month. He was on his own and self-supporting.

He enjoyed his first teaching experience. He liked working with children and was touched by their devotion to him. Some of them cried when he told them he would not return the following fall, but he was sure he could do better. With his hunger in the head driving him and the habit of the farm strong within him he saw no need for a summer vacation, so he spent the summer months in college study and teaching. Hewett's dedication to summer schools was to last the rest of his life and to play a large part in his later teaching and archaeological career.

The first year that he enrolled for a four weeks' session of Teachers' Institute at Tarkio College he was invited to join the staff, and taught several classes in exchange for $40—enough to cover his expenses. By working, reading and studying eighteen to twenty hours a day (he never seemed to need as much sleep as most people) young Hewett put himself through high school, followed by two years of teaching in one-room country schools and a business course in Burlington, Iowa. After two years of student teaching at Tarkio College he was given the title of Professor. Anthropology was among the subjects he studied at Tarkio in 1886; the professor was a Dr. Dodds, whose influence Edgar often acknowledged in his later career. At Tarkio Hewett taught commercial courses as well as history and literature. It was at a Tarkio summer session that he formed a momentous friendship with a young woman named Cora Whitford, just graduated from college. Her charm, he always said, was indescribable.

In the wealth of brash new colleges springing up all over the West at the close of the nineteenth century, opportunities for the young educator were many. But Hewett was not yet sure of his profession. He left Tarkio to read law in the office of Jeremiah Perkins Blood, counsellor-at-law in Sioux City, Iowa. Although Edgar would have preferred to sit quietly reading Blackstone, his employer demanded a more active pursuit of the law. Much of his apprenticeship was spent in debt collection and petty lawsuits tried in the lower courts in and around Sioux City. He did not participate in criminal practice, but he saw enough to know it was not for him. Although he granted every accused person the right to good counsel, he came to the conclusion that much defense of criminals was designed to defeat order and justice.

Hewett found in Attorney Blood a man who was more interested in a just decision than in winning a case for a client. Writing of him later Edgar said, "If anything would have anchored me to the law as a life interest, it would have been the influence of that modest attorney, who was in my estimation exactly what a lawyer should be, even though he didn't arrive via Blackstone."[2]

No villains appear in Hewett's autobiographical *Two Score Years*. When he

Edgar Lee Hewett, college student, 1887. Photograph by M. F. Phillips. Courtesy of the Museum of New Mexico.

looked back he saw only heroes. His high school teachers and college professors; the presidents of the colleges where he studied and taught; the lawyer under whom he read Blackstone — these mentors form a fine procession of admirable men. His praise for them is characteristic. Although he was to engage in many notable controversies throughout his long career, he let those for whom he had little respect sink from his memory, or after commenting with humorous disparagement about them in private, considered them beneath his public notice.

About the time Hewett was ready to go up for his bar examination he was offered the school principal's job in Fairfax, Missouri, where his parents still lived. The salary was an inducement, especially when weighed against the uncertainties of the law. His parents were getting along in years, and could use a little financial help. An even larger necessity, however, was the urgency for courting Cora Whitford, the young teacher whose charm he could only describe as indescribable. Other men found her charming, too, and the competition could not be ignored.

He accepted the teaching job and never regretted the choice. Like Morgan and Bandelier, he turned his back on the legal profession but paid tribute to its training. "Superficial as my study of law was, I must attribute to it a profound influence over all my subsequent thinking," he wrote later.

> The evolution of law came to mean the evolution of history. As man formulated his rules of action he shaped the human events that constitute history. As primitive culture evolved into civilization, he found it more and more necessary to control society of which he was a part with rules of conduct, and in the fullness of time he arrived at the ultimate achievement of human freedom, that of government of the people, by the people, for the people. What a tragedy we are witnessing in the acute disturbances of our time![3]

Edgar and Cora came to an understanding: they would marry when his income reached a thousand dollars a year. He began his principalship in Fairfax in 1889, and two years later a simple wedding card announced the marriage of Cora Whitford and Edgar Hewett on September 16, 1891, at Denver, Colorado.

Cora had graduated from Lindenwood College, St. Charles, Missouri, in the class of 1886. The record shows that her lowest grade was an 85 in Ancient History; a character reference describes her as "faithful in all her studies, and uniformly ladylike in her deportment." At the time of their marriage she was twenty-two to Edgar's twenty-five. She had been teaching in Canon City on an advance certificate obtained the previous February.

During their courtship, which Edgar called a "reasonable period of acquaintance and impatient waiting," the young couple had a chance to learn how much they had in common. Both preferred outdoor rural life to city pleasures. They shared a passion for reading the classics and for horses. From childhood Cora had been taught to ride and manage horses; her love of them matched Edgar's.

When they started life together their most important possession was a pair of

Cora Whitford Hewett, Edgar Lee Hewett's first wife, ca. 1891. Photograph by Leon. Courtesy of the Museum of New Mexico.

ponies, Don and Dot. Their first investment, beyond the basic necessities for keeping house, was a camp wagon that Edgar designed. Starting with a sturdy wagon, he made sure that the top was waterproofed. Sleeping accommodations in the wagon bed consisted of springs, a thin mattress, and ample blankets. Under the driver's seat was a packing box with tools and repair supplies. A whole summer's commissary of staples could be stored under the wagon body; at the end and back of the rear axle was the dustproof packing case to hold cooking utensils. Opened out, the back leaf could be used as a table for two, with the camp chairs drawn close.

Guns, fishing tackle, and extra personal supplies were strapped to the bows of the wagon. When all was in order the young couple was ready for a whole season of riding and camping in the open.

At the eastern base of the Rockies where they lived, the world was wide and vastly unpopulated. They could spend weekends on short jaunts in the foothills, and at the beginning of the long summer vacation they headed for the mountains. It was a time when fifty to a hundred dollars would carry a couple with their inclinations and equipment through an entire summer. Grazing for the ponies was good in the mountains, and could be supplemented with oats procured for a few pennies from a rancher or a small-town feed store. They carried the basic flour, bacon, ham, and coffee with them. Trout from the stream, rock pigeons or quail, a young cottontail — such delicacies were free and easy to get in the days before game seasons and fishing licenses. Edgar was a good shot, although he had no taste for hunting beyond the immediate need for food.

Wild berries were gathered on the hillsides; fruit, vegetables and eggs could be purchased for little cost from the scattered ranch houses or in the towns along the road. Often such delicacies were proffered as gifts by hospitable people who would never miss the small amount the young couple could use. Travelers like Edgar and Cora were rare in the remote settlements. Whole families visited their camps to learn their names and their news, bringing fresh milk, berries or vegetables from the farm garden and taking companionship in exchange.

As the campfire glowed down to ashes Cora and Edgar curled up in their blankets under the stars when the weather was fair and the wind soughed gently in the pines around them. When it stormed they were snug inside the wagon while the rain drummed a rhythm on the waterproof top. To be young, in love with one's companion, and endowed with three months of freedom to wander in some of the world's most beautiful wilderness was, as Edgar pointed out, the peak of complete living. They came to know every pass, park and valley from Yellowstone to Chihuahua. In their journeying Edgar paused to note and make casual exploration of ancient ruins, caves and pictured rocks, with an increasing curiosity about their significance.

As he progressed up the teaching ladder, each move took the Hewetts to a larger and more rewarding job. Edgar was superintendent of schools at Florence, Colorado and then accepted a position in the training department of the new state normal school at Greeley. Everywhere they made new and lasting friendships. Although his interests were putting him at a greater distance from his family each year, Edgar kept in touch with them. He tried to visit his mother at least once a year, and as he matured he found a quiet respect for his father who had struggled hard but never quite succeeded in restoring affluence to the family. The older brothers went their independent ways, staying for the most part with the land as ranchers and farmers. The sister remained unmarried and always close to the mother she idolized.

From time to time he heard from Charley Wallace, who continued to climb toward his goals. Charley kept on writing poetry, combining it with a study of literature, yet when he took a bachelor of science degree from Western Normal College at Shenandoah, Iowa he was majoring in geology. He went on to a bachelor of arts degree from the University of Iowa where he met and married his wife, Hulda. To many it might have seemed that Charley had the easier road, but Edgar was not jealous of his friend. He was glad for Charley's opportunities, and eagerly reported his own progress. Life for both young men was rich and filled with promise.

4

*THE TEACHER BECOMES
AN ARCHAEOLOGIST*

*With me, learning meant exploration—adventuring
into the unknown; teaching, a matter of scouting —
taking young people along if they cared to go and didn't
mind the hard road.* — ELH

During the years he spent at Teachers College in Greeley, Edgar formulated a basic philosophy of education which evolved as he studied; he also developed his public speaking skills in the classroom and by entering the college contests popular at the time. By June 1893 he had completed his credentials for a bachelor's degree. His graduation oration, entitled "Master Motives," was published in the Greeley *Tribune*. During the next four years, while he taught and worked on his master's degree, he prepared a series of reports on the Department of Child Study for a periodical called *The Crucible*.

Although he was quick to yield superiority to Charley Wallace as a poet, he had not given up altogether. The only publication he listed for 1897 was a poem, "Dream Clouds," and the following year "Mist Wings" also appeared in *The Crucible*. Styles in poetry change with time; at the end of the Victorian era poetry was expected to be romantic and a bit mystic. However, the year that saw his second — and last — publication of a poem also brought his first publication of a paper in the field that was now attracting Hewett: "The Study of Anthropology" appeared in *The Crucible* two months after "Mist Wings."

Hewett was popular with his students. He was young, vital and knowledgeable about things that interested them. If he tended to moralize and even to preach, those qualities were expected in pedagogues. He also had a quiet humor and tremendous zest for life. He was searching history and philosophy for the truth about mankind, and the young are always concerned about their own identities. The friendships and associations he developed with faculty and students at Greeley were lasting.

Hewett had been raised in a Bible-reading family during a period when intellectuals dared to challenge fundamentalist dogma. He had firm principles of right and wrong, but no narrow conviction that one man's religion was necessarily better than another man's. Some of his good friends were followers of Mary Baker Eddy, and in his search for understanding Hewett became interested in a man who evidenced extraordinary powers of healing. He first heard of Francis Schlatter when the man left his shoe-repair shop in Albuquerque and, like the disciples of old, went to fast forty days in the desert wilderness beyond the Rio Grande. It was rumored that this man had performed miracles.

Charles Fox of North Denver, whose family had evidence of a remarkable cure at the hands of Schlatter, invited the healer to become his guest and minister to the many people who sought his faith-healing. During Schlatter's stay in Denver, Hewett went to observe the powerfully built European peasant who stood each day at the gateway in front of the Fox home. From six in the morning until six in the evening, with only an hour at noon for rest and food, Schlatter quietly met all those who came. The crowd waited in an orderly queue several blocks long; as each one passed in front of Schlatter, the healer grasped the hand of the suppliant firmly between his palms and murmured a prayer. In response to any gratitude that was expressed he said simply, "Thank the Father, not me."

Hewett learned that the healer took no pay from the thousands who waited for his words, and that he made no pretensions to special powers. Everything Schlatter did was simple, straightforward and without hocus-pocus. He had only one piece of paraphernalia besides his Bible — a copper rod about the size of a baseball bat, encased in a leather holster, which he kept always near him. The newspapers built him into a nationwide sensation, and the crowds came from great distances to be touched by him.

When the cold winter weather came to Denver in December, Schlatter announced that his mission was ended there, even though the waiting line was still blocks long. His host gave him a large white horse which Schlatter was seen riding southward. Hewett learned later that the man stopped for a few days' rest at the home of a friend, Don Mariano Larragoite, in the little settlement of La Joya in northern New Mexico. He next traveled over the old trails, avoiding the cities, until he reached the ranch at Datil owned by a woman who had gone to the Fox home to meet him and who later became a warm friend of the Hewetts — Ada McPherson Morley, widow of railroad builder William Raymond Morley. Years later Mrs. Morley's daughter, Agnes Cleaveland, who was a young girl living with her mother in the log ranch home known as The White House in Datil at the time of Schlatter's visit, wrote a chapter about it in her book *No Life for a Lady*.

As that story relates, during the time Schlatter remained at the hospitable Morley ranch it was as if he needed to hide from the notoriety that had been built around him in the national press. During the three months that he remained secluded in an upper room, Schlatter recalled that the Healer and His disciples had often found it necessary to retreat into the wilderness when the throngs pressed too closely for too long. He told Mrs. Morley, "The Father has directed me to a safe retreat. I must restore my spiritual powers in seclusion and prayer."[1]

Schlatter kept his mind active by dictating to Mrs. Morley a manuscript, *The Life of the Harp in the Hands of the Harper,* which she later caused to be published. He kept his powerful body in good physical trim by daily twirling his copper rod like a baton. The ranch people estimated that the rod must weigh at least forty pounds, but it seemed to require no effort for the man who swung it tirelessly. He was eventually recognized by a Mexican washerwoman who promptly spread the news, and the people from miles around began to camp in the Morley dooryard. Schlatter, knowing that the press would soon learn of and advertise his reappearance even in this remote spot, told Mrs. Morley, "I must go."

He saddled his white horse Butte and tied the leather case with its brass rod to the saddle, then asked Mrs. Morley to walk with him that he might talk with her. When she returned hours later she was in a state of ecstasy. To her daughter Agnes she reported that the healer had promised he would return to Datil, and in the meantime she was not to be misled by false evidence of his death. Mrs. Morley, who became more and more immersed in mysticism, quoted him as saying, "The Father has told me that Datil is the place He has selected for the New Jerusalem. Wait for me."[2]

After his departure a strangely bent cross about ten feet high, seemingly painted with whitewash, appeared on the log wall of the Morley ranch house. Mrs. Morley insisted that no one knew how it got there. No tracks, no ladder and no whitewash on the ranch explained it. Agnes Morley Cleaveland's chapter concludes with the statement that they learned some ten years later from the newspapers of Schlatter's death, but for the rest of her life Mrs. Morley behaved as if in the presence of the unusual man. "The home life went on around her, but she was no longer interested in it. She was now sure that a shortcut to the Eternal City was to be opened through the tortuous mountains of human struggle."[3]

Actually, it was Edgar Hewett who uncovered the ultimate adventure of the healer with the copper rod. His account of it will appear as the events unfolded.

During Edgar's years as superintendent of teacher training at Colorado State Normal School the Hewetts continued their summer journeyings, and as he talked of his discoveries among the ancient ruins Edgar began to be known as an amateur archaeologist. He earned his Master's Degree in Pedagogy in 1898, the same year that Charley Wallace garnered his Bachelor's at the University of Nebraska and proceeded to graduate work. Edgar was one step ahead at this point, but Charley soon overtook him in graduate studies at Nebraska and the University of Chicago.

Among the ancient sites that fascinated Hewett were the ruins found on the Pajarito Plateau of the Jemez Mountains in north central New Mexico, the setting for Bandelier's *The Delight Makers.* Centuries before, a volcanic eruption had left a

Edgar Lee Hewett, high-school principal, ca. 1889. Courtesy of the School of American Research.

great crater, now softened to a vast meadow where streams wandered into small lakes, the curling heads of gramma grass ripened into rich feed for deer, antelope and cattle, and the winter snows lay until late spring under the bordering pines.

The ashes laid down by the ancient eruption formed a broad rim of soft, friable grey-brown tufa which eroded through the years into valleys between steep cliff faces. The north-facing sides of the valleys were covered by scrub oak and pine; the south-facing sides were usually more sheer and barren except for tiny, sparse plants. In the cliffs where the southern exposure was warmed by the winter sun, the Ancient Ones had found shallow caves. Deepening the caves and adding outside rooms, the cliff dwellers occupied many favorable places on the Pajarito Plateau. These ancestors of modern Pueblo people also built the multistory houses that lay in rubbled ruins on the valley floor at El Rito de los Frijoles and on the jutting mesas of Puyé, Otowi, Sankowi'i, and Tsirege.

These were the sites Bandelier had visited and made his own. In the years while Hewett was acquiring his start in the teaching profession, Bandelier was struggling to build support for American archaeology in the learned societies and museums of the eastern seaboard. His father's bank in Highland, Illinois had failed, and after his father fled the scene Adolph was actually indicted as being partially responsible for the failure, though he had never been an officer of the bank and knew little of its operations. When his brother-in-law, Maurice Huegy, committed suicide as a result of the financial fiasco, Adolph found himself responsible for two young cousins, Lizzie and Emma. He moved the entire family to Santa Fe in 1885 and established them in a rambling adobe house on De Vargas Street. More relatives and friends came to visit there, putting an added strain on Adolph's precarious resources. Bandelier supplemented his stipend of $1,200 a year by writing articles for newspapers and reports for scientific journals. When the Archaeological Institute, short of funds, dropped him from the payroll, he offered lessons to Santa Fe townspeople in Spanish, French and German, but found few takers. At one time he considered turning to the law through apprenticing himself in the office of Eugene A. Fiske, but he soon gave it up. Even his novel, *The Delight Makers,* which eventually became a classic, never made much money for the author.

Beginning in late 1885 and continuing through 1886, Bandelier's financial condition was improved by several commissions. Archbishop Salpointe of the Santa Fe archdiocese employed him to write a history of the missions for presentation to Pope Leo XII, and two friends involved in the Hemenway Expedition at Zuni, Frank H. Cushing and Frederick W. Hodge, secured funds for him to go to Mexico City to pursue some archival investigations that would supplement their work. From that time on, although he still maintained the Santa Fe home, Bandelier's activities centered in Mexico and, later, South America.

In the years between 1890 and 1896, when Hewett's travels in southern Colorado and New Mexico were developing in him a lively interest in the history and preservation of the ruins he visited, several of Bandelier's publications strengthened his knowledge. The English version of *The Delight Makers* appeared in 1890, and Bandelier's *Final Report of Investigations among the Indians of the Southwestern United States, Carried on Mainly in the Years from 1880 to 1885* appeared among the papers of the Archaeological Institute, American Series for 1890-1892. Both were stimulating and must have whetted the appetite of the budding archaeologist Hewett had become. He discussed his interest with his academic colleagues and soon was being invited to lecture about it. Among those who heard of his explorations and were stimulated by his knowledge was Frank Springer, a wealthy landowner in northeastern New Mexico.

Springer was a native of Iowa who had migrated to New Mexico while Edgar was still a boy on the family farm in Illinois. He established a legal practice in the village of Cimarron and shortly became a leading member of the New Mexico Bar. As attorney for the trustees of the famed Maxwell Land Grant, Springer was influential in drafting legislation that led to the establishment of the Court of Private Land Claims for adjudicating the tangled titles to Spanish land grants. In addition to the law, Springer had been trained as a paleontologist, and found his adopted state a rich field for research and scientific study.

When the scientific community living in Las Vegas (then the most important town in the Territory of New Mexico) became interested in the ancient ruins of the area, Springer told them, "There's a professor in Greeley who knows more concerning these ruins than we do. Suppose we invite him to give us a course of lectures."[4]

Hewett accepted, and out of that lecture course a friendship developed that was to be a significant influence on Frank Springer and Edgar Hewett for the rest of their lives. Because of the admiration and trust between the two men, they were able to promote some of the most important institutions in the Southwest. The first of these was a new state normal school for the training of teachers in Las Vegas, New Mexico. Springer was named by the governor to the board of regents, and he persuaded them to accept the young educator from Greeley as head of the college.

In October 1898, Edgar Lee Hewett became the first president of the Normal University at Las Vegas. His contract, dated August 5, 1898, called for a beginning salary of $2,000, payable in twelve monthly installments, and was to run for five years unless previously terminated by mutual consent. He agreed to accept no other paid employment unless permission was given by the regents. Hewett was thirty-three years old; in the move from Greeley to Las Vegas he came of age as an educator. Up to this time he had worked under older men whose views colored his thinking. Now he had a brand new institution of his own to shape, and he set about it with enthusiasm. The president was a busy man as he recruited promising young instructors and stimulated enrollment.

Among the instructors was Kenneth Chapman, a young Indiana-born artist who came to Las Vegas for his health. After graduation from high school, Chapman had been enrolled at the Chicago Art Institute for five months when the death of his father brought an end to his studies. He then became a commercial artist and was employed by several firms — including a farm journal published in St. Louis — before he suffered a breakdown which forced him to quit his job and go west. Unable to find employment in Las Vegas, he began to paint watercolors of the New Mexico scene which he exhibited at the Harvey house in Las Vegas, La Castañeda, for sale to tourists. Hewett liked Chapman's work and, although the young man had no teaching experience, offered him the position of art instructor at the Normal University. Chapman gratefully accepted and thus began his long association with Hewett and Frank Springer.

Hewett had ideas that were not in accord with current academic practice. He thought young people could gain more from field trips than they learned in classrooms and libraries; he believed that the one-to-one relationship between professor and student was essential. In faculty recruiting he sought advice from colleges where the departments were outstanding, and when he was persuaded to accept young women as heads of science departments he was delighted to find that they were quite capable of leading their students into the surrounding countryside to learn geology or botany firsthand.

The Normal University included a high school department. The entire course of study was under the president's guidance, and thus he felt that the basic philosophy was his responsibility. He must plan the budget and persuade the Territorial Legislature to accept it. The staff was so small that the details of daily administration must cross his desk; and just to be sure that he did not lose touch with the classroom, he scheduled himself to teach courses in archaeology and anthropology.

With a young president and teachers who were recent graduates, the small student body enjoyed the give-and-take of one big happy family. They loved it, but some conservative observers were critical of a college that encouraged young people to traipse around the countryside in pursuit of education. How could picnic lunches contribute to scholarship?

Edgar and Cora lived modestly in Las Vegas and, because their early training had taught them thrift, saved enough to buy a summer place in the beautiful narrow valley where the headwaters of the Pecos River formed a rushing trout stream. Since their little ranch was only a few miles from the ancient pueblo of Pecos which had been the destination of Bandelier's first field trip, Hewett could easily continue his summer work at the ruin of the village which had once been the northern outpost of the Pueblos against the Plains Indians.

Pecos had been a multistoried communal village, built high-walled against invaders and stepped down to interior plazas and kivas. It was still inhabited by a remnant of its people when the Americans first drove their wagons over the rutted Santa Fe Trail and bivouacked in the lee of its bulk. Its long abandoned Franciscan mission had been one of the most awesome in the Southwest. Now the massive walls were crumbling, though they still stood out as a landmark against the sky. A huge, rounded mound covered with weeds and wildflowers was all that was visible of the ruined town adjoining the mission. Hewett later summed up his feelings for New Mexico's old missions and his desire to preserve them:

> ...our archaic missions — Pecos, Jemez, Gran Quivira, Quarai, Abo — these are monuments of religious fervor that recognize no limits of time and distance, and hardship. They were hoary with age when California's well-advertised missions were being founded; they were ancient when our Declaration of Independence was being signed. They are period-markers in the history of our great Southwest and if a commonwealth that owes its characteristic charm to that crusading spirit will enable us to do it, we will preserve not only the stones of these venerable monuments, but the atmosphere of sanctity which should be their best protection. We will allow no vandal hands to destroy or restore them, and let their noble walls testify to the spirit that built them. In short, the preservation of these monuments means the establishment of sanctuaries where a spirit of reverence may

abide. We will not put back a single block of stone more than necessary to arrest destruction, and we will let no work of our hands deface the work of theirs, nor belie the spirit that wrought them; for that spirit lives in every chapel in the Southwestern land and blesses simple native homes with a peace more precious than worldly wealth. When it is important for the information of the public, make a model of a building or a restoration on paper, clearly indicating where it is conjectural, and let it go at that.[5]

On their visits to Santa Fe Edgar and Cora usually stayed at St. Vincent Sanitorium, which was a sort of hotel-adjunct to the town's only hospital. Cora was frail—her health became a matter of increasing concern. In Santa Fe, Edgar found friends who shared his interest in New Mexico's vast wealth of prehistoric remains, and in the living Indians descended from the Ancient Ones who built those ruined habitations. In 1898, about the time he moved from Greeley to Las Vegas, Hewett helped to found the Archaeological Society of New Mexico. Among its members he discovered some associates whose friendship would be lasting, and some whose later opposition would be formidable. Among the friends were John R. McFie and Paul A. F. Walter.

McFie was an Illinois lawyer who had been appointed registrar of the U. S. Land Office in Las Cruces, New Mexico in 1884. He later formed a partnership and practiced his profession until President McKinley appointed him as associate justice of the territorial supreme court. This appointment necessitated a move to Santa Fe, where he first established his living quarters on the top floor of the old Palace Hotel. McFie's rooms became a rendezvous for the growing group of "lay archaeologists" whose happy hunting ground covered the whole Southwest— Bandelier, Charles Lummis and Hewett among them. Judge McFie was elected president of the newly formed Archaeological Society of New Mexico, and held the position for the next thirty-two years. Probably the idea for forming the organization incubated in his rooms.

Paul A. F. Walter came to Santa Fe in 1899 to serve on the editorial staff of the city's prestigious newspaper, the *Santa Fe New Mexican*. Except for a brief abortive move to California in 1912, he was to call Santa Fe home for the rest of his long, productive life. The association that began in the judge's rooms and was carried on later in the McFie home, after the family moved to join husband and father, grew into a bond that made McFie, Walter, Hewett, and Springer a quartet that shaped much of the cultural life of Santa Fe for half a century.

The members of the Archaeological Society, including Bandelier, were addicted to prolific note keeping from which many of them developed impressive bibliographies, but there seems to have been no Boswell among them to record the gossipy details of their interactions as friends. The contrast in their output is interesting. Judge McFie's writings were largely official, in the form of legal opinions or as letters written to colleagues about projects of mutual concern. Bandelier kept a journal, which only recently has been published in segments. It is strongly colored by the state of his health or his mental attitude at the moment. He was given to complaining about his associates, and no doubt worked off a lot of his dissatisfaction with the state of the world by confiding it to the diary. Except for *The Delight Makers*, his writing prepared for publication was intended for specialists interested in factual data about the current state of archaeological material or in the archival background. Charles Lummis was a journalist by inclination and a photographer by trade. His writings were for popular consumption — enthusiastic, dramatic and often somewhat imaginary accounts of his adventures in the Southwest. Although he had many quarrels with his associates through the years, he is generally laudatory in his published work. Paul A. F. Walter spent a large part of his career as an editor; most of his writing is sober, factual reporting. Whenever he wrote an account of an associate it was carefully composed, never gossipy or scandalous in any way. Hewett kept notes on everything: descriptions of ruins, conversations with Indian guides, anecdotes heard on the trail and around the campfire. They were intended merely to refresh his own memory, and once he had used them for scientific reports or informal essays he destroyed them.

One can imagine the lively interchange of information and opinion when these men met. Santa Fe has always been a yeasty place for ideas, and these young, ambitious men originated a continuing series of projects, stimulating one another to work for their accomplishment.

In its roles as the capital of a Spanish and later a Mexican province, and then of a newly accepted territory of the United States, Santa Fe was also a center for political intrigue which overflowed into social and business associations. Frank Springer and his brother Charles were political activists; Hewett soon discovered that he needed legislative support for his struggling new college although he had no great desire to show a high political profile; Judge McFie and Paul A. F. Walter preferred to play roles as powers-behind-the-throne, motivating others to play the leader's part.

Among the members of the Archaeological Society was a former chief justice of the territorial supreme court, L. Bradford Prince, who had received his legal training and begun his political career in New York State. After a stormy period as chief justice, Prince resigned and was out of political office for several years until President Benjamin Harrison appointed him governor of the territory, a post he held from 1889 to 1893. During this time Governor and Mrs. Prince lived in the old adobe Palace where Lew Wallace was writing *Ben Hur* when Bandelier first came to Santa Fe. Prince, whose ancestors had come over on the Mayflower, was an ardent student of history and a leader in the Historical Society of New Mexico. Some of the space in the eastern end of the Palace had been set aside for the territorial library and the Historical Society. When Prince moved out of the governor's apartments he continued to visit the society's rooms almost daily. He shared with Hewett an interest in the mission churches of New Mexico, although the two were to clash bitterly for control of the Palace.

Among the president's duties at Las Vegas Normal University was a considerable amount of speech-making, and Edgar Hewett was ready for it. He started off with an inaugural address, then, to his first graduating class of thirteen members in 1899, he spoke on *Man and God*, which was a subject large enough to cover almost anything he might want to say about his developing philosophy of life. The two speeches were published in a magazine called *The Southwest*. Having found a format that seemed to work, he used broad themes for his baccalaureate addresses to succeeding classes: *Man and Nature* (1900); *Man and Man* (1901); *Man and Self* (1902); and *Man and Destiny* (1903). His five addresses, published by the Arts and Crafts Press, San Diego, became his first bound volume.

During these same years he prepared three articles for incorporation in the annual territorial report sent by the Governor of New Mexico to the Secretary of the Interior: *New Mexico Normal University* (1900) was an account of the beginnings of the new college; *Archaeology of New Mexico* (1902 and 1903 reports) was an overview of the territory's resources in this field. (Hewett's first anthropological paper, entitled "A Zuñi Creation Myth," had appeared in *The Southwest* in 1899.) He was building a professional reputation that would serve him in the academic world.

From the knowledge gained on his summer vacation travels he had built a hobby which was becoming a profession. Out of his enthusiasm for the ancient places grew the conviction that action must be taken to save them or they would vanish forever. He and his friends succeeded in arousing the concern of federal authorities. In the spring of 1903, Congressman J. F. Lacey of Iowa, chairman of the House Committee on Public Lands, accepted Hewett's invitation to come and look. The two men spent a couple of weeks in the saddle, traveling from one prehistoric ruin to another. As an outgrowth of this concern Lacey prepared a bill providing for the protection of American antiquities on public lands, and solicited support in Congress.

About 1900 Hewett made his first trip to Washington, seeking to meet important national figures in the scientific world. One of his early encounters was with John Wesley Powell, on whom Bandelier had paid an initial call twenty years earlier. Powell, who had lost an arm in Civil War combat, had never allowed his handicap to slow him down. He headed the strenuous Grand Canyon Expedition mounted by the Smithsonian in 1869, and was later placed in charge of that institution's anthropological investigations. Beginning in the year in which Bandelier met him — 1880 — Powell had for fourteen years been director of the United States Geological Survey. When Hewett first met him he was in his late sixties, and had become a legend among Southwestern pioneering heroes.

In Washington Hewett came to the attention of Alice Cunningham Fletcher, a quiet, mild-mannered woman who was one of the country's leading anthropologists although she had not taken it up as a serious study until she was forty years old. He also met William H. Holmes and Frederick W. Putnam, two nationally known leaders in the scientific field. All of these people helped to strengthen Hewett's feeling that his future lay in the study of mankind. He wanted to take back all they could teach him to his students in Las Vegas.

5

SOME BRIDGES ARE BURNED

When I decided to specialize in the study of humanity, I concluded that I must seek first-hand knowledge of my subject. So my work has taken me into many lands and into contact with most of the peoples whom we call civilized and many that we consider backward. — ELH

Some friendships formed through national organizations during Hewett's tenure in Las Vegas were to help launch him as a professional archaeologist; the association with Alice Cunningham Fletcher and William H. Holmes provided his most steadfast supporters.

Alice Fletcher came into scientific study by way of such philanthropic works as were considered proper for a Victorian lady. One of these organizations was the Women's Indian Association, dedicated to the proposition that Indians should be helped to purchase land of their own in order to build homes away from Reservation life. Alice Fletcher was appointed administrator of the funds the women raised for this purpose, and became a dedicated leader in the cause. It has been a deep irony in the history of western Indians that so many of their staunch admirers and defenders have failed to understand their cultural approach to the ownership of land. With the Plains Indians as well as the more sedentary Pueblos of New Mexico and Arizona, land was for tribal use, not for individual possession. Fields for growing maize and squash were assigned to individuals and used by them, but were not owned as Europeans and Americans understand land ownership. The vast prairies with their uncounted buffalo, deer and antelope herds had invisible subdivisions into traditional hunting grounds for tribal groups as long as they could hold off trespassers, but the concept of taking title, paying taxes, buying and selling — in short, making the land a basis for a family's prosperity or poverty —

43

Alice Cunningham Fletcher, ca. 1890, chairman of the managing board, School of American Archaeology, 1907-1912. Courtesy of the School of American Research.

simply did not exist in the Indians' inherited consciousness.

In the course of promoting Indian integration into the white man's concept of land ownership, Alice Fletcher met Thomas Henry Tibbles, an experienced frontiersman, minister, journalist, and do-gooder in the cause of Indian rights. Through him she arranged to get some firsthand knowledge of how Caddoan, Sioux and Pawnee Indians lived and thought. She had never camped out in her life when she arrived in Omaha, Nebraska on September 1, 1881 and was met by Tibbles and Bright Eyes La Fleche, an educated woman of the Omaha tribe who later became Tibbles' wife. They proceeded to initiate Fletcher into Indian ways.

Alice bore the hardships of her introduction into tribal life gamely, making friends among the Indians who sensed her respect for their cultural achievement. The women knew that her delight in their gifts — horn spoons, wooden bowls, artifacts made from buffalo hide — was genuine. If they had reservations about her enthusiasm for basing their economic future on individual ownership and cultivation of land, they did not succeed in destroying her conviction that it was the only way.

Back in Washington to work on the Indians' behalf through her influential social and political contacts, Alice Fletcher helped to draft and secure passage of the Dawes Severalty Act of 1882. This legislation granted apportionment of Omaha lands among the tribal members, to insure "both their land and their future citizenship rights." Surplus unapportioned land was to be sold to the government for the benefit of the tribe, and the proceeds used to buy seed, livestock and farm machinery. A year later she returned to the Omahas with a government assignment to supervise the allotment of the land. Her assistant was Francis La Fleche, brother of Bright Eyes, who was to become her collaborator in numerous Indian studies.

During the next ten years Fletcher was employed by the government to supervise land allotments among the Omaha, Pawnee, Winnebago, and Nez Perce tribes. Among them she came to be known as the "Measuring Woman," whom they deeply respected. An illness that may have been rheumatic fever left her with a permanent limp, but she did not allow it to slow her down. Indeed, she turned a period of enforced invalidism on the reservation into an opportunity to study Plains Indian music and its role in religion and social life. Her ethnographic studies, each detail faithfully recorded and checked for accuracy, became early classics of American anthropology, but her zeal for solving the Indians' economic plight in a manner totally foreign to their culture tended to discredit her for many years with later students after it became evident that the allotment of lands was a failure.

As her approach to the Amerindian cultures turned from an amateur's enthusiasm to the more critical study of a professional, Alice Fletcher became the protégé of Frederick W. Putnam, who was curator of the Peabody Museum and a leader in the American Association for the Advancement of Science. Putnam, who had approved Bandelier's first foray into American research, arranged in 1891 for a special fellowship set up by Mrs. Mary Copley Thaw of Pittsburg that would enable Fletcher to pursue Indian studies for the rest of her life; for his help Fletcher considered Putnam the fairy godfather of her ethnological career. It will be remembered that Fletcher and Putnam were two members of the executive committee of the fledgling Archaeological Institute of America who were strongly influenced by Morgan in the decision to sponsor Bandelier's research in the Southwest. By the time Hewett met them some twenty years later in Washington the Institute had grown much stronger, though it was still plagued by lack of funds adequate for its ambitious undertakings and by the tug-of-war between the traditional classicists like Dr. Norton and the growing body of specialists in ancient American cultures.

The most influential person Hewett met in Washington at this time, however, was William H. Holmes, who was soon to be appointed chief of the Bureau of Ethnology at the Smithsonian (1904). Hewett developed for Holmes the same kind of deference that characterized his admiration for his boyhood teachers. Holmes was The Chief, and needed no other identification. Edgar joined the American Association for the Advancement of Science and was invited to read a paper at the annual meeting in Washington in 1902. Most members of the Archaeological Institute also belonged to the AAAS, and because their leaders formed a sort of interlocking directorate it is sometimes difficult to remember which organization sponsored a certain cause or spawned a certain controversy. Membership in professional groups was essential, and papers presented to their assemblies often were later published in scientific journals. Hewett's maiden effort was politely received and promptly forgotten.

By this time the president of Las Vegas Normal University had developed for classroom use a syllabus of lectures in anthropology, which he prepared for publication in 1903. It formalized a course of twenty lectures, with a foreword emphasizing what he regarded as the two main lines of scientific study: the science of life (biology) and the science of man (anthropology). This material was published in 1904 in the *American Anthropologist* under the title, "Anthropology and Education."

Edgar Hewett was now thirty-eight years old, and the twin branches of his life interest were firmly established. For twenty-five years since his enrollment in high school he had been soaking up and testing the ideas that his teachers offered. Now he entered the next period of his life — the building of institutions — for which his five-year contract at Las Vegas had been an apprenticeship.

New Mexico's governor during Hewett's years at the Normal University was Miguel Antonio Otero, a lively political partisan whose family mercantile firm had brought him to Las Vegas with the coming of the railroad. The reports written by Hewett on the archaeology of the Territory were incorporated in Otero's official reports to the Secretary of the Interior for the years 1902 and 1903. In them Hewett urged that the entire Pajarito Plateau be set aside as a national park, preserving the extensive ruins for posterity. The proposal brought Hewett to national political attention.

In the Territory's shifting struggle for political power Governor Otero and

Hewett's supporter Frank Springer sometimes found themselves working together, but they were more often opponents. Both were deeply interested in the fledgling college at Las Vegas but in firm disagreement as to how it should be run. Although Hewett had built and strengthened the institution every year during his tenure, some people thought his philosophy of education too liberal. Many thought his preoccupation with summer archaeology, in which he was involving his students, was a waste of time. His notion of withdrawing enormous acreage from private use to form national parks met with resistance from stockmen and big landowners. In 1903 Governor Otero's partisans on the board of regents decided not to renew Hewett's contract.

Hewett had surrounded himself with a faculty of excellent young scholars, most of whom were loyal to him; the student body made few complaints. He might have made a fight over the regents' decision, but he recognized that it would not be in the best interest of the school; even if he won, his future usefulness was impaired. He submitted his resignation without protest. It was the first serious defeat of his career.

No matter how unjustified the dismissal, it is a jolt to any man to have five years' work judged inadequate. As soon as he could put aside his private disappointment, however, Hewett took stock of his assets. Behind him were fifteen years of teaching experience, bolstered by the hard-won bachelor's and master's degrees in pedagogy. He had enjoyed being president of the small college. It provided prestige, a reasonably good, safe salary, and the heady feeling of building a viable institution. He had gained a background in New Mexico politics, and savored the sense of power that comes with behind-the-scene battles with the legislature. These were plus considerations in seeking another position as a college administrator.

On the other hand, he considered his growing absorption in archaeology and anthropology. He had felt himself at a disadvantage in the scientific societies dominated by Easterners and centered around the distinguished group at Harvard and the Peabody Museum. He had seen Bandelier often on the defensive in seeking support from that group and knew that his friend alternated between an eager, almost abject appeal for sponsorship and annoyance that the leaders should be so irritatingly uncooperative.

Edgar had never lost sight of the goal he had set at the end of his high school years, and he still kept in touch with Charles Wallace. Even as Cora had accompanied him on his field trips and loyally helped him as the wife of a college president, so had Hulda Wallace worked with her husband in his literary studies and geological explorations. Now the Wallaces were about to embark on the next step—a doctorate from a German university. Edgar and Cora talked over the possibilities of a similar step. It would take money and daring to cut loose from all they had built to date. Would the gamble be too risky?

Edgar had tasted the thrill of archaeological research, the satisfaction of organizing his material into college courses and finding his name in print as an author in reputable scientific journals. Those things might well be combined with a job in some other college. Reluctance to cut himself off from a regular salary, plus the natural desire to continue in a field he found congenial, probably were the determining influences in his decision to seek another college presidency. He sent letters of application and sought references from those who had known his work at Greeley and Las Vegas. Included in the schools to which he applied were the universities of Arizona, Illinois and Wyoming and the Girls' Industrial College at Denton, Texas.

The record does not show how many interviews Hewett was granted in response to his applications, or whether he was given the opportunity to accept any offers, but it became increasingly clear to him that his background in small, little known Western colleges was not very impressive. Although the lack of a doctorate was not crucial, it was still an important consideration. He was no longer an aspiring young teacher, he was a mature administrator. If he was to go up instead of down, he must fortify his credentials.

Edgar and Cora decided to gamble on a European doctorate, even though it meant the sacrifice of most of their possessions. They had some small savings and they owned the little ranch on the headwaters of the Pecos River which had served as a retreat from college responsibilities. They owned household furniture, a team of horses, and a carriage. They decided that they must sell all their possessions except clothes and books.

The one sacrifice Edgar was most reluctant to make was the team of horses, Spider and Snoozer, that had replaced the ponies, Don and Dot, who used to draw the camp wagon in their honeymoon days. While Snoozer was just another horse among the many that Edgar had enjoyed, Spider was a special treasure, with a place in his master's affections exceeding even the favorites of his farm childhood. Spider later became the subject of an entire chapter in Hewett's book of anecdotes, *Campfire and Trail.*

Spider's gangling build and long legs had suggested the name Hewett gave him when he acquired the three-year-old to be used chiefly as a saddle horse. As the bay rounded out to maturity, he developed the proportions of a graceful thoroughbred. Although he teamed with Snoozer in pulling the camp wagon or the Hewett carriage, it was as the saddle companion of Edgar's solitary explorations that a close rapport developed between Spider and his master.

In the years between 1897 and 1902 when Hewett spent many summer weeks exploring and mapping the ruins of the Pajarito Plateau, Spider was often his only companion. Describing the role of the horse in these adventures, he wrote:

> If I had to work on foot, Spider followed like a faithful dog. If it meant
> a stiff climb out of a canyon, he negotiated it with the agility of a mountain
> goat. In hundreds of miles of that rough travel, I never knew him to
> stumble. If my day's stint took me twenty miles from camp and the return
> trip reached far into the night, I never needed to touch the rein. If, instead

of going back, I unsaddled, made my little camp fire, and started to prepare my bacon and coffee, Spider nipped his supper on whatever grass he could find, then came up to me to claim his two lumps of sugar — his sure reward for a task well done.[1]

Spider had been his partner when he made his tentative, preliminary excavations at Puyé, Tsirege, Sankowi'i, and nearby smaller sites where he scarcely scratched the surface enough to justify his survey observations. Now, after ten years of close companionship, Hewett felt that the horse had earned the right to "eternal pasture in the Vales of Paradise," and he could not bring himself to sell him. Instead, he arranged for the purchaser of the Valley Ranch on the Pecos to provide a life tenure for Spider. When Hewett was an old man he wrote, "Would that the primitive belief were valid and that you might accompany your master to the Happy Hunting Grounds or the Elysian Fields, or wherever we may find ourselves in the Hereafter."[2]

Many years later in a leaflet entitled *Call of the Spade,* Hewett summarized the feelings that impelled him to change the course of his career:

> Toward the end of my first two score years I burned my bridges. Through all the preparatory years, something had been tugging at me along with my various preoccupations. A knowledge of what man had thought and done in the past seemed vital to any sure vision of his future. In that I saw the cave man cracking stones together to set free flame to warm his cheerless world, and inching on "from dream to shining dream" through millenia to a day when men cracked an atom open to set free a world-shaking force. I saw the crude painting in his cave evolve through the slow march of time into the ceiling decorations of the Sistine Chapel; the pile of unhewn stones in front of his rock shelter into the miracle of a Parthenon; the homely clay idol on his altar into a Venus de Milo. There was nothing of all this in the history textbooks, but there were fragments of it in museums and art galleries and under refuse heaps and sand dunes and tropic jungles. I had to take part in recovering those lost glories of human existence. The call of the spade became too imperative to be resisted.
>
> I had been a picture-book archaeologist from the time I could devour old woodcuts and steel engravings of wonders of the ancient world, and could name the pictures long before I could read a caption. Through early life books supplied exciting adventures in human history and set aflame the passion to touch the soil from which great men and events had sprung. But the time came when experience at second hand was insufficient. I became a "dirt archaeologist."[3]

In addition to the call of the spade there was another feeling. Only dimly felt but steadily taking more definite shape was the growing conviction that he must burn his bridges because he was disenchanted with teaching. As he wryly commented, "I came to think that the Science of Pedagogy was trying to function without much basic knowledge of its subject matter."[4]

An additional tenet of his philosophy was expressed after his doctor's degree was safely secured: "Knowledge and reverence of nature, and respect for human values are well balanced in the great school of outdoors; and one who has the earth for his Alma Mater doesn't find academic credentials indispensable."[5]

Back in 1903, however, Edgar and Cora Hewett felt that two ventures had become essential to their progress — the academic credentials of a Ph.D. and extensive European travel.

In his letter of application to the University of Geneva listing his academic background, Hewett added that he had already done original research in geology, paleontology, anthropology, pedagogy, and archaeology. Perhaps that was laying it on a bit thick, but he could back up his claims with some evidence, and he was never a man to underestimate his ability to accomplish any task he set himself. Experience to date had convinced him that when he made up his mind to accomplish something, a way would open.

In cutting loose from a regular salary he had only himself and Cora to consider; as always Cora was willing to share any stringency their circumstances dictated. There were no children to be fed; Hewett's parents were not dependent on him for basic support — the older siblings who stayed close to the parental home were quite capable of helping there — and Cora's relatives made no demand on her.

When the sale of their assets had provided the necessary capital, the couple was ready to sail for Europe. The Hewetts were readers — they knew which literary shrines they would visit on their journey. Edgar had always been envious of Bandelier's fluency in languages, so useful in research. He now expected that the European experience would help to sharpen his language skills as well as enrich his general background. Cora's health was frail, but Edgar's robust strength could compensate for her weakness. He planned to carry her in his arms up steep flights of stairs, and for the more strenuous expeditions they could rent a wheelchair which he could push. The change of climate might be very beneficial for her, too.

Early in 1904, a few months after Edgar's contract at Las Vegas expired, they set out on the adventure that was to be both romantic and practical.

6

※ ¥ ※

THE DOCTORAL DEGREE AND
THE FELLOWSHIP YEAR

Can faith actually move mountains? Yes, it can bring
Alps and Andes to you. — ELH

The record of Hewett's first European venture is scattered in fragments throughout his writings, and it is not always possible to determine whether some of the experiences he describes occurred in 1904 or on subsequent trips. Charley Wallace went to Freiburg for his doctorate, but Hewett did not like the rigid German approach to higher learning. In the more relaxed and democratic freedom of Geneva he found graduate work an exciting adventure. Louis Wuarin and Edouard Naville became for him two more heroes of academic leadership whose lectures were not to be missed. Still smarting from the criticism of his innovations at Las Vegas, he was pleased to find that at Geneva men and women were equally accepted as students and professors, and a social commingling made for warm relationships. He wrote of the experience, "You climbed the Alps with them; with rucksack on back went on walking tours into Germany, France or Italy. You sat down with them to a lunch of wine and pretzels; and in their libraries and gardens you got what formal classroom lectures never convey."[1] He must have left Cora behind when he went mountain climbing or hiking, but she could enjoy the garden parties.

For his doctoral thesis Edgar submitted a proposal to write about the ancient communities of the American Southwest desert country — a topic in which he was already much more knowledgeable than his instructors. They would fill in his background in classical archaeology, however, and their teachings would broaden the base of his philosophy. Once Hewett had established himself with his mentors he worked out his own program. The university did not record classroom attendance or grade a candidate's progress. Achievement was measured in academic conference, so Hewett could free himself to take Cora to the places they had read and dreamed about.

The couple managed as much continental travel as time, funds and strength allowed, visiting archaeological sites and art museums as well as the literary shrines known through their classical reading. Frail Cora could not possibly match her husband's energy, but he divided his strength with her as he pushed the wheelchair to the places they were determined to see.

Back at the family home in Hopkins, Missouri, Edgar's father died in 1904. The older sons and the daughter had always remained farm people with no such unappeased drive as possessed Edgar to satisfy the hunger in his head. Hansen Hewett had been proud of his youngest, although his reticence would not allow him to praise. Edgar knew that his father had often been present in the back of the auditorium when he was making a public appearance in high school, and he treasured the memory of the excitement he had felt when his father was the most important and successful man he knew. Hansen Hewett was never able to rebuild the family fortunes after they moved to Missouri, but the obituary in the local newspaper described him as a good, kindly, God-fearing man, admired by all who knew him. It was one of the few clippings that Edgar could never bring himself to throw away.

On their return to the United States Edgar and Cora went to Washington, D.C., where Edgar began work under the auspices of the National Museum. He found his friendships there congenial, as he carried out the tasks assigned to him and tried to continue his own various projects. At the annual meeting of the American Academy for the Advancement of Science in Philadelphia during the holiday season late in 1904, he read a paper on "Ethnic Factors in Education." His bibliography shows the acceptance of several articles by archaeological and historical publications, for which he probably received some small remuneration. But the great concern of this period was with his wife's failing health.

Cora Whitford Hewett died in Washington in 1905. During the fourteen years of their marriage Edgar had been blessed with unstinting comfort and support from his wife. She joyously shared their early camping adventures, and when she found it necessary to remain at home while he went alone on the more strenuous expeditions she was no nagging, complaining invalid. In their last years together when it was sometimes necessary for Edgar to carry her from the house to the carriage, his tenderness for her was constant.

Cora was buried in Fairmount, Missouri. Among Hewett's correspondence is a copy of a letter addressed to a "little friend" who had sent him a rose from Cora's grave. It is one of the few letters of an intimate nature that he did not destroy:

> I remember once when we stood by Keats' grave in the lovely little
> cemetery a short way out of Rome, she spoke of the words of his

friends, that "It almost made one in love with death to think of resting in so sweet a place."

I think that way about Fairmount. Flowers and bird songs tell of life and joy. I believe in surrounding our loved ones with them while they are with us and when they go away for a little while, fill up the vacant places with the loveliest things that remain, and around everything and place that keeps them in our memory and us in their love throw all the beauty and fragrance that made our lives together joyous and blessed.[2]

The letter goes on to quote from Carlisle, "We have nothing to fear but fear."

With Cora's death something of his youthful exuberance went out of Edgar's life. As a memorial to her he established a scholarship; the first two recipients were a young brother and sister, children of a Greeley friend, whose need was brought to his attention.

Meanwhile Hewett plunged into filling the vacant place in his life with hard work. He stretched his slender resources to further his apprenticeship under the Eastern-based leaders in the scientific field; he worked on his doctoral thesis, trying to distill the essence of his studies and observations, wrestling with the translation into French which was required of him. Cora's death left him lonely but it also left him free of family responsibilities. He had always worked long hours. His rugged constitution could take sixteen, eighteen, even twenty hours a day of sustained effort, and he now drove himself with a sort of desperation.

While he had been informally associated for some eight years with the leaders in the Archaeological Institute and the Academy for the Advancement of Science, there is no evidence that they felt any special deference for his views or were impressed by the modest papers he had presented. However, the Annual Report of the Smithsonian Institution for 1904 which appeared about the time of Cora's death included Hewett's paper, "A General View of the Archaeology of the Pueblo Region," which was a spin-off of his work for his doctoral thesis. It recommended him to scholars as a man knowledgeable in a field that was wide open for exploration. Respect for him increased.

The Archaeological Institute of America, which was to play such a large part in Edgar's life, had been founded in 1879 by Charles Eliot Norton of Harvard. Professor Norton had a broad concept of education; he described teaching as "an activity directed for forming men's lives as a whole; not to impart narrow training for professions, not to inculcate masses of useless facts, nor again to preach moral goodness barren of the inspiration which beauty can give."[3]

Norton did not see the Institute as an academic conclave but as an active group to carry out expeditions in the field, gather new information and sponsor publications to disseminate what they found. The Institute ranks as one of the oldest of the country's continuous cultural organizations. For the first twenty-five years it was oriented toward Old World sites. The first daughter school was in Athens, then others were established in Rome, Jerusalem and Baghdad. There was never quite enough money to mount all the expeditions and explorations that the

founders yearned to carry out in traditional areas. They were reluctant to believe
that anything of cultural value could be found in the Americas, and most of them
felt that an expenditure of funds for ventures in the New World would be a total
waste. It seems likely that Edgar Hewett was first tolerated and then accepted
because his philosophy of education coincided with that of Norton and other
leading classicists, even though they never lost their reservations about the
importance of his field.

In an age when disciplined depth in study and a far-ranging breadth of

Balcony House, Mesa Verde, Colorado, 1907, before stabilization. Photograph by Jesse Nusbaum.
Courtesy of the Museum of New Mexico.

knowledge were the goals of an educated man, many of the pioneers of American
archaeology were perforce self-taught and came into the profession by way of
youthful hobbies. Morgan, Bandelier and Fletcher had all reached middle age before
they made the transition to professional status in anthropology, and the classical
men were inclined to some condescension about their importance. At the time when
Hewett moved onto the national scene in Washington, however, the
Americanists Alice Fletcher and Frederick Putnam were well accepted.
Fletcher was elected president of the American Anthropological Society in 1903
and president of the American Folklore Society in 1905. Putnam, a pupil of
Louis Agassiz, was by now in his mid-sixties. For some thirty years he had played a

leading role in popularizing American anthropology as a university study. His Peabody Museum provided a model and an inspiration for museums established across the country by his former associates and students.

After the Institute dropped Bandelier's stipend, its support for American exploration had languished. The committee on American Archaeology included members with prestige, however, and in 1905 they managed to pry loose a $600 stipend to finance a fellowship for a man working in the Southwest. The job may have been set up with Hewett in mind. In any case, he was available and eager to

Balcony House, Mesa Verde, Colorado, 1910, after repair and stabilization. Photograph by Jesse Nusbaum. Courtesy of the Museum of New Mexico.

undertake it, although the leaders were not very clear as to how they expected him to earn it.

Thomas Day Seymour, president of the Institute at that time, left the supervision of the new fellow entirely up to the American committee. Charles Bowditch, the committee chairman, passed the responsibility for setting up Hewett's duties to Fred Putnam, who served as temporary chairman while Bowditch went abroad. Bowditch did make a couple of suggestions. He proposed that Hewett's energies be spent to promote the growth of the local archaeological societies in the West. (This should in turn swell the Institute's coffers and membership roll.) Any time left could be spent working for the preservation of the cliff ruins in Colorado for which there was a growing favorable sentiment.

Putnam wrote to the other committee members, seeking advice. William H. Holmes, by now chief of the Bureau of Ethnology, had received a mandate from the Department of the Interior to designate an archaeologist qualified to investigate and report on Mesa Verde, and he thought that Hewett fitted the description. H. Walter Fewkes (who had been one of the witnesses to Cora's simple will) felt that in Hewett they had the man needed to combine respect for both the classical and the Americanist schools. From the Midwest, classical scholar Francis Kelsey at Ann Arbor sent along some informal instructions about developing the archaeological society in Colorado, and urged encouragement of the Southwest Archaeological Society in California where Charles Lummis was trying to promote a research project in northwestern Arizona.

Hewett consulted his friend Alice Fletcher in Washington. Her prime interest was in the humanist aspect of helping living Indians rather than in exploring ancient ruins, and she urged Hewett to follow his concern for studying Indians as *people* rather than as examples of esoteric cultures. Franz Boas (who was not always so tactful) wrote Putnam that since Hewett had already demonstrated considerable ability as a self-starter, he might be trusted to choose his own activities.

With all these mentors to guide him, Hewett spent January and February of 1906 preparing for work in the field and awaiting definite instructions. He went to the Mesa Verde area but found the snow too deep for travel and returned to Santa Fe to wait for more propitious weather. Putnam finally sent instructions that Hewett should start work as soon as possible, making a comparative study of the culture — especially the art and architecture — of the Pueblo sites he already knew and those of the ancient sites in Mexico. The object was to ascertain whether there was any ethnical connection between the two groups. This decision provided a definite goal, yet was broad enough to let Hewett choose his sites.

The new fellow was quite willing to try to please all members of the committee, particularly where their suggestions coincided with his own pet ideas. The American Antiquities Act, presented by Congressman Lacey after their horseback trip, was before the Congress; the preservation of the Mesa Verde area naturally interested him. Holmes wrote that there was urgency about making his recommendation on Mesa Verde, because the U.S. Land Office had ordered a survey of the northern boundary of the Southern Ute Reservation. Unless proper steps were taken the ancient ruins might be sold to unsympathetic private ownership. As for building the local societies, Hewett liked working with people and was a natural organization man. When the snow melted he hied himself back to Mesa Verde and made some notes on the desirability of putting it beyond the reach of private greed. To back up his report he entrusted responsibility for a field survey to a friend, George Mills of Mancos, Colorado. Proceeding to Colorado Springs and Denver, he enlisted the interest of people who would be locally influential and would promote the federal government's acquisition of the property. Two groups soon became vocal on the subject: the Colorado Archaeological Society and the Colorado Federation of Womens Clubs, which listed conservation of antiquities high among its priorities.

Hewett touched base at the Arizona project Lummis was promoting, dashed to Washington for consultation, went back to outfit himself in Santa Fe, and took time for a quick return trip to Denver. It was hard to keep track of his whereabouts, and Bowditch commented in some irritation that Hewett appeared to be dissipating his energies, trying to do everything and accomplishing nothing. He underestimated his man. Hewett never squandered either time or energy.

Through the years Edgar had been storing up fragments of knowledge about Pueblo culture gathered from his surveys, from the folksay heard at Indian firesides, and from his reading. He now set about organizing this material and filling in the gaps. After Bowditch's outburst he knew it was time to move into his new field. He proceeded to Casas Grandes, Chihuahua and set out to find the material he needed for the regional comparison. One of his unfinished chores was to forward a preliminary report on Mesa Verde. He apologized for the lack of the final map he had been unable to complete in the field but which Mills was completing for him, and summarized his recommendations: "There can be no doubt as to the advisability of having the government assume control of this great archaeological district and opening it to the public."[4]

Some time later, in one of the rare flashes of humor that Hewett permitted to creep into his correspondence, he wrote Mills: "I am glad to learn from the General Land Office that your survey has at last been approved and I trust that the money for the same will be available at least by the time you need it for old age."[5] Mesa Verde became a national park in 1906.

Hewett next proceeded to wander through northern Mexico, much as he had surveyed the field on the United States side of the border, by wagon, horseback, or on foot. He hired local guides and listened to local folksay. In his reconnaissance of the Piedras Verdes River valley on the eastern slope of the Sierra Madres, he used a local youth as a guide and thus learned the second chapter in the story of the healer, Francis Schlatter, who had ridden away from the Morley ranch in Datil some ten years earlier. The guide pointed out a grave marked by a wooden cross under a lone pine tree, and told Hewett that as a boy he had herded the family cows in that valley. Early one winter morning he saw a man covered by a grey blanket, apparently asleep under the pine tree. Hobbled on the hillside nearby was a big white horse wearing a fine saddle, ready to be ridden. When the boy drove the cows down the valley in the afternoon the man had not moved, and on drawing nearer for a better look the boy saw that he was dead. The child raced to the village and notified officials. At the ensuing inquest they decided that the man had died of freezing and starvation.

Intrigued by the story, Hewett asked his guide to describe the man and was told that he was very large and wore his hair long. The combination of such a man riding such a fine white horse brought Schlatter to remembrance, so Hewett asked to be taken to the *jefe politico* of the village. There he learned that the white horse had been ridden by the children until he died of old age, but the big saddle bearing the trademark of a well-known Denver saddler remained, as well as a worn Bible found in the pocket, with the name of Francis Schlatter on the flyleaf. In the village, also, was the strange object found attached to the saddle — a solid copper rod about the size and shape of a baseball bat, encased in a leather holster.

It was evident why the healer had been unable to keep his promise to return. Hewett jotted down in his notebook the account of the Alsatian peasant's lonely death on a Mexican hillside and put it away. It would be sixteen years before he once again took up the story of Schlatter and his copper rod.

When he camped alone among the pines on the crest of the Sierra Madre, Edgar lived again the days and nights of his life with Cora. He remembered how they had worked, planned, played, and traveled together, sharing tasks, pleasures and disappointments. With him Cora had always been happy, always filled with courage. Everyone who knew her loved her. As Edgar brooded by his little fire, he had to fight off desolation and convince himself that he must carry on as he and Cora had planned.

When the 1906 summer fieldwork in Chihuahua was completed, Hewett returned to Santa Fe and thence to Washington. For the next year he was a traveling representative of the Institute, visiting societies, lecturing, working his notes into formal reports, and most important of all, promoting the idea that it would be a good time for the Institute to locate a headquarters of Southwestern Archaeology in Santa Fe. Congressman Lacey had persuaded Congress to pass the Antiquities Act in 1906, and constant vigilance would be needed to carry out its mandate.

Meanwhile, Hewett incorporated his survey material into articles published in the *American Anthropologist* and continued to put his doctoral dissertation into "acceptable French." It won for him, two years later, his coveted degree; he had the cherished parchment framed to hang on his library wall. Without Cora to share it his success didn't seem quite as important as it had when they sold their security to seek the degree, but it was a bulwark against his critics. Once, when he mentioned to Frank Springer the failure of his presidency at Las Vegas, Springer rejected the idea, assuring Hewett that he had outgrown the college post and was ready to move on into his true life work. Springer was a source of steady support for Hewett's career; throughout their long friendship Hewett sought his advice on every important project, keeping a confidential file of their correspondence so that they might freely exchange ideas.

It was during Hewett's fellowship year that a controversy arose in Colorado which provided a sort of comic relief (though nobody thought it was funny at the time). A group of promoters decided to move a whole cliff-dwellers' village from its original site to become a tourist attraction in Manitou, Colorado. The project was challenged by those who sought a broad application of the Lacey Law, and they wanted Hewett to help them enforce it.

7

THE CLIFF DWELLINGS
OF MANITOU SPRINGS

*They [the archaeologists] are the conservationists of
culture. They may seem to be doing an infinite amount
of disputing over things that are of little importance
whichever way they go.... These are gropings in the
wilderness.* —ELH

A modest news story that appeared in the *Colorado Springs Gazette* for May 1, 1906
precipitated an argument that, oddly enough, was to be remembered in connection
with Hewett for the rest of his life.

CLIFF DWELLINGS TO BE PUT IN CANON
CLOSE TO MANITOU

Colorado Springs and Ohio Capitalists Plan Novel Scenic
Feature for Edification of Summer Throngs of Tourists
Will Spend $50,000

The announcement stated that one of the most picturesque canyons in the
Manitou area, currently belonging to a gentleman named James James, had been
chosen as the site for the new attraction and advised:

The plan of the promoters is to secure cliff dwellings from Southwestern Utah, near the state line, bring them to Manitou, and rebuild
them in the cañon which they are prepared to buy. These relics will not
be imitations. They will not be reproductions, but the rude and prehistoric
buildings themselves. The towers, block houses, pottery relics, ladders,
places of worship, and everything that remains of a cliff dwelling will be
brought to Manitou...on freight cars, stone by stone. Each stone will be

59

numbered, and a surrounding diagram will be kept which will enable the builders to erect the structures just as they now stand in the cañon. They will not be restored. It is the idea of the promoters to have ruins, actual ruins, here in Manitou.[1]

Some opposition evidently was anticipated, as the story included the assurance that the ruins which the promoters intended to move were located on private land, outside the Indian reservation and not under control of the federal government. No legal difficulties were anticipated.

The Manitou citizen backing this scheme was W. S. Crosby, who, it was stated, had been commissioned by Ohio Capitalists to work out the details. Probably the idea originated with Crosby, since he had been visiting ruins in the Mesa Verde area as early as 1892 and had previously sought financial backing for this grand idea. With the help of the Ohio group the Manitou Cliff Dwelling Ruins Company was incorporated, having an initial capitalization of $100,000. The ruins Crosby procured were located in a canyon twenty-five miles north of Cortez, Colorado, a distance of more than two hundred miles from Manitou.

Interest in the ancient cliff dwellings was intense in Colorado at the time. The state's Federation of Womens Clubs had worked for several years to have the Mesa Verde region designated a national park. The Colorado Archaeological Society naturally felt a vested scientific interest in all ruins within the state. Howls of protest arose over this proposal to move a whole village to an alien site. No matter that the promoters insisted they would exactly duplicate the original setting in their Deadman's Canyon site close to Manitou, opening almost directly off the streetcar line for convenience of access. They claimed the attraction would stimulate interest in the Mesa Verde ruins and at the same time edify the hordes of tourists who came to Pike's Peak but did not have the time or money to venture into more remote regions. The rebuilt village would make possible wide knowledge of a civilization more ancient than that of Egypt or Greece for many who would otherwise remain unenlightened.

Since Hewett had recommended that Mesa Verde be made a national park, it was natural that those opposing the Manitou project should seek his help. He was bombarded with letters from the leadership of the Colorado Archaeological Society. In February 1907 he wrote Professor Noyes agreeing that the removal of the cliff dwellings would be a serious loss to science, and that once removed from the original site they would be of little or no scientific value for teaching. He suggested that a replica would do as well and recommended that the promoters be urged to accept this substitute.[2]

Since the proposed ruin was on private land, persuasion and the pressure of public opinion were the only weapons Hewett knew to use, but both were unavailing. Public opinion was swayed by the local businessmen who were fired by the promoters' idea and had bought into the Manitou Cliff Dwellings Ruins Company. A large sum would be spent in the community to install the ruins, build a café nearby, and blast a handsome sightseeing road into the canyon. Furthermore, a rich by-product became available when blasting uncovered a fine deposit of fire clay available for quarrying.

In March 1907 Hewett wrote to Mrs. Lucy Peabody, secretary of the archaeological society, "I understand the Colorado Springs cliff dwelling matter has proceeded beyond recall, and so far as I can tell the parties have not acted in violation of the law."[3]

The first units of the new attraction opened with fanfare on Sunday, June 2, 1907 and drew a large crowd. When Hewett inspected the work some time later he admitted that it had been carefully supervised, and while in his opinion a replica would have served equally well, once the ruin had been removed from its original site nothing would be gained by further bemoaning its loss to science. Indeed, he was against publicizing this successful act of vandalism.

The promoters moved forward. Through the years the Manitou Company developed its original 120 acres until it could boast of an extensive attraction for visitors, offering "an example of vanished prehistoric civilization." Deadman's Canyon was renamed Phantom Cliff Canyon; the museum, curio shop, reconstructions, and real live Indians performing "authentic ceremonies" flourished under a management which became a member of the Colorado Springs and Manitou Springs chambers of commerce, Pikes Peak Motel Association, and Colorado Visitors Bureau. Of the thousands who still visit it annually many have no further interest, but others are motivated to visit Mesa Verde and other sites in the Southwest which are now accessible through a network of modern roads.

At the same time the Colorado Archaeological Society was opposing the Manitou project it was also involved in controversy over the naming of a superintendent for the new Mesa Verde Park it had helped to create. A Mrs. McClurg, who was Lucy Peabody's arch rival in scientific circles, wanted the appointment. Lucy felt her rival to be vastly unqualified and set about blocking her. In a series of letters to Hewett she referred to the machinations of Mrs. McSnippity or Mrs. McStinger, and urged Hewett to arrange the appointment of some other candidate.[4]

Members of the chauvinistic congressional delegation from Colorado were not eager for a woman's appointment, regardless of her qualifications, and indicated that they were willing to go along with the recommendations of the Colorado Society. Several men who could have been appointed, declined. It was hard to find a qualified man willing to undertake the responsibilities of the new park in exchange for the salary offered—"$1,500 a year and provide your own horse." In the meantime some women belonging to a group known as the Colorado Cliff Dwellings Association were urging the appointment of Mrs. McClurg.

Hewett steered a discreet course during this tempest. He had no favorite candidate and was only concerned that the park be well administered. Without committing himself, he conducted a quiet investigation into the qualifications of the nominees and made some careful suggestions to his scientific colleagues. When

Major H. M. Randolph accepted the post he was satisfied that the problem was solved.[5]

Lucy Peabody continued to write letters about Mrs. McStinger, however. She sent Hewett a rumor that the long delay in securing Randolph's appointment was caused by Mrs. "McS," who had secured the endorsement of President Theodore Roosevelt (whose support for conservation and preservation was well known); thus the congressional delegation, faced with the dilemma of conflicting loyalties, had procrastinated in its sponsorship. Furthermore, the ladies of the opposition were still active; even though Major Randolph's appointment was confirmed, they were trying to run the park through Mrs. McS's committee. The Colorado Cliff Dwellings Association, according to Lucy, had got rid of all the Democrats in their midst and was now exclusively a Republican organization. Did Major Randolph, they asked, wish to ignore the recommendations of four hundred Republican women who knew exactly how the park should be run?[6]

Hewett did his best to avoid taking sides in these Colorado politics and at the same time live up to his mandate to encourage interest and growth of the local archaeological societies. Those who were disappointed by failure to halt the project blamed him for "the rape of the Manitou Cliff Dwellings," however, and the partisans of rejected applicants for the superintendent's post accused him of meddling in national park affairs. He decided to concentrate his attention elsewhere until things simmered down, but there were some who would never be convinced that he had done all he could for their cause.

In 1906 and 1907 Hewett established the pace for handling a multitude of research, lecturing, organizational, and administrative activities which was to be the pattern for the rest of his life. From the moment that he plunged into the projects requested by his fellowship committee, his method of operation awed his admirers and exasperated his opponents.

When the fellowship year was behind him, he had succeeded in meeting most of the leaders concerned with archaeology in the western states; he had lectured before learned and amateur societies, sometimes to large, respectful audiences and sometimes to a handful drummed up at the last minute by a local promoter of a fledgling organization. Hewett had engaged in a field survey from Arizona to Mexico City. As his critics later pointed out, it was very superficial in nature, but the field was so vast and the depth of scientific ignorance so great that at least he had taken a first step, to be followed by others through the years.

Most of Hewett's interest had been concentrated on pre-Columbian sites, but he was now to plunge into the job of saving a building that owed its importance to historic times — the old governmental palace which served the capital in Santa Fe. Much has been written about this building; for a reader who does not know the background, the next chapter will include a brief summary of its history.

8

THE OLD PALACE

*The primitive emotions upon which human character
has been built are still potent.* — ELH

At the beginning of the seventeenth century, the Spanish Empire decided to build a fortress as headquarters for the government of its Kingdom of New Mexico. The place chosen was a small settlement in the valley of a snow-fed stream at the point where it emerged from a canyon in the foothills of the Sangre de Cristo Mountains. Approximately ten acres were marked off on the valley floor, with the town plaza to the south, a spring-studded marsh on the east, sloping ground rising to a commanding bluff on the north, and firm, level ground to the west. The middle of the plot was designated as a space for a parade ground and vegetable garden, and a system of ditches was dug to carry water from the river to the fortress.

Around this central square, massive walled structures were gradually built of the material most available and most widely used in the province — mud. The Indians used mud for their multi-storied houses in a type of construction that has come to be called "puddled adobe," which was achieved by mixing the grey-brown clay with small stones and water and piling it up layer on layer, allowing each addition to dry before the next was applied. This system required a very broad base for a wall, gradually tapering as more height was achieved. When the wall had reached the desired height, pine logs were laid at intervals to bridge the width of the room and a lattice of aspen saplings was laid across these to form a mat on which more mud was spread to harden into a roof. The second, third and sometimes a fourth story were set back to form a sort of truncated pyramid — an aboriginal stepped, set-back "skyscraper."

When the Spaniards came they brought an easier method of making walls out of sun-hardened bricks of clay and straw. The bricks were laid up with mud plaster; the work went more quickly and the base was not so thick as required by puddled adobe.

The fortress town was called La Villa Real de Santa Fé de San Francisco de Asís, with St. Francis as its patron. The structures built around the periphery of the ten-acre site were the *casas reales* — the royal houses — necessary for the governance of this province so far from the central authority in Mexico. They included rooms for government business, living apartments for the governor's family and servants, military barracks, and stables for the cavalry. On the south the massive building fronted the road along the north side of the town plaza, and terminated at either end in large square lookout towers. The western tower served as a military prison, with room for the storage of gunpowder; the eastern tower was used as a chapel and thus became the first church in Santa Fe. The entire complex was known as El Palacio Real. Although it has undergone many vicissitudes, much destruction and frequent remodeling, it is standing today as the oldest government building in the United States.

For some seventy years after its building, the fortress knew periods alternating between intense activity and contented sleep under a rich, semi-desert sun. It was a place of lively bustle when a caravan arrived from Chihuahua, far to the south, or when a detachment of raggedy cavalry rushed forth to pursue marauding Indians; it was a place where lovers met at gay parties, where governors lived with their wives or mistresses, where children were conceived and born, church services were held, and prisoners flogged. Busy with their own intrigues, the Spanish of the province ignored the sullen defiance of their Indian subjects until on August 10, 1680 the ungrateful natives renounced their forced allegiance to the Christian God and the King of Spain in a rebellion that broke out by prearranged signal throughout the province. The terrified colonials gathered inside Santa Fe's fortress, rolled out the gunpower from its tower storage, and tried to defend themselves. Bands of Indian warriors swept in from every direction after killing the settlers, plundering the little settlements, and defiling the missions established in the villages along the watercourses of the Rio Grande drainage. Defense in Santa Fe ended abruptly when the besiegers cut off the water supply flowing through the acequias into the fortress.

Under protection of darkness the men, women and children led by Governor Otermín fled southward, covering their retreat as best they could. Along the route they gathered up the stragglers who had survived the uprising, until they numbered about a thousand. They continued south until they reached El Paso del Norte, where they halted, regrouped and established a small settlement that became the nucleus of Juarez, Mexico and for which adjacent El Paso, Texas is named.

During the next twelve years no written records were kept of events in Santa Fe, where the victorious Pueblo Indians occupied the government buildings. Excavation has revealed that some walls and roofs were burned, others apparently allowed to deteriorate in the weather, but a researcher can only speculate on activities. By 1692-93 the Spanish colonials were strong enough to reconquer the province under the leadership of General Diego de Vargas. Bringing their banners and the little statue of the Virgin Mary which has come to be known as *La Conquistadora,* they marched back to the ruins of their fortress. Much of it was rubbled, but the southern portions had been raised to a multistory pueblo with its lower walls repaired by puddled adobe. The chapel had been converted into a ceremonial chamber similar to the kivas of the Indian villages.

Once the Indians were ousted from the building, the Franciscan friars who came with De Vargas reconsecrated the chapel, and it is believed that when De Vargas died some eleven years later he was buried under the altar. In 1714 the religious observances of the town were moved to the new parish church at the eastern end of the plaza as it then existed; a century later the first archbishop of New Mexico built there the cathedral which stands today.

The royal palace continued to be the home of the governor and the administrative seat of government. New Mexico was under Spanish rule until 1821, when the Mexican revolution changed the ownership of the province. The rule of Emperor Maximilian lasted scarcely long enough for messages to come up the Chihuahua Trail, and then the Republic of Mexico replaced the Empire. Governor Manuel Armijo was living in the old Palace when the U.S. Army under General Stephen Watts Kearney arrived on its transcontinental junket in 1846. Under Kearney's direction the Mexican flag came down and was replaced by the Stars and Stripes, which has flown there ever since except for about a month in 1862 when the Stars and Bars of the Confederacy ruled over the old Palace.

Summaries of legislative activities in the early American days give a picture of the life and times centering in the Palace where the sessions were held. At the first session of the Territorial Legislature the capital was confirmed at Santa Fe, where it has remained in spite of occasional rumbling threats from Albuquerque. Among the acts regulating the financial and moral affairs of the Territory were many relating to the venerable building. Congress early granted $20,000 for the erection of public buildings, and the New Mexico Assembly, appropriating another $20,000 for the expense of government, decided that a new capitol should be built. The foundations were laid for a building described by the historian Bancroft as "an awkward and ill-planned structure,"[1] and with the help of an additional $50,000 appropriated in 1854 the building rose to a story and a half — then stood unfinished for the next thirty years, when it became the federal courthouse.

In the meantime the New Mexico Assembly was concerned with getting the jail out of the old Palace; a memorial was introduced in the second session recommending $50,000 for a penitentiary. Provision was also made for a manager of the Territorial library, to be housed in the Palace, at a salary of $100 a year.

Gambling had always been a legitimate amusement of the people, and games of chance were a regular part of entertainments in the old Palace. With the coming of the Americans, however, the Puritan influence of some governors raised new issues. The first session of the Territorial Legislature limited legalized gambling to the county seats (for an annual fee of $600), but the fourth session, deciding that it was discriminatory to let people gamble only in the county seat, authorized probate judges to issue licenses in the other towns as well.

The early records show concern for public education, suppression of marauding Indians, and settlement of Mexican land claims — issues that were to occupy the Territory for years to come. Although education, Indians, and land ownership still preoccupy the lawmakers a century and a quarter later, one decree of the second session does seem quaint: a pimp was ordered to be punished by thirty lashes, with the additional disgrace of having to ride an ass in public on the next feast day, accompanied by the town crier to call attention to him. How many such parades ever took place in front of the old Palace is not known.

Meanwhile, as the sovereignty changed and political fortunes fluctuated, the governors moved their possessions and their entourages in and out of the Palace, which continued in use for all public purposes. Attempts to secure money for needed repairs were either unsuccessful or inadequate. The importance of preserving archives was noted from time to time, especially after the New Mexico Historical Society was organized in 1859 and 1860. In 1850 Congress appropriated $500 to be spent on a Territorial library, but with the librarian's salary set at $100 per annum the post was vacant most of the time and no one was responsible. In 1863 Governor Henry Connelly urged and secured the passage of a law providing for the custody and preservation of the archives, but Governor William A. Pile, who came in 1869, created a scandal when he was accused of selling a lot of musty old documents for waste paper, or even using them to light the Palace fires! Historian Ralph Emerson Twitchell thought the amount of such vandalism was exaggerated, as many records were later recovered, but there were those who believed that the losses were deliberately planned to cast clouds on land titles.

Five thousand dollars were spent on repairs to the Palace immediately after the Civil War, but the roof soon began to leak again, the outside plaster melted away, and the small, inconvenient rooms could only be described as musty and dusty. Secretary of the Territory William G. Ritch wrote in 1875, "It is safe to say no other legislative body in the United States outside of New Mexico, ever met inside of such disgraceful surroundings."[2]

Just before General Lew Wallace arrived to take over as Governor of the Territory on September 29, 1878, some $2,260 was expended to tidy up the governmental buildings, but it was scarcely adequate for essential repairs. Although an appropriation of $40 was voted for library shelving, the Territorial archives were still sadly neglected. General Wallace was making the best of his quarters when Adolph Bandelier arrived in Santa Fe on August 23, 1880. He called at the Palace to pay his respects and found that the governor had gone to visit his mining holdings at a plaza forty miles away. It was the vicar-general, Father Eguillon, who told Bandelier that the government archives were in a sorry state and that many thought the loss Governor Pile insisted was purely accidental had indeed been designed to obscure Spanish land grant titles. He said that valuable documents were still being purloined by visitors; a report prepared by De Vargas and belonging to Tomas Cabeza de Vaca was alleged to have recently been stolen by an "American."

Among the newcomers trying to preserve the historical documents was L. Bradford Prince, who two years previously had been appointed Chief Justice of the Territorial Supreme Court. The New Mexico Historical Society, founded just before the beginning of the Civil War, had lapsed into inactivity when its leaders chose sides for the conflict. In 1880 Prince helped to reorganize the society, and together with Territorial Secretary Ritch and a few others, began the systematic preservation of relics and records. Two years later the Territorial Legislature memorialized Congress, asking that the old adobe Palace be ceded to the Historical Society as a relic of antiquity. Nothing came of that, but the legislature then passed an act regulating the Territorial library. The librarian, Samuel Ellison (who had been laid up with a broken leg when Bandelier first came to town), undertook the labor of classifying the archives and keeping the library in order. His report the following year lists 1,810 volumes and 144 pasteboard boxes containing the classified archives.

When Supreme Court Justice Prince was forced to resign in May 1882, he turned his legal talents to several personal pursuits, including an interest in acquiring title to some New Mexico land grants. His historian friend Twitchell says tactfully that Judge Prince resigned "to engage in other matters."[3] One of these matters was furthering the Historical Society. Although the Congress took no positive action on ceding the old Palace, in 1884 the Territorial Legislature voted to permit the Historical Society to occupy some rooms in the building and made a small appropriation for the purchase of relics.

It was a time of cataclysmic change in the Territory. Governor Lew Wallace and Judge Prince, together with the current military commander General Edward Hatch, had been the three dignitaries who drove the last spikes to complete the branch of the South Pacific Railroad (later the Atchison, Topeka and Santa Fe) into the capital city. Those spikes marked the end of Santa Fe Trail days and the beginning of quick development that led to wild speculation in land and mining claims. It was taken for granted that officials appointed to govern the Territory would promote and profit from these gains.

From his desk in the old Palace, Governor Wallace carried on a five-fold program. Three of his duties were official: managing a legislature composed of the most contentious and jealous elements; directing an Indian war; and quelling the civil strife that had broken out in Lincoln County and led him to several encounters with Billy the Kid. Two of his activities were personal: trying to finish a novel he had begun before his appointment to the governor's position, and, most exciting of all, prospecting for a fortune in mining claims. He would surely have been astonished had he been told that history would remember him chiefly for the novel — *Ben Hur*. Although he acquired holdings wherever mining property seemed most promising — in nearby Cerrillos, and, with his son Henry, in Grant, Socorro and San Miguel counties — and at one time offered his holdings for several hundred thousand dollars, he never realized his dreams of wealth.

The Lew Wallace papers in the New Mexico Record Center and Archives (where all that have been salvaged of official archives are now housed) provide a good description of the Palace of the Governors when he occupied it:

> A rambling, one-story adobe structure, with the walls in places six feet thick.... The walls were grimey, the undressed boards of the floor rested flat upon the ground; the cedar rafters, rainstained...over-weighted by tons and tons of mud composing the roof.... Nevertheless in that cavernous chamber I wrote the eighth and last book of Ben Hur.
>
> My custom when night came was to lock the doors and bolt the windows of the office proper, and with a student's lamp, bury myself in the four soundless walls of the forbidding annex...there at my rough pine table, the Count of Monte Cristo in his dungeon of stone was not more lost to the world.
>
> The ghosts, if they were ever about, did not disturb me; yet in the hush of that gloomy harborage I beheld the Crucifixion and strove to write what I beheld....Long before I was through with my book I became a believer in God and Christ.[4]

Wallace wrote to his wife Susan, who had not yet joined him, that one day when he was free of interruptions he was able to write from 10 a.m. to 10 p.m. He sent completed portions of the work for her criticism and duly acknowledged her reactions.

After Susan Wallace joined her husband in New Mexico, he took her with him on an official journey to Lincoln County to attend a court of inquiry dealing with the civil strife in that area. They stayed at the post trader's house, which Susan found even more primitive than the governor's residence in Santa Fe. She wrote to their son, Henry, quoting General Sherman's famous remark that the United States should have another Mexican war and make them take back New Mexico. She worried about Billy the Kid's reported threat to kill the sheriff who caught him, the judge who passed sentence on him, and the governor who had tried to save him. Susan quotes Billy as saying, "I mean to ride into the plaza at Santa Fe, hitch my horse in front of the Palace, and put a bullet through Lew Wallace."[5]

Friends in Santa Fe warned Mrs. Wallace to keep the Palace shutters closed in the evening, "so the bright light of the student's lamp might not make such a shining mark of the governor writing until late on Ben Hur."[6]

This, then, was the condition of the old Palace when Bandelier came to Santa Fe to be told that the archives were in a sorry state. Lionel A. Sheldon succeeded Wallace as governor about a year later, and he was followed by Edmund G. Ross. Neither of these men seems to have done anything notable about the old building, but in the spring of 1889 Judge Prince, returned to political favor, was appointed Governor of the Territory by President Benjamin Harrison. The new governor had, of course, been a frequent visitor to the Historical Society rooms in the east end of the Palace; now he followed tradition by moving his living quarters and office into the building.

Prince had been married twice. His young first wife had died a few months after he brought her as a bride from her New York home to New Mexico. The couple had gone in midwinter on an excursion promoted by the new railway, during which the bride developed pneumonia. A stained-glass window in Santa Fe's Episcopal Church of the Holy Faith commemorates her short life.

Some two years later Judge Prince married Mary C. Beardsley of Oswego, New York. The second Mrs. Prince came from a socially prominent family and had a highly developed sense of Victorian taste. The Princes brought many family heirlooms from the East, including china, silver and furnishings.

Refurbishing of the Palace for the use of the incoming governor was carried out under the direction of the Territorial Secretary, B. M. Thomas. When the executive family moved into the Palace in late December 1890, a local newspaper account described the improvements:

> ... rooms have been finished in hard plaster, rough coat and calsomined
> with the most exquisite tints, and many of the dwelling apartments to
> be used by the governor have been rather handsomely finished with
> rich paper ceilings, broad friezes and painted to match. For instance, in
> the reception room a soft tint of yellow predominates, in the dining
> room everything tends to be pea green, in the main hall the colors are
> more somber, while the family bedroom is a bright blue, and the library
> dark maroon.[7]

In February 1893 the governor held a reception for members of the Territorial Legislature about which the Santa Fe *Daily New Mexican* rhapsodized:

> The many rare and historical decorations of the spacious rooms
> were supplemented until the scenes were fairy-like, elegant and
> beautiful. Exquisite paintings, ancient armor, idols, arms and shields,
> highly interesting relics from church, pueblo and cliff dwellings, Aztec
> and Mexican tapestry, Navajo blankets, were tastefully commingled, and
> in a mazy web, flower, leaf and delicate lace made a background for the
> host of guests.[8]

Among other much admired Chinese objets d'art was a full dinner service of Medallion Ware, but it is not known whether or not it was used on this occasion. The governor's friend, Colonel R. E. Twitchell, observed many years later that no occupant of the old Palace, before or since, had so elaborately entertained the people of all classes.

However smooth it may have been socially, Governor Prince's tenure was tumultuous politically. Dedicated to securing statehood for New Mexico, the efforts of Prince and his associates were destined to be thwarted. In order to apply for statehood, the Territory convened a constitutional convention which hammered out a document proudly proclaimed to be the best in the United States. But a Democratic Congress was not interested, and an effort to have the constitution ratified by a vote of the people failed two to one. Life in the capital city was marred by a series of murders and assassinations that read like a story of modern gang warfare; the underlying cause was the struggle for political power among various local factions. Reports of the unrest were quoted to prove that New Mexico could not govern her own affairs.

The Princes lived in the Palace for four years, then (when his successor, William T. Thornton, was appointed shortly after the grand reception described above) moved their belongings and the social headquarters of Santa Fe to a home of their own on Palace Avenue. It was a block east of the governor's residence but conveniently close to the rooms of the Historical Society in the east end of the Palace.

The historian Bancroft, who relied heavily on contemporary informants and on resumes prepared for him by assistants, described Santa Fe as it appeared in 1889 when the population was about 8,000, and this must have been the way it looked when the Hewetts first came to town in the late 1890s:

> During the past decade its quaint, old Mexican, one-story adobes have given way to a considerable extent to brick blocks and residences of the modern style. It has gas and sewer works, good hotels, and fine churches and schools.... Among relics of antiquity the old adobe *palacio* holds first rank, while the old foundations of the more modern capitol and penitentiary [which had been destroyed by fire] are also interesting ruins. That town has an altitude of 7,044 feet and is noted as a sanatarium. With this advantage, its fascinating reminiscences of past centuries, its central position, its modern spirit of thrift, its extensive mercantile establishments, and its half-dozen newspapers, Santa Fe looks forward to a future of prosperity, and has not the slightest idea of ceding its supremacy, political, commercial or in any other respect, to either Albuquerque or Las Vegas, its most ambitious rivals.[9]

In the years 1898-1903, when Hewett was president of Las Vegas Normal University, he came at frequent intervals to the capital. When he made Santa Fe his headquarters during his fellowship year (1906), he must have been well aware of the proprietorship that L. Bradford and Mary Prince felt for the old Palace and the hope ex-Governor Prince cherished of securing the entire building for the Historical Society.

9

≈⁂≈

THE SCHOOL OF AMERICAN ARCHAEOLOGY IS ESTABLISHED

My instruction was to found a School of Research for the purpose of "giving field work and training" to students in archaeology and ethnology. — ELH

Hewett's frenetic efforts during his fellowship year paid off. Francis W. Kelsey became president of the Archaeological Institute and Alice C. Fletcher chairman of the American committee. Frederick Putnam was impressed by Hewett's achievements in the field and his success in cementing friendships with such mercurial men as Charles Lummis. Because these members of the American committee felt justified in their choice of Hewett and their instructions to him as a fellow, they persuaded the classicists that there was sufficient material awaiting exploration to warrant the appointment of a full-time director of American research.

In 1904 when the Bureau of Ethnology published its 23rd Annual Report (covering the years 1902 and 1903), director John Wesley Powell could point to more than twenty-five years of pioneering scientific work in ethnology, archaeology and anthropology under the sponsorship of this government bureau, either alone or in collaboration with other institutions. In the West the Bureau's research activities extended from Alaska to Chihuahua, and by now Hewett knew personally many of the men and women involved. He sought advice and guidance from The Chief, William H. Holmes, as well as his other close Washington friends, Fletcher and Fewkes. There were others whom he knew more casually. Franz Boas of Columbia University acted under an honorary appointment to supervise the Bureau's linguistic research. Ales Hrdlicka of the American Museum of Natural

History, Roland B. Dixon of Harvard, and A. L. Kroeber of the University of California collaborated on Bureau projects. While two pioneering giants at Zuni pueblo, Frank H. Cushing and James Stevenson, were no longer alive, Matilda Coxe Stevenson had stayed on to complete the work she and her husband had started. Her monumental report on the Zuni ceremonials was published in the Bureau's 23rd Annual Report (mentioned above). Hewett respected her firsthand knowledge.

Hewett's survey of Pueblo cultures had been built on the work of his predecessors; Powell, Fewkes, Russell, and Bandelier were all known to him. The scholastic respectability of these researchers could not be gainsaid by the most rabid classicist. After his initial work in the Southwest was no longer sponsored by the Archaeological Institute, Bandelier had gone on to the archives in Mexico and South America, where European scientists were making research history. The time was ripe for the Institute to establish at least a cautious toehold in the Americas if it was not to be crowded out of a field preempted by others, and therefore its leaders ventured to launch a school of archaeology in Santa Fe, baby sister to those in Athens, Rome, Jerusalem, and Baghdad.

The decision was described many years later by Judge McFie's archaeologist son-in-law, Lansing Bloom:

> To develop adequately this new field of research, a well-qualified leader, a comprehensive and well formulated program, and an organization were needed. The first was found in Dr. Hewett, who on January 2, 1907, was made director of American research for the Institute; the program which he drafted at the request of the committee has stood the test of thirty years; and in December of that year the Institute created a school for work in the American field, similar to its earlier foundations for work in Greece, Italy and the Oriental field.[1]

The next step was to convince the Institute that Santa Fe was the proper headquarters for the new school. Hewett's enthusiasm for the riches of archaeological material in the area strengthened his powers of persuasion. A two-week field trip on horseback had convinced Congressman Lacey of the need for federal legislation to preserve this heritage. Hewett used the same tactic to indoctrinate the Institute's American committee members. Alice Fletcher was almost seventy years old when she paid her first visit to Frijoles Canyon; getting there involved a wagon ride over rutted dirt roads to the canyon rim and a taxing walk down the winding cliffside trail to the primitive camp beside the Rito. She cheerfully limped around the ruins, joined the discussion at the evening campfire, and the following morning refused the offer of a horseback ride back to the top. Santa Fe and Frijoles Canyon became two of her favorite places, and she returned to them as long as her strength permitted. She was one of those who urged the choice of Santa Fe as headquarters for the School of American Archaeology.

Members of staff and managing board, School of American Archaeology, on ladder leading to cliff ruins, ca. 1910. Courtesy of the Museum of New Mexico.

As Hewett set about organizing his school, he had the staunch backing of three longtime New Mexico friends: Frank Springer, Judge John R. McFie and Paul A. F. Walter. They had encouraged him to promote Santa Fe as the logical headquarters for the new school, and they were soon in accord that no better home could be found for it than the old Palace.

The idea of using the Palace may have originated with Justice McFie. Like

Justice John R. McFie, a founding father of the Museum of New Mexico and the School of American Archaeology. Courtesy of the Museum of New Mexico.

Prince, he was active in the affairs of the Historical Society, though relations between the two men were not always cordial. In any event, McFie became the active lobbyist for acquisition of the Palace during the 1907 legislative session.

Hewett was busy commuting from one to another of his projects when, early in February, McFie wrote him that two bills concerning the future of the old government building had been introduced in the Legislature. One proposed to give the building to the city of Santa Fe for a hall. Another, backed by ex-Governor Prince, gave that portion of the building known as the "Judge Laughlin rooms" to the Historical Society. Judge McFie found no strong sentiment for either, and arranged to have both bills delayed until Hewett could come home from Washington for consultation. McFie warned that the legislators generally felt title to the building should be retained by the Territory, regardless of the use to which it might be put. He therefore proposed that Hewett's new school might take a long-erm lease at a nominal fee, which would have the same effect as a lease in perpetuity if the school continued to occupy the building.

Hewett took the matter up with the Institute and on February 14, 1907 wrote McFie, "Your proposal to endeavor to secure the use of the old Governor's Palace as a home for the School was received with profound attention by the officers of the Institute."[2] In order to assure that the building would be preserved for future generations (and perhaps to relieve some legislative concern about the cost of upkeep), McFie next proposed that the Palace be designated a national monument.

Several people watched these activities with considerable concern for the future of their own pet organizations. Ex-Governor Prince and his wife naturally thought that they had a vested interest in the old building and viewed the machinations of these upstart newcomers with considerable annoyance. Prince insisted that the Historical Society had been legally housed for many years in the Palace, and said that he was prepared to expand its occupancy.

W. G. Tight, president of the University of New Mexico in Albuquerque, thought the new research school might more properly become part of the university. On February 22, 1907 he wrote Hewett:

> It seems to me that it would be a decided advantage to have the
> school located where students could have the advantages of other
> college work. I notice the resolution has already passed the House to
> transfer the Old Palace. If, however, such a resolution should fail in the
> Council [of the Institute] and the whole proposition in Santa Fe fall
> through I should be very glad to renew the offer I made you in New
> York, to have the University furnish the school with a building fully as
> good as one of the buildings of which I am sending you prints today,
> which will amount in value to between six and seven thousand dollars.[3]

President Tight went on to make the tactful suggestion that if university students were received in the school, the head professor would rank as a member of the faculty with privilege of a vote.

In his reply Hewett ignored the implications of the term "head professor" and, cordially noncommittal about Tight's proposition, asked permission to use the prints of university buildings to illustrate a brief comment on the proposal that he was writing for one of the official journals. President Tight was not about to have his proposal publicized as long as no decision had been made, however, and stiffly refused permission, using as his excuse that he had already arranged for the prints to be published elsewhere.[4]

There was a further complication concerning that portion of the old Palace currently used by the U. S. Government as the town's post office. This lease would soon expire, however, and McFie learned that there would be no difficulty in moving the post office to another location.

Prince's proposal was that the eastern half of the building be granted to the Historical Society and the western half designated for use by the School. Hewett countered that he must advise his superiors that such a suggestion was unacceptable because it did not provide for the growth of the School. He offered the use of the three rooms then occupied by the Society and tried to reassure the members that it would be advantageous to accept. "The Institute is incorporated by Act of Congress and its officers can bind it to leave the Historical Society undisturbed in the rooms designated," he promised.[5]

It looked like a stalemate for a time, but in order to move the matter forward Judge McFie helped to draft House Joint Resolution No. 6, which was introduced into the Legislature by R. L. Baca, a most respected and influential member. This resolution proposed that the Territory give the old Palace to the United States as a national monument, and that if accepted "the use and custodianship thereof be granted to the Archaeological Institute of America as the home of its proposed School of American Archaeology."[6] The resolution further provided for disposition of the rental paid by the post office during the balance of its lease, which had only a few months to run, and for continued use of the rooms currently occupied by the Historical Society. In his role as president of the Archaeological Society of Santa Fe, Judge McFie duly forwarded the proposal to Hewett for Institute approval.

Prince continued to push for more space in the building, until Hewett agreed that it might be granted on a temporary basis while his school was being established. Concerning Prince's lobbying activities, McFie wrote, "Of course we do not care what favor may be shown him if he rises above his own personality — pretty hard to do — and works for the advancement of the cause here."[7]

The Institute was quite willing to house its Santa Fe school in a building supplied by the Territory of New Mexico, but the matter was not resolved until 1909, when the Legislature established the Museum of New Mexico (vigorously promoted by McFie, Springer, Hewett, et. al.) and decreed that the old Palace should be home for both institutions. The Hewett forces moved into full occupancy of the building, with suffrance granted to the Historical Society.

As Hewett understood his mandate, the old Palace was to be placed in the custody of the School on condition that the School would repair it and restore it to its ancient architecture, preserving it as a monument to the Spanish founders of Southwestern civilization. The Legislature expressly stipulated that the School should conduct therein the Museum of New Mexico, with operational expenses contributed by legislative appropriation. Under the sponsorship of the Institute the School was to be controlled by a national Board of Managers, appointed by the Institute, which meant that its membership would be drawn from all parts of the country. The Museum, on the other hand, like other tax-supported educational institutions, would be under the control of a Board of Regents appointed by the

Governor of New Mexico.

Such a hydra-headed complex could only be operable if all was directed by one man, a benevolent dictator. Hewett did not think it was beyond his powers to combine the double directorship. He promptly developed a policy which was to be continued throughout his life: the Director would recommend appointments for both boards, and the chairman of the Regents would also serve on the Managing Board to provide an interlocking directorate. He had learned a hard lesson at Las Vegas. Any time the governing authorities could appoint an unfriendly majority the administrator was doomed and the edifice he had built so carefully could quickly crumble. For the next thirty-five years he would need all his political skill to guide the policies of the groups in the channels he favored. A first step must be to convert the living quarters and neglected areas of the old Palace to serve their new functions.

In his 1911 official report Gov. William J. Mills says:

> The most important work of the museum during the past year has been that of putting in repair the Old Palace of the Governors, which, under the stipulations of the legislative Act, has been made the home of the museum and of the School of American Archaeology. The funds for the repair of the building have been furnished largely by public spirited citizens of New Mexico. The work of repair has consisted in the removal of modern wood work from the doors, windows and fireplaces, and the restoration of those interesting architectural features to their original form as nearly as can be determined. The modern plastering and papering of the walls have been replaced by cement work of the most durable character, simulating as nearly as possible the original finish of the rooms. The modern cloth and wall-paper ceilings have been removed, laying bare the ancient *vigas* and hand-chopped slabs of centuries ago.
>
> The rooms, thus repaired, present much of the appearance which they had before the modernizing of the past half century was done. All of the building, which has been turned over for the use of the Museum of New Mexico, has thus been put in repair, and now affords facilities for the school and museum, a number of excellent exhibition rooms, and a large room, formerly occupied by the United States post office, for the purpose of library and lecture hall...[8]

So much for the Victorian era and the elegance the Prince family installed in the Palace. Hewett had indeed achieved a coup when he was appointed director of both the Museum and the School, with financial backing from the Territory and the Institute. Thus began a period of incredible management feats when he would cheerfully commingle the activities and the funds of both organizations in what he considered a vital stewardship necessary to the survival of each. He always knew what was going on and could account for funds and accomplishments of his charges, but his opponents likened his activities to a dictatorship not always benevolent and did not hesitate to accuse him of playing off one sponsor against the other. Governor Mills' report on the state of the Museum continues:

> The museum has during the past year been visited by a large number of travelers. Almost without exception, artists, scientists, historians and travelers have spoken in highest approval of the spirit in which all the alterations of the building have been made and the plan upon which the museum is developed. The museum is kept open every day of the year and the number of visitors is constantly increasing.
>
> The relations between the museum and the School of American Archaeology have been all that was contemplated by the act of the legislature. There is perfect unity of purpose and harmony of action. The collections of the museum have accumulated rapidly, and at present rate it can be but a matter of a little time until the capacity of the building is overtaxed to accommodate the collections on hand.
>
> It is the purpose of the regents and the director to make this

Palace of the Governors, Santa Fe, ca. 1900-1910. Courtesy of the Museum of New Mexico.

museum display the history of the Southwest for the past thousand years. No other part of the United States is so rich in archaeological remains, and the history of the Southwest is full of dramatic interest. It will be the function of this museum to preserve all that is best in New Mexico's historic past, and especially it is the intention to preserve the Old Palace of the Governors as a monument to the Spanish founders of the civilization of the Southwest, as provided in the organic act.[9]

Edgar Hewett could not have said it better. Indeed, one might suspect that this portion of the Governor's annual report was drafted by the Museum Director himself.

The renovation of the Palace, which took place between 1909 and 1913 under the direction of Hewett's protégé, Jesse Nusbaum, was not without trauma. Ina Cassidy, wife of painter Gerald Cassidy, told of being invited by the former Governor and Mrs. Prince to a tea given by the Historical Society in *their* part of the old Palace. The party was held on the same afternoon that Dr. Hewett was to

Palace of the Governors during renovation, 1913. Courtesy of the Museum of New Mexico.

lecture in *his* part of the Museum. When Mrs. Cassidy, on leaving the tea early, explained to her hostess that they wished to hear Dr. Hewett, Mrs. Prince attempted to dissuade them. "You are newcomers to Santa Fe and should not get mixed up in our local controversies," she told Ina earnestly. "There is no need for you to hear Dr. Hewett."[10]

The Cassidys not only wanted to hear Dr. Hewett, however; they realized that he was in a position to do much more for Gerald's future career than the Princes, so they went on to the lecture. They did, nevertheless, manage to remain friendly with both factions. Mrs. Cassidy was much amused by the direct action taken by Hewett and Nusbaum to unify the building. For some years the portion occupied by the Historical Society had had no direct access to the rest of the old Palace, and the Princes steadily refused to allow doors to be cut between their bailiwick and the Museum proper. One weekend after the custodian had gone home, while former Governor and Mrs. Prince were occupied elsewhere, Nusbaum moved in a crew of workmen who chopped two doorways through the thick walls, installed lintels, frames and wooden doors, and plastered the broken walls neatly so that one scarcely realized that the work had been done. When Monday morning came, there was nothing the indignant leaders of the Historical Society could do to seal themselves off once more.

To build a school, students are needed. Although Hewett had already developed friendships with most of the older scientists working in the Southwest, he needed young people to train in field techniques. In 1907 he asked Frederick Putnam to help him recruit students receiving academic training at Harvard who would be interested in field experience. Putnam tacked up a notice on a college bulletin board proclaiming that Dr. E. L. Hewett of the Archaeological Institute of America was seeking three volunteers for an expedition to the Indian lands of the Southwest. The appeal was ignored by older, more experienced students, but three young men who had only begun to study science promptly offered their services. Hewett accepted all three — Sylvanus Griswold Morley, Alfred Vincent Kidder and John Gould Fletcher.

Several versions of that first summer's fieldwork have been told, and incidents of the initiation were campfire talk for a generation. That the hardships the young men claimed to have suffered were real enough is attested by Hewett's own account of his philosophy about field training, as set out in his chapter about making archaeologists in *Campfire and Trail.*

It seems that in his own youth Hewett had been much impressed by a Chicago waterfront tough who declared that the best way to teach boys to swim was "to push 'em off de pier." Remembering the success of this pragmatic pedagogy and well aware that the great pioneers in archaeology were largely self-trained, Hewett took his recruits to camp at Holly's Ranch on the San Juan River in southwestern Colorado and put them on their own. His description of the initiation there sounds as sadistic as any fraternity of the day might have devised:

Edgar Lee Hewett in Guatemala, 1909. Courtesy of the Museum of New Mexico.

Sylvanus G. Morley in studio for research workers, School of American Archaeology, ca. 1910. Courtesy of the Museum of New Mexico.

Kidder's first workout was a fifty mile ride across the mesa with me on the roughest bronco I could find for him. He came through it a chastened man, but game. Fletcher was horse wrangler in charge of the team, a venerable horse and a wicked looking mule. A run-in with the latter resulted in his getting tangled in the mule's picket rope and dragged a quarter of a mile or so over the rocky terrain. He was not favorably disposed to this first phase of his "training." Morley undertook the commissary; put plaster of Paris in his biscuit dough in lieu of baking powder; spread the camp beds in the dry irrigation ditch (water turned on at four in the morning); moved their Harvard crimson blankets to Mr. Holly's haystacks where in the early morning downpour the colors "ran" copiously over Mr. Holly's new mown alfalfa. The next transfer was to a neighboring group of anthills. A high wind scattered their note paper and garments over the valley...

I planned their work so they wouldn't lie about camp; told them to make a complete archaeological survey of McElmo mesa and have their report ready in six weeks. I had to join a group of western students two hundred miles down the San Juan. Helplessly they watched me ride off into the sunset."[11]

Hewett saved the first letter he got from that camp, a penciled scrawl from Fletcher, saying that it was impossible to accomplish anything on the riding stock provided and asking for help. Morley and Kidder were made of sterner stuff, or else they had a more steadfast dedication to archaeology. They thought they could cope and asked no favors. At the end of the six weeks the trio had produced a two-hundred-page report from well-kept notebooks, and could fend for themselves very well in their camp situation. Although Hewett's rough treatment may have been in some measure inspired by the Westerner's characteristic scorn for the Eastern dude, he made amends. Vay Morley ultimately became a trusted assistant nurtured by Hewett in his first archaeological work in the Maya world of Middle America — a field in which Morley became eminent. Vincent Kidder became the outstanding authority on the excavations begun by Hewett at Pecos Pueblo. John G. Fletcher, more poet than scientist, gave up archaeology for good, although he was always an *aficionado* of the Western country and through the years returned often for visits under more comfortable auspices.

After that first experiment Hewett received more applications than he could accept for summer fieldwork under his tutelage, and although some were mere curious dilettantes, he gave a starting push to an increasing number of dirt archaeologists and field-trained ethnologists who went on to become eminent in their professions.

During the next two years Hewett continued to build his School of American Archaeology and the Museum in Santa Fe, and to supervise summer camps on the Pajarito Plateau and elsewhere in the Southwest. Much of his time and energy was spent in seeking financial support for the proliferating activities of the School, and when he saw an opportunity to move into the Middle American field he was ready for it. The country was Guatemala; the site chosen was the jungle-covered ruins of Quirigua.

The carefully worked out sponsorship and financing for the winter season of 1910-1911 at Quirigua set the pattern for many later ventures. The ruins lay on land owned by the United Fruit Company, which granted permission for the work, helped to procure the necessary government permits, and contributed $2,500, partly in cash and partly in services. Transportation from New Orleans for men and supplies was arranged on a ship owned by the Fruit Company, which also furnished many of the amenities at the site. Matching funds were contributed by the St. Louis Archaeological Society, whose members were invited to visit the expedition. The staff was made up of young eager beavers pleased to have the experience and the adventure in exchange for a pittance above their maintenance. Among them was Sylvanus Morley, promoted to director's assistant at a stipend not much larger than was paid the native diggers.

The first season's work went slowly. Jungle had to be cleared and the techniques of archaeological digging taught to native workmen. The tropical climate debilitated the staff, who were subject to fever and in constant peril of dysentery. All the time it rained — and rained. By the end of the season the expedition had overspent its budget and found little to show beyond the preliminary groundwork. There were no artifacts to reward the St. Louis financiers with tangible evidence of their money's worth. Hewett and Morley explained that the really important finds were in the nature of heavy stone facings on buildings and monuments, some huge carved figures, and some undecipherable hieroglyphics. They began their long campaign to persuade sponsors that it was better to leave discoveries at the site, carefully restored or housed in small museums, than to carry their loot to some distant city, even if it were transportable, which many Mayan remains were not. Sponsors were not always convinced.

To add to the problem Hewett, like most active scientists, was always behind in his paper work. There was neither time nor energy to organize field notes into scientific papers or even to write popular reports that would publicize the work and encourage future sponsors.

Back at headquarters in Santa Fe's old Palace, Kenneth Chapman was left to mind the shop during Hewett's absence. Primarily an artist, Chapman had been among the young faculty members Hewett recruited for Las Vegas Normal University. He had left the school and entered the employ of Frank Springer, making maps and drawings on a part-time salary; when Hewett asked him to join the Museum staff in Santa Fe he wangled a small stipend to supplement what Springer paid.

Governor Mills did not exaggerate when he said that the Museum's collections threatened to swamp the building. An unorganized jumble of material arrived faster than it could be accessioned — bowls, arrowheads and other hunting tools, fragments of ancient weaving, bone artifacts — anything obtained as the School's share of its own excavation in the Southwest, by purchase, or in exchange with other museums. Chapman did his conscientious best to enlighten important visitors, handle the correspondence, and store the input, but administration was not his long suit and many problems could not be solved by anybody until Hewett himself returned. Through the years Chapman was to become an outstanding authority on Pueblo ceramics, but at this point in his career he was doggedly trying to carry on in Hewett's absence, with little time left for any work of his own.

Throughout 1910 and 1911 a mounting pile of appeals found their way to the Director's desk: applications for summer schools conducted at various excavations; requests for lectures, not only to the Western societies but for scientific meetings and college groups in the Eastern states; appeals to do something about the deplorable condition of the ruins at Uxmal and other ruins in Mexico and Central America; applications for jobs; letters concerning exchange of artifacts or purchase of pothunters' loot; and correspondence about literature published by the School. It was Hewett's earnest intention that all this mail receive proper consideration, but often the stack on his desk, requiring decisions no one else could make, became so far in arrears as to be obsolete.

Because he spent part of his year in Washington, Hewett rented a room at 210 E Street, N. E., at the home of A. F. Barrett, a member of the Capitol police force and a devout amateur archaeologist. Barrett collected "pottery dishes" and took care of Hewett's possessions, including a special chair in which Hewett sat and worked during his Washington visits. An increasing amount of the work load centered in Santa Fe, however, and Edgar finally gave up his room in the Barrett home.

10
⋙❧

THE SCHOOL BROADENS
ITS ACTIVITIES

I spent a good deal of time identifying counterfeits in large collections. I found that the only way to learn to know counterfeits was by studying the genuine. — ELH

Hewett's schedule of operations for 1911 shows the planning of an ambitious man who never gave a thought to the limits of his own energy and expected his associates to perform equally well. From January through May he was the leader of the expedition to Quirigua where the previous season's work had cleared a relatively small area from the clutches of the jungle. Such an expedition was an exercise in logistics, requiring months of previous planning detailed down to the inclusion of thirty-six gallons of mineral water for the staff. Hewett had to wheedle funds from the dissatisfied sponsors of the St. Louis Society and apologize for delays in preparing formal reports. He wrote to the secretary, "You see I am accountable to the St. Louis Society, the Fruit Company, the Institute, and the School of Archaeology, so it [the money] makes quite a circuit before being handed out to the peons at Quirigua."[1]

The United Fruit Company was generous about supplying the use of its equipment; one list forwarded by Hewett stipulated ten wheelbarrows, forty long-handled grading shovels, four dump cars of the same gauge as the plantation railway system, sufficient iron for track leading to the ruins, a one-thousand-gallon "Panama" tank (whatever that was), and a motor car. In addition the company procured necessary permits for visas and for digging on its land, local manpower to wield the long-handled shovels, and adequate quarters for the visiting staff, and supplied the expedition's transportation to and from Guatemala on a company fruit boat.

The staff Hewett recruited was made up of young scientists who were willing to serve in any capacity required. In spite of all precautions about food handling and the best living quarters that could be arranged, the men inevitably came down with "Guatemala fever" which plagued them off and on for years afterward. Jesse Nusbaum's hearing was permanently impaired, and even Hewett, who always

Jesse Nusbaum and Charles F. Lummis, Gua-temala, 1911. Courtesy of the Museum of New Mexico.

Quimu and Charles F. Lummis at Stela K., Quirigua, Guatemala, 1911. Photograph by Jesse Nusbaum. Courtesy of the Museum of New Mexico.

boasted of his good health, brought a bout of fever home with him. His friends and associates, especially the Regents of the School, worried that he was undertaking too much for one man, and for a brief period he actually considered giving up further excavation at the site for a time.

In the end the three seasons' work was undoubtedly worthwhile, although Quirigua was not an outstanding archaeological site. The work there provided valuable experience and fired the ambitions of several young men who would make names for themselves in the field. Sylvanus Morley, paid $100 a month as "the director's assistant," laid the groundwork for his future preeminence in the field. Earl Morris, a student at Boulder, Colorado, applied for the 1912 expedition, as did Neil Judd, then enrolled at the University of Utah in Salt Lake City. Hewett was subsequently able to further Judd's career by helping him apply for work at the National Museum in Washington where, although the salary was a bare maintenance of between $75 and $100 a month, Judd could advance in his training Later, Hewett arranged for Judd to be offered the troublesome job of superintendent at Mesa Verde — a postion that paid $1,500 a year and was worth far more for the work accomplished.

During Hewett's absence from Santa Fe, incidents that might have been easily smoothed out had he been present grew out of all proportion. One of these involved a well-respected scientist.

Colleagues of the scientific fraternity as well as aspiring students were encouraged to visit and study the growing collections at the Museum of New Mexico. Among them was a staff member of the American Museum of Natural History in New York. He asked permission to examine the Santa Fe material and was accorded free access. It was a time when the artist Carl Lotave was engaged in painting murals to decorate the rooms of the old Palace. After the visitor left, word reached Hewett in Guatemala that a valuable piece of ancient pottery as well as one of Lotave's original sketches for a mural were missing. Perturbed, Hewett wrote Chapman for his evaluation of the problem. Chapman replied that the man had been troublesome, very nosy, and too curious about all Museum affairs. Convinced, Hewett wrote to Clark Wissler, director of the National History Museum, that no further invitations would be extended to the accused staff member. Wissler's reply was a stiff denial that his man had been guilty of any impropriety. He went on to say that the Lotave painting was a reject sold to him by the artist, and that a search of his artifact collection failed to turn up the missing pot. Wissler wound up by assuring Hewett that the staff of his museum would not seek any invitations from Santa Fe in the future — indeed, that they would try to avoid the place. The resulting ill feeling returned to plague Hewett in later years.[2]

The Director of the Museum of New Mexico and the School of American Archaeology was not so completely immersed in his duties that he found no time for social life. In Santa Fe he was in constant demand for dinner parties and other functions. Since he was an eligible widower, mothers of charming young ladies regarded him with favor and encouraged their daughters to become interested in science, even to the extent of taking fieldwork in archaeology at the summer sessions or joining horseback trips organized by the School to visit the more remote spots of interest in the Pajarito area.

It became apparent, however, that Hewett was showing a preference for a young divorcee who had no social pretensions. Donizetta Jones Wood had first come to Santa Fe as a teacher on the staff of the Allison-James School, a Presbyterian mission effort devoted to helping young Spanish Americans from the rural part of northern New Mexico to obtain an education. It was a time when the schools of the mountain villages were one-room affairs, usually taught by a teacher of limited training and little command of English. Hewett first came to know Donizetta and Mrs. Jones (a matron in the school where her daughter taught)

Donizetta Jones Wood Hewett, Edgar Lee Hewett's second wife, ca. 1912. Courtesy of the School of American Research.

Frederick W. Hodge with Indian helper, ca. 1910. Courtesy of the School of American Research.

because Donizetta had been a classmate of his wife Cora when both young women were taking their teacher training at Lindenwood College.

Donizetta's marriage to a railway mail clerk named Wood was not a happy one. Wood was a religious zealot, so filled with missionary enthusiasm that the postal service finally dismissed him for stamping such texts as JESUS SAVES on the mail he handled. Although Donizetta and her mother believed in a reasonable amount of religious fervor, as Wood behaved in an increasingly erratic manner family and friends convinced Donizetta that she must seek a divorce.

Thrown on her own resources, she asked Hewett's assistance; he employed her as secretary-receptionist at the Museum where she could help him with his correspondence, and in his absence take some of the load from Chapman's shoulders by showing visitors around. In November 1911 Mrs. Wood resigned her position at the Museum to marry the Director.

A letter of appreciation for her services, signed by Governor Mills, by Judge McFie as President of the Board of Regents, and by Nathan Jaffa, Secretary and Treasurer of the Board, read in part: "We feel that to your conscientious, painstaking service is due in a very great measure the popularity that our Museum has attained with the public."[3]

Edgar L. Hewett and Donizetta Wood were married in Red Oak, Iowa (her mother's home town) on December 30. If some young socialites in Santa Fe were disappointed they soon turned their attention to other men, while Doni Hewett moved quietly from her position as Museum receptionist to that of gracious hostess in the home of the Director. As Hewett's reputation spread, he was invited to lecture in colleges both in the United States and abroad. He accepted an invitation from Oxford University, since he planned to be in England anyway for a scientific congress, but turned over a proposal for an extended lecture trip in Canada to an associate. Doni, who went with him when his schedule permitted, was easily accepted by his friends and associates.

Much of Hewett's time and thought had to be spent on the problem of promoting his institutions and their projects among patrons and sponsors who could lobby for his budgets and contribute additional funding. Publications offered a channel not only for making scientific reports available to other scientists but for public relations with interested laymen. The ponderous Bureau of Ethnology annual reports usually came out after the work of an expedition had been completed and evaluated; they made valuable reference works and could help to document and justify Congressional appropriations, but they had little circulation among the general public. Publications of the Institute, the American Academy for the Advancement of Science and other learned groups were directed to their membership. Hewett needed a more popular vehicle to promote the proliferating activities directed from his office in Santa Fe. He consulted his old friend Paul A. F. Walter, whose newspaper experience made him the ideal choice to edit such a magazine. They named it *El Palacio* and established its publication headquarters in the old Palace. It gave them a press for articles and reports that soon had a wide readership among the public concerned with local, national and international items in art and archaeology.

Among the protégés for whom Hewett first sought sponsorship during this period was John P. Harrington, whose specialty was linguistics. Hewett arranged for Harrington to be funded jointly by the Smithsonian and the School of American Archaeology in a research grant to study language and customs of the Mohave and Yuman Indians of Arizona and California. The deal was for Harrington to be supported during the 1910-11 and 1911-12 seasons for a total of eighteen months. At the end of that time he was to send in a report prepared for publication by the Bureau of Ethnology. The work went more slowly than anticipated, however, and Hewett was urged by Dr. Frederick Hodge at the Bureau to speed up the report. Hodge was in the difficult position of being forced to come up with tangible results for the money advance, thus justifying his requests to Congress for continuing support, while giving his scientists enough time and encouragement to do creditable work. Urged to complete the project, Harrington complained that he had been delayed because Hewett did not forward to him the funds he needed. Hewett countered with the assertion that Harrington had overspent his budget and was not entitled to more money. Harrington promptly complained to Hodge that Hewett was thwarting his work by failure to cooperate, so Hodge wrote to Hewett inquiring as tactfully as possible whether Hewett had indeed undertaken to supervise more projects than he should have assumed, and whether the funding had been properly planned.

The correspondence among the three men finally led to an uncharacteristic outburst from Hewett, who, whatever he may have revealed in private conversation, was usually carefully discreet in his written communications. A long letter to Hodge dated June 19, 1911 ends with this summary:

> I do not want his [Harrington's] shortcomings to be made more widely
> known than necessary. Some way we must get control of him. I got for him
> practically every opportunity he has ever had in research and every
> opportunity he asked for. He begged for a start in the Southwest and I
> arranged it. He pleaded for a chance to go on with his Mohave work and I
> arranged it. He begged for some money for Yuman collections and I got it.
> He begged for the Finch library and I managed that for him. He professes
> undying loyalty, profound gratitude and everything that is possible to
> human achievement in return, and yet continually fails to keep his
> promises, no matter how serious the consequences to himself and others.
> Do you wonder that I find him trying? And do you wonder that I still have
> faith in him?[4]

The letter demonstrates very well the dilemma in which Hewett often placed himself; he was enthusiastic over proposals to further human knowledge and sought to encourage the scientists who asked for help, but the funds were often inadequate and the results delayed to the point where his protégés turned back on him and blamed him for failing to anticipate their needs. With his philosophy of

Julian Martinez of San Ildefonso Pueblo at El Rito de los Frijoles. Courtesy of the Museum of New Mexico.

Early excavation of Tyuonyi, El Rito de los Frijoles, ca. 1908. Courtesy of the Museum of New Mexico.

giving them "a push off de pier" he sometimes threw them into swifter currents than they could conquer, and when they yelled for help he had to find some way to rescue them. Nevertheless, his patience was great, and with most of them, as with Harrington, he managed to find a way for them to keep on swimming and remain his friends. When one became an opponent or even an enemy, he bore no rancor. It was all part of the job.

After the 1911 season in Quirigua closed, Hewett went on to fieldwork in the Pajarito that centered in a summer school session at the Rito de los Frijoles during July; work at Cochiti in August; some survey work in the Chama region in September; and a commitment to teach at the University of Colorado during September. Then it was time to sandwich preparations for the next Guatemalan season between catching up with the backlog of reports and other work on his desk. Throughout the year there were train trips for consultation with Washington colleagues and meetings of the Board of Regents and the Managing Board (often scheduled back to back). It was probably fortunate that Doni Wood was working with him in the Museum, or he might never have found enough time for his courtship that culminated in their marriage just before he was to take off for the 1912 season at Quirigua. Morley was with him once again there, as well as some of the other young men who were sufficiently experienced by this time to keep the operation running without the Director spending full time on the site.

It was during this period that Hewett acquired some important material in the Mayan field for the School's library. For this job he employed a woman named Alice M. Kurty, who undertook to find ancient books and manuscripts that would be valuable reference material. Hewett placed a sum of money in her hands, with instructions that the School would buy such of her discoveries as he could use and that she would be free to sell the rest elsewhere. The arrangement resulted in some valuable acquisitions.

During these years Hewett had not been completely successful in keeping his governing boards happy with his operations. Franz Boas, a member of the original Managing Committee of the American School, resigned in December 1909, expressing his disapproval of both the scientific and administrative methods of *Mr.* Hewett and complaining that Hewett was not fit to head the School because he was not thorough, covered too much ground, and dissipated his energies.

Boas' criticism was set out in a letter to Francis Kelsey in which he explained that he believed the progress of science required slow and steady work by trained observers. He deplored the participation of local interests that could not possibly be well supervised and felt that such amateurish work was little short of criminal. Ruins would be safer left untouched until competent men could save them.[5]

Hewett must have been stung by Boas' criticism. He had made surveys and talked to many informants before he drove a spade into the ancient sites. As he later commented, "It took me quite a while to disturb the soil that I felt was sacred; longer still to spoil the scene with scientific papers."[6] He was careful to leave untouched portions of every ruin in order that those who came after him (and must therefore be wiser) might find pristine evidence for their own interpretations.

The philosophical approach followed by the two men in their work among the Indians was worlds apart. Boas, attempting to find reliable informants among the Northwest tribes with whom he worked in the 1880s and 1890s, complained in letters to his wife that the natives were unreliable and uncooperative. Thwarted in his efforts to coax information from them, he grew arrogant and angry. Commissioned to take anthropometric measurements (a task he did not relish anyway), he was irritated when the natives refused to become his guinea pigs. Finally Boas was compelled to use Indians in prison and children in mission schools for his subjects, and in despair after his sixth field trip to the Northwest he told his wife that in the future some young student must be found for such lowly work. "After this trip I shall never do it again. All this measuring, or rather the talk connected with it to get the Indians, is really repulsive," he wrote.[7]

In contrast, Hewett enjoyed the hours he sat in relaxed communion with his Pueblo friends, stowing away in his mind every crumb of understanding. While Boas insisted that the Indians owed it to science to assist in describing themselves, Hewett would sit all night in a crowded kiva or stay awake by a campfire, quietly listening. He commented, "When the storytelling began, there was no evasion or restraint. It was like the 'Uncorking of the Rain Jars' of their own mythologies."[8]

During the years of his horseback explorations of the Pajarito Plateau, the Indians who guided him and lived with him in the wilderness came to trust his sensitivity. He made lifelong friends of such men as Weyima (Antonio Domingo Pena); Potsonutsee (Diegito Roybal); Oyegepi (Santiago Naranjo); and Agauono (Juan Gonzales). He said they were the best teachers he ever had.

Although he was piqued by Boas' criticism, Hewett still respected the accomplishments of his fellow scientist, and the matter of Boas' resignation would have ended there if Boas had allowed it to drop. In the way that gossip follows bad friends, however, Boas was convinced that Hewett made derogatory remarks about him. Believing that he had been charged with dishonesty in accepting double payment for some of his fieldwork, Boas wrote Hewett an angry note, accusing him of libel.

Under date of May 11, 1911 Hewett replied briefly, "I am in receipt of your note of the 27th ult. In reply I beg leave to state you have been misinformed — the statements attributed to me have not been made."[9]

Hewett's denial did not mollify Boas. He called Hewett a prevaricator and said that he would bring the director of the American School to court if he could afford the expense. In a rather remarkable letter he asked Hewett to place himself under the jurisdiction of a court more convenient (for Boas) than Santa Fe, to which Boas might more easily bring his own witnesses. Hewett, with a dozen projects claiming his attention, had little patience for such bickering. The majority of his two managing boards believed in him and backed him. Indeed, he had been early placed under mandate to encourage local participation as much as possible. He went his busy way, for the most part ignoring his detractors, which only further infuriated

Boas. As usually happens in the struggle for professional prestige, each man had his partisans.

Ex-Governor Prince continued to oppose Hewett at every opportunity, although the two men maintained surface amenities. Other Santa Fe historians, like Ralph Emerson Twitchell, were more friendly. Twitchell was a Board member who served as attorney for the Atchison, Topeka & Santa Fe Railway. In seeking financial support for the School, Hewett asked the attorney to approach railway officials, but Twitchell replied under date of February 28, 1911 that the time was not propitious. He had served as both president and vice-president of the New Mexico Historical Society, and was engaged at the time in compiling his monumental *Leading Facts of New Mexico History,* for which he was also seeking funding. In his letter to Hewett he commented that he found ex-Governor Prince "a thorn in the flesh; I can see sprouting in his intellectual garden some plants of the jealousy species; first time, however, that I have detected anything of the sort so far as efforts of mine go."[10] Twitchell thought it strange that some people would rather reign in Hell than serve in Heaven. As for himself, he preferred a golden mean — he was not much on reigning, and he had always been a poor server.

In the meantime Hewett continued to assist the careers of the younger men who sought his help. Jesse Nusbaum was entirely happy with an appointment to the staff of the National Museum in Washington that Hewett wangled for him. This apprenticeship was usually open to an appointee of Hewett's choice, and Nusbaum, like other incumbents, was acquiring some college credits while earning a small stipend. He wrote breezy letters, usually asking Hewett to hurry with his past-due check as he found life in Washington more expensive than he had anticipated. He kept a lively contact with Santa Fe affairs through letters from friends and in turn relayed the gossip circulating among the scientific community in Washington. Early in December 1911 he commented, "I hear that our museum is to be the booze joint for the Inaugural Ball [which was to be held in the adjoining Armory Building]. Bet the smell remains until summer. Guess Roque [the janitor] will manage to slip aside about a six months supply."[11] Of the scientists with whom he was working, Nusbaum confided his appraisal to Hewett: "Holmes I like very much, altho he is a little gruff I believe, and Judd is the same good fellow. Hough is a dandy, and although they all dislike Hrdlicka, guess I will like him O.K."[12]

One of the opportunities offered Nusbaum in Washington was to learn how to make masks. He described his progress and then commented, "The only problem on my return will be to get the permission of Antonio Domingo and a few of the fast disappearing Indians to let me plaster them in the face."[13]

Another protégé who became a close friend was Barbara Friere-Marreco, an English woman whom Hewett sponsored by introducing her to Santa Clara Pueblo, where she was soon deeply involved in local politics and ran afoul of Clara True. The redoubtable Miss True was a prim woman who had enjoyed a controversial career in the Indian Service. President Theodore Roosevelt had arranged her appointment under Indian Commissioner Francis Ellington Leupp to be superintendent of the Mission Indians in California, where five reservations were under her jurisdiction—the Morongo and the Mission Creek near Banning, Martinez-Torres and Palm Springs in the desert, and Twenty-Nine Palms in Mohave country. She was soon embroiled with the bootleggers who supplied liquor to *her* Indians, and stirred up so much opposition by her peppery prosecution of them that her enemies finally succeeded in having her dismissed from federal service.

She then transferred her sphere of influence to New Mexico and was soon battling the liquor interests there. Miss Friere-Marreco found Santa Clara in such ferment that she wrote Hewett on September 13, 1911: "Miss True has got seven Indian policemen and one white man to keep the Indians from drinking. Donaciano had a bottle last Monday week and these new policemen took it away from him. Santiago wants something definite to tell the Indians about these policemen as they have nothing to do with Mr. Crandall [the Indian agent] and *his* police."[14]

Hewett did his best to steer a course acceptable to the Indians, Agent Crandall and Clara True; perhaps his mediation helped a little, for he succeeded in remaining friends with all of them.

Friere-Marreco also appealed to him when their friend Santiago had a chill. Would Hewett please send a message recommending quinine? In another letter she reported that the local missionary, Dr. McCurdy, was suffering from eye trouble, and asked Dr. Hewett to take a look at his eyes.

There is nothing in the record to indicate how Hewett responded to these appeals to supply medical information. It seems unlikely that Friere-Marreco, who moved in English academic circles, could have mistaken his Ph.D. title for a medical one. It was customary for the scientists who were trusted by the Indians to assist with their health problems, however. Bandelier went about the country innoculating for smallpox and suffered a cruel bout with it himself, his recovery being little short of a miracle. Doctors were scarce and often mistrusted, and all frontiersmen had to dispense medicine at some time or other. Whatever action Hewett may have taken in response to these appeals, they point up the esteem in which he was held by his Indian friends.

It was about this time that Hewett's advice was sought on a very different matter. He had become an influential member of the Masonic fraternity in Santa Fe where the Scottish Rite was making ambitious plans for a fine new building. Sumner P. Hunt of the Los Angeles architectural firm of Hunt, Eager & Burns appealed to the Museum of New Mexico for a photograph of the proposed site at Washington Avenue and Federal Place, stating that "through the interest of Mr. Hewett we have been commissioned to make plans for the new Scottish Rite Cathedral in Santa Fe."[15] The building that resulted became a landmark, although enthusiasm for its architectural style (which was said to have been inspired by Spain's Alhambra) has waned somewhat through the years.

11

HEWETT TAKES ON THE SAN DIEGO EXPOSITION

A land of wheat, and barley, and vines, and fig trees, and pomegranates; A land of olive trees and honey.—
Deuteronomy 8:8
[Inscribed on the California Building in Balboa Park]

In Santa Fe it had been decided to devote two central rooms of the old Palace respectively to the excavations of Puyé and Frijoles. The artist Carl Lotave was employed to make a mural above the exhibit cases in each room. It was one of his sketches that had gone to spark the rift with the staff of the Museum of Natural History in New York, and Lotave was now indirectly responsible for Hewett's making another enemy who was to work against his schemes.

In 1910 Bronson Cutting, a wealthy young Harvard man from New York, moved to New Mexico seeking a cure for tuberculosis. His sister came to visit him, and, like several other young ladies, found Lotave very attractive. He, in turn, paid her marked attention. The couple created gossip, as they often rode together in a carriage around the plaza and Miss Cutting frequented the Museum to watch Lotave at work. When word got to Hewett that his artist employee was using the Museum as a place of rendezvous he sought out Cutting, explained that Lotave's reputation as a ladies' man might be damaging to his sister's reputation, and suggested that perhaps Cutting would like to do something about it.

Cutting was neither grateful nor amused. He curtly told the Director of the Museum to mind his own business. In later years, as the rift widened between Hewett and many of his former Harvard associates, Bronson Cutting often led the opposition. Cutting's power grew steadily from the year of his arrival, 1910, to the time of his death in 1935. A later student of his life, New Mexico's Governor Jack

97

Campbell, said of him, "I believe most political scientists would agree that this wealthy, simple, calculating, unpredictable, idealistic, ruthless, generous, self-centered and shy individual, known among his Spanish-American followers as the 'Don of Santa Fe' held the balance of power in almost every election from 1912 to 1932...in New Mexico."[1]

Since Hewett had to go to the well of legislative appropriations every two years to sustain his growing empire, Cutting's opposition was no small thing. Indeed, it grew in strength as the power of Hewett's Republican friends in the state gradually declined, until Cutting's forces might have vanquished him utterly had it not been for the politician's untimely death.

In 1911, however, Hewett was riding high and seemed in complete command of his future. In the autumn of that year he received a request from Col. D. C. Collier, Director-General of the Panama-California Exposition which was being planned for San Diego, to accept the post of Director of Exhibits. Hewett promptly relayed the request to the School's executive committee, seeking their approval and telling them that Alice Fletcher, the chairman, would undoubtedly ask for a vote on the proposition at their next meeting.

"He [Collier] is for doing the most substantial scientific work such as has never been done before in connection with an Exposition and believes in putting into our hands ample means for the purpose," Hewett wrote, and continued:

> I talked over the work with him at great length, and I find that practically everything that he desires can be accomplished in connection with the expeditions that we have all along proposed to put in the field when funds permit. On the technological side the large number of tribes from which they desire us to secure representation, would afford admirable facilities for study during the year at San Diego, for the Exposition will be open from January 1, 1915 to January 1, 1916. Our expeditions would have the great advantage of first studying the tribes in the field, and afterward in settled quarters at San Diego.
>
> The arrangement would enable us to increase the salaries of our men, who are sorely underpaid, and also to take on some good new men who have not yet found openings in our work such as Mr. Kidder and Mr. Bushnell. The plan as laid before us by Mr. Collier meets with my fullest approval.[2]

Replies from the committee members ranged from disapproval to enthusiastic support. Among those who opposed the idea was Dr. Frederick Hodge, who wrote that he felt Hewett was already overextended and should concentrate on the projects already under way, rather than expand to meet this new opportunity. He warned that the St. Louis Archaeological Society was withdrawing support for the dig at Quirigua, since they did not feel it had been sufficiently productive. Hodge, of course, knew of Hewett's difficulty in getting John Harrington to finish his proposed publication, and found it hard to reconcile his own need for planning with Hewett's tendency to rearrange projects whenever a more convenient or rewarding suggestion opened up. The previous summer Hodge had written in some agitation, "There seems to have been a revision of your summer's plan all around. When does the summer school begin and end? Please let me know about this, since with the proposed Jemez work in July, the Cochiti work in August, and the Chama researches and your University of Colorado work in September, I cannot see when the School comes in."[3]

Hewett needed as large an allotment of financial assistance as he could coax out of the Bureau, and it was usually granted in anticipation of reports that would be ready for publication when Hodge needed them. During 1911 he wanted to keep Harrington happy in his Mohave work even though the final report would be later than the original agreement (the material promised for January 1 had not been received by June); he hoped to schedule Morley's *Introduction to the Study of Maya Hieroglyphics*; and he sought space for reports on progress of continuing work in the Rio Grande pueblos, the Pajarito Plateau and the Jemez Valley. In addition Hewett's encouragement of Barbara Friere-Marreco's research among both the Yavapai and the Santa Claras included the hope of eventual publication.

And now he proposed to add men like Alfred Vincent Kidder and David Bushnell to the list of field workers for whom he would solicit support, and to undertake immediately several expeditions that were only in the dreaming stage — all in order to secure exhibits for San Diego. Fred Hodge had reason to think him overambitious.

Hewett was not easily daunted once he had made up his mind. He set about soothing the St. Louis Society into supporting the Quirigua work for another season, proposing that Earl Morris be taken along as an assistant in exchange for his expenses and that Morley be paid his usual $100 a month for at least six months. To the St. Louis people he wrote, "I am quite hopeful that with the jungle cleared from the buildings as at present, the rains will not be as detrimental to the work as heretofore."[4] He was able to tell them that the United Fruit Company would continue its support, and thus finally put together the third and final season.

In the meantime the setup of the School in Santa Fe was taking on a complexity that was perfectly clear and logical to Hewett, but confusing to most outsiders. He kept himself reasonably free of New Mexico political obligations by arranging that as Director of the Museum he receive no salary, so the job was not exactly a plum. As Director of the School, he was paid whatever he and the Executive Committee could scrounge from the Institute. Staff members were carried on the payroll of one institution or the other as the budget permitted, but often worked half time for each, depending on where the money was available. So long as Hewett remained firmly in control there was no great problem, although those who opposed him saw the combination as a two-headed monster, or better, perhaps, as Siamese twins whose bodies could not be separated without permanent impairment or death. Now, in suggesting that he take on responsibility for a big job in San Diego, Hewett was further extending his jurisdiction.

Nevertheless, he succeeded in convincing a majority of the School's board that this new opportunity was a logical expansion of the Americanist work. Congressman Lacey was among those who believed the venture would be a good one. The School and the Museum soon agreed that Hewett could undertake the new job, provided he did not neglect the duties he already carried.

From Washington, Jesse Nusbaum sent congratulations. Alice Fletcher had told him of Hewett's appointment to the post in San Diego and the School's plans for cooperating with the exposition. "I think it is the best you have ever pulled, and am sure glad you got ahead of Dixon and some of the others of Spinden's and Tozzer's and Boas' stamp," he wrote.[5]

The city of San Diego had begun preparations for the Panama-California Exposition in 1909 when G. Aubrey Davidson, banker and civic leader, suggested that an expansive future awaited the quiet little town when the Panama Canal was completed in 1915. Since it was the southernmost port in the United States at the western end of the canal, the potential was enormous, and something big should be done to tell the world about it. As San Diegans tell the story, the idea of a world's fair came first to them, was approved by the city fathers, incorporated as an organization, and duly registered in Sacramento six months before San Franciscans woke up to the possibilities of such a public undertaking to promote *their* city.

When Congress appropriated five million dollars to celebrate the completion of the canal, both West Coast cities set forth their claims to receive the money as a subsidy for their respective exhibitions. San Francisco maintained that San Diego was not large enough to support a show of sufficient magnitude, but Col. D. C. Collier, who had been appointed Director-General for the San Diego Fair, went to Washington to convince Congress that San Diego could do it.

In his presentation he pointed out that San Diego, with a population of 40,000, had the summer climate of Siberia, Alaska, Newfoundland, or Nova Scotia, while the winter weather rivaled the Gulf Coast of the United States, with a variation of only ten degrees between the average temperatures for January and July. To put her fair together San Diego had employed the finest talent money could buy. Insisting that the people of San Diego were the pluckiest, nerviest, gamest in the United States or in the world, Collier told the Congressional committee that the citizens had already raised a million dollars on their own to help finance the exposition and that the 400 acres of Balboa Park set aside for the site were already being improved.

Unfortunately for Col. Collier's promotional effort in the national capital, it was a political reality that San Francisco, with a population of close to half a million, had more clout in Congress. When he continued to get the runaround in spite of all his efforts, he decided to give up and come home. "To hell with Congress," he is reported to have said in disgust, "San Diego has already raised three million dollars on her own; we won't fight over the lousy five million. We'll stage our own Fair."[6]

Which they proceeded to do. Eventually a tactful solution was reached. San Francisco would have the World's Fair, with the big exhibits from leading foreign nations invited by the Federal Government. San Diego would concentrate on quality instead of quantity, with exhibitions from many of the Latin American nations. Congress would give each some financial assistance, and the two fairs would be complementary. Visitors would be encouraged to attend both.

As a theme for the exposition, the planners decided to publicize methods of agricultural development in their area, demonstrating the resources and showing the possibilities for the future in the Southwest and Latin America. Special invitations were extended to the republics to the south and to the nearby Southwestern states. Emphasis was placed on the development of mankind, with the life of Mayan, Aztec and Southwestern Indian tribes to be stressed.

Whether the special emphasis on Central American and Southwestern mankind was first proposed by Hewett or the fecund Collier matters little. Probably the two sparked each other. The scientific aspects of man's history were certainly Hewett's special field, and once the two had cleared the groundwork, Collier sent his formal offer asking Hewett to develop the exhibits. On November 11, 1911 he wrote Hewett, explaining that the purpose of the Panama-California Exposition was to demonstrate the progress of the human race and its future possibilities. He proposed that representative tribes of North and South America be brought together in a congress of the native tribes of the Western Hemisphere, and that a permanent building be erected for the purpose of this demonstration.[7]

Once Hewett had convinced his governing boards that this was an opportunity to broaden the scope of their activities and open new doors to gaining their objectives, he was ready to plunge into organizing the work. Ground breaking for the exposition had taken place on July 1, 1911, inaugurating a four-day fiesta with speeches by dignitaries, industrial and floral parades, the crowning of Queen Ramona by King Cabrillo, and an elaborate historical pageant. The genesis of many subsequent Southwestern celebrations might be traced to San Diego's with its exuberant variety. Banker Davidson, as president, was quick to point out that San Diego began to reap the benefits of the exposition on the day of breaking ground for the administration building. Bank deposits were up nearly $200,000 that week. New population was already pouring in, seeking and finding construction jobs and the related industry that came with new people.

"We do not need to wait until 1915 for benefits," President Davidson boasted in the *Exposition News* for December 1911, and continued:

> The $5,000,000 spent in Balboa Park begins earning money at once. Money is spent at the rate of $1,250,000 per year. This project has resulted in an improved harbor, an extra trolley system, street pavement, new buildings for the City, a new depot of Spanish Colonial design built by the Santa Fe Railroad for the Exposition; thousands of new homes are built or planned, apartment houses, restaurants and so on are planned. There is a twenty million dollar layout. In the meantime, there is work for every type and trade.[8]

Money was indeed begetting money in San Diego. Every time anyone spoke or wrote of the exposition the amounts were doubled, trebled or increased fivefold.

The permanent building that Collier promised in his invitation to Hewett turned out to be the California Building, which became headquarters for the Science of Man exhibit. As the San Diego *Exposition News* of October 1912 described it, "The theme running through the exposition will be Progress of Man and his achievements in the completion of the Panama Canal, evidence of what has been done on the American continent for a period of 3,000 years before Christ, the reproduction of monuments and temples in Yucatan and Cliff Dwellers from New Mexico and Arizona as discovered by Coronado in 1540."[9]

In persuading his boards and other backers that it would be advantageous for him to serve as director of exhibits, Hewett claimed that the projected activities connected with the exposition would offer a wonderful opportunity to enlarge the activities of the School, particularly in research, and to promote the education and salary of the staff, for whom he was always seeking advancement.

As the plan progressed, however, it became evident that the School lacked the financial resources and manpower to accomplish so much in the brief time allotted. Rather than bite off more than he could digest or shrink the size of his plans, Hewett turned to colleagues in other institutions. He had always been in close touch with the leaders at the Smithsonian, and his sponsorship of a series of young apprentices kept him well acquainted with its staff. Although he had, as Jesse Nusbaum bragged, "put it over" on some eminent eastern scientists when he secured the directorship, Hewett now needed and sought their help. The Smithsonian granted an appropriation of $100,000, which gave the enterprise quasi-governmental backing, and Ales Hrdlicka was given responsibility for accumulating an exhibit to be the most comprehensive ever attempted in the field of physical anthropology. With such prestigious backing, noted scientists from the Anthropological Institute of Prague, the Anthropological Institute of Warsaw, Georgetown University, the National Museum, and others began to scurry around the world, procuring casts of skeletal material. Expeditions went to areas near ancient mounds and caves, seeking sculptured busts of contemporary types for contrast and comparison.

Hewett was soon so deeply involved that in order to give necessary attention to the exposition he and Mrs. Hewett found a residence in San Diego. He retained his desk in Santa Fe where Paul A. F. Walter and Kenneth Chapman were kept busy pinch-hitting for him, carrying out the directives prepared on his frequent visits or sent by mail from San Diego or Washington. He simply could not squeeze in a working session for himself in Central America, but he kept in constant touch with his friends there as his plans developed to display material discovered in recent excavations.

Monuments were brought to the Museum of Man from Guatemala. More than 5,000 specimens of ancient pottery, wearing apparel and other articles of ethnological value were garnered from various expeditions. The first condition set by the exposition was that specimens would remain the property of the San Diego public after the exposition was over. Since articles on loan from the Smithsonian

Paul A. F. Walter, Associate Director, Museum of New Mexico, 1914. Courtesy of the Museum of New Mexico.

Kenneth M. Chapman, authority on Indian design. Courtesy of the Museum of New Mexico.

and other museums must be returned, Hewett arranged for replicas, copies or molds to be made for the permanent exhibit. Failing these, paintings had to suffice, or, as a last resort, photographs.

The "noble California building, greatest of all in the Exposition City," was entirely devoted to ancient America. Writing of it, Hewett said, "Never before have the Mayas been given such a setting as here . . . and never before have they been presented in such perfection. Some of us dare to hope that this is the beginning of a general awakening to the importance of a great people, possibly to the opening up of a veritable treasure-house of knowledge, long obscured, but not destined to perpetual oblivion."[10] Among the models on exhibition was the Temple of Sacrifice at Chichen Itzá. Photos of sculptured monuments from Quirigua and Copán, as well as a tablet from the Altar of the Sun at Palenque, were displayed.

The New Mexico Legislature accepted the invitation to erect a building at the exposition, voted an appropriation and gave enthusiastic support to the whole idea. Col. Ralph Emerson Twitchell was appointed to head the committee in charge, and I. H. Rapp was chosen as architect. Twitchell's two-volume history of New Mexico had brought him a wide following, although some critics carped that the amount of space allotted to contemporaries was weighted by the amount of their subscription to help pay for the work. Twitchell also founded and edited a periodical called *Old Santa Fe—A Magazine of History, Archaeology, Genealogy and Biography* in which he continued to publish information along the line of his special interests. He seemed properly qualified to take charge of the New Mexico exhibit. Rapp drew his inspiration for the building from paintings made by the artist Carlos Vierra which depicted the facades of New Mexico's mission churches; the structure erected in Balboa Park became, in turn, the model for the New Mexico Art Museum a few years later.

Several men recruited by Hewett built international reputations on the work they produced for the Science of Man exhibits, which spread over five large rooms. The first room told the story of man's evolution; the second illustrated the development of the human body from birth to old age; the third contained illustrations of physical variations of various races and subraces; the fourth centered on prehistoric pathology and surgery; and the fifth room became an anthropological laboratory.

Two struggling Santa Fe artists, Gerald Cassidy and Carlos Vierra, were commissioned to paint murals for the rooms. Cassidy had been well established as a lithographer in New York when he decided that he preferred to be a painter of fine art in the Southwest. Perhaps he originally came because of the delicate health of his first wife. After her death he married a Denver widow, Ina Sizer, who encouraged his ambitions. They remodelled an old adobe house on Canyon Road in Santa Fe and traveled the Indian country of New Mexico and Arizona. Cassidy drew the strong faces of Indians who interested him and caught the delicate nuances of the desert in his landscapes. In the early years of his struggle for recognition important sales were not frequent, so he was glad to sell his work for a few dollars to

Carlos Vierra at work on mural for Central America exhibit, Panama-California Exposition, San Diego, California, 1915. Courtesy of the Museum of New Mexico.

New Mexico Building, Panama-California Exposition, San Diego, California, 1915. Courtesy of the Museum of New Mexico.

cover necessities. He was trying to build patronage in California when his friend John P. Harrington became aware of his financial plight and urged Hewett to commission Cassidy as a muralist.

Carlos Vierra, a Californian of Portuguese ancestry, had been a sailor before he became a full-time painter. The murals he painted for the exposition were done on huge canvases in his Tesuque, New Mexico studio and prepared for shipment by railway freight to be installed on the walls of the California museum. Two Santa Feans built models of Indian sites for the exposition — Wesley Bradfield made replicas of Mayan monuments, and Jesse Nusbaum constructed models of the living pueblos with which he was familiar.

As the deadline for installing exhibits approached, the pace of all concerned, most especially the director, became frenetic. Payments for materials were slow, and those tied to government finances could not proceed without temporary subsidy. Carload shipments were arranged from Washington for the material prepared at the Smithsonian and the related museums; another carload was assembled in Santa Fe to take the Vierra murals and the commissions assembled by the Museum and School staff, as well as the exhibits Twitchell had assembled for the New Mexico state building. Hewett was constantly tested as he begged for money and made loans from his own pocket when all else failed, spurred the laggard, encouraged the disaffected, and coordinated the whole project. If there were times when he doubted that his grand schemes would ever be completed, he gave no sign. The theme of the show — The Science of Man — was the thread that bound his whole career together, and he was determined that his fine showcase would live up to its billing.

When the exposition opened on New Year's Eve — December 31, 1914 — Europe had been embattled for five months in World War I, but there was no trace of that struggle in San Diego. One lyrical observer wrote,

> The soft, balmy air of Southern California, the exquisite brightness of the full moon, the incomparable site, and the handsome buildings all complete (and this is the first Exposition in the United States of which this can be said on the opening day), the distinguished guests, the gay throngs, of whom thirty thousand passed through the gates on the opening night — all contributed to make the event memorable and worthy of the occasion which it celebrated, namely the opening of the Panama Canal.
>
> New Year's Day dawned bright and clear, not a cloud in the sky, the birds were singing, the flowers were in bloom — for all the world it was like a day in June, and the city and the Exposition gave a right royal welcome to their thousands of guests. At the Exposition there were speeches and congratulations.... San Diego had taken her place as a new-orld Mecca; she had won her right to be regarded as one of the earth's most favored spots...
>
> One can look forward a thousand years and imagine man here, grown to the stature of his surroundings, under the influence of spiritual ideas,

having laid aside the modern restlessness, jerkiness, angularity, crudeness and intense greed and grown *quiet,* a little reverent and sincere, with the beauty of the sunlight and the mountains soaked into his consciousness. Then there will be great Art, great and astonishing poetry, a civilization worthy of the name. Our descendents may attain to the majestic dignity of the Egyptians, the clearness and poise of the Greeks, the magical insight into nature of the great old Chinese of Tan and Sung times — plus something peculiar and Californian of their own; in all, a richness and beauty of culture of whose like history has no record. It is a long way ahead, to judge by the screaming, tearing, screeching ugliness of our present life; but here is promise of it.[11]

Sixty years later the prophecy of that exuberant New Year's Day seems fulsome and simplistic, but the prophet gave it a span of a thousand years for fulfillment, and it surely reflected the buoyant optimism of all those who had assisted in making the Science of Man exhibit a thing of wonder.

The official exposition colors were yellow and red. More than forty thousand poinsettia plants were in full bloom, and their vivid red contrasted with the yellow of blossoming acacias. Bougainvillea of red and yellow festooned the buildings; the workers wore Spanish costumes, carrying out the color scheme. San Diego had justified Col. Collier's most extravagant boast. Not only were the buildings complete and everything in readiness, but the Panama-California Exposition was out of debt.

Not everything was sober education or science. Many features were designed for sheer entertainment. There were Spanish dancers costumed in red and yellow. Some months after the opening their ballerina, La Belle Savilla, sent the exposition management a bill for $600 to cover the cost of her dancing slippers. Her dainty feet required custom-made slippers only seven inches long; she was employed for thirty weeks, and estimated that she danced fifteen miles a day.

There was other entertainment. A street of concessions offered the usual varied choice — scary rides, mazes and roller coasters. Night life was not neglected. "Paris After Midnight" and "The Grizzly Gulch" were two favorite spots. "The Sultan's Harem" was considered so naughty that a local minister complained to the newspapers. Representatives of the exposition were sent to check and were assured by the promoters that what they saw was the regular show, not something cleaned up for their benefit. H. J. Penfold, exposition secretary, wrote to the San Diego County District Attorney Spencer M. Marsh suggesting that opinions concerning decency or indecency reflect the mental attitude of individuals. The charges were dropped, and the show went on.

In the three years of final planning and carrying out the exposition San Diego's population trebled, reaching 100,000. The city bragged that she never had labor troubles, and with the present system of government she never would have. Her men, women and children were declared to be the happiest, healthiest lot of people on the West Coast, and that, of course, meant in the entire United States.

The impetus was given by the men and women who dreamed up the exposition, struggled to realize their dream, kept it going for a second full year, and then built on that splendid beginning. No wonder San Diegans are protective of those old buildings, and battled to save them long before historic preservation became nationally fashionable.

For the planners of the exposition, many good things came to pass immediately. Collier and Hewett realized their ambition for a permanent building for the Museum of Man. From the moment he established a residence in San Diego Hewett encouraged the local archaeological society, and before the show was closed a group of public spirited citizens was ready to help establish a museum of archaeology, anthropology and ethnology. Out of this local interest the San Diego Museum and San Diego Museum Association developed, with Edgar Lee Hewett as the first director. For him it was not a matter of making a difficult choice between Santa Fe and San Diego. He simply used one to spark the other, and henceforth was official director of three busy institutions.

12

❧✦❧

HEWETT TAKES ON THE
SANTA FE CHAMBER OF COMMERCE

We refuse to have any enemies. Such, I believe to be the
spirit in which all of us must go on to our future
work.—ELH

Three years elapsed between the time Hewett secured permission to work on the San Diego Exposition and the night of its grand opening. His governing boards had stipulated that he should not neglect his jobs in Santa Fe, and in dividing his time between his dual headquarters he never let anyone forget that he was *the* Director.

In Santa Fe life in the Palace was often contentious, in spite of the best efforts of Paul A. F. Walter and Kenneth Chapman to mind the show and keep everything running smoothly. They handled the day-to-day flow of visitors and correspondence that deluged them, made as many decisions as Hewett would permit them to make, and kept him as well informed concerning their problems as his busy schedule permitted. Both men were supposed to be developing careers of their own — Walter as a writer and editor, Chapman as an artist specializing in Pueblo pottery. The Historical Society still maintained its rooms in the east end of the Palace, and Prince tried to assert his rights against encroaching Museum interests, even though his influence was steadily waning. Mrs. Prince spent much of her time in their Long Island home. Eventually the couple made it their residence, although they kept many ties with Santa Fe through old friendships and extensive real estate holdings.

New Mexico's long battle for statehood was finally won in 1912 when it became the forty-seventh state, so the energies of its people could be directed in other channels. During the summer of 1913 Santa Fe was sparked with new ambition which was spearheaded by the Chamber of Commerce, with Harry Dorman as president. Under the curious title of the New-Old Santa Fe Movement, a publicity program was inaugurated for the city with the avowed object of encouraging owners and builders to retain, as far as possible, "the old Spanish style of architecture, including the stucco finish, which is part of the ancient mode that has come down for centuries." Santa Fe was to be made so distinctive in character that both tourists and permanent residents would be attracted.

The September 1913 *Santa Fe New Mexican* headlined: "SANTA FE DECLARED 'THE OLDEST CITY' IN THE UNITED STATES. Santa Fe Chamber of Commerce Vote to Have That Legend Printed on 68,000 Envelopes to be Used by the Merchants and Others to Strive to Swell the Tourist Crop." The article under this banner admitted that there was some question concerning the authenticity of the slogan, but continued:

> Some one who had heard of St. Augustine's claim to the "oldest city" suggested that the slogan be changed to "second oldest city" but the merchants who had ordered the envelopes said, "Nay, Nay. After all, what is the use of taking second place and telling the world about it?"
> So the matter was aired at the meeting last night. Colonel Ralph E. Twitchell, historian and lawyer, and former Governor L. Bradford Prince, President of the New Mexico Historical Society, rallied to the support of the oldest city boosters and declared,
> "There is no documentary proof there is any city in the United States that is OLDER than Santa Fe."[1]

Sylvanus G. Morley, trained by both Harvard and Hewett to be careful of facts, offered his opinion that Santa Fe lacked evidence that it is the oldest European city in the United States. His careful emphasis on the term *European* was overlooked in the heat of the debate. Hewett, who was present at the meeting, maintained a calm silence.

Encouraged by the enthusiasm of most of its members, the Chamber order for 68,000 envelopes was increased to 125,000. Hewett went quietly home from the meeting, considering his best course of action. He was already in a sensitive position with reference to the Chamber and its president. Two years previously he had given permission for the Chamber to headquarter in a small room in the west end of the Palace, with the understanding that 1912 should be rent free but in 1913 the Chamber would pay $375, which would help defray some staff salaries and other operating expenses (expenses from which the Chamber also benefitted). Chamber memberships and contributions had been slow, however, the $375 had not been paid, and the Museum was hard pressed to pay its utility bills.

After thinking it over, Hewett took two steps which so antagonized Dorman that all hell broke loose. Hewett asked the Chamber either to pay up or vacate the room in the Palace. Also, he supported Morley's position that Santa Fe should not advertise itself as the Oldest City. Mindful that some people did not regard him as the ultimate authority on the history of the United States in general and the

Southwest in particular, Hewett wrote asking for opinions on Santa Fe's claim from the best sources he knew—Bandelier, Lummis, F. W. Hodge, and the local historian, Benjamin M. Read.[2]

Part of the argument centered on semantics. Santa Fe, known as *La Villa Real,* had apparently never been dignified in the old documents by the name *ciudad,* and thus some claimed that it had not been a city at all in the earliest days. Everyone acknowledged that several settlements on the East Coast took precedence in founding, but it seemed that only St. Augustine, Florida, could lay claim to having been *continuously occupied* from an earlier date than anything Santa Fe could document. Some historians brought up the delicate question of whether Santa Fe's claim to continuous occupation by Europeans should begin as late as 1692, since there was that twelve-year hiatus between the Pueblo Revolt in 1680, when the Spaniards were driven out, and De Vargas' reconquest in 1692. Might this not invalidate Santa Fe's claim in any case?

The authorities whom Hewett consulted sent prompt replies. B. M. Read stated that for Santa Fe to claim seniority "would be substituting historical fiction for true history," and declared, "Truth blushes and history frowns on the persistence of some people in giving by mistake to the world of fiction for facts." Frederick W. Hodge commented succinctly, "It would hardly seem to be wise to play the iconoclast in view of the just claims of Saint Augustine." Bandelier's reply was received about the same time. "Sir," he wrote formally to his old friend Hewett, "The fact is well established that Santa Fe was founded as late as 1605. San Gabriel (Yunque or, now, Chamita) was the first Spanish settlement in New Mexico but abandoned in 1604. The earliest settlement and one still extant is Saint Augustine in Florida, which was established 1559 or 1560." Lummis concurred in Saint Augustine's priority. Twitchell's support for the Chamber viewpoint was silenced when critics pointed to his own writings, citing 1605 as the earliest possible date for Santa Fe.

Instead of scrapping the Chamber's discredited envelopes, Dorman, backed by Bronson Cutting's *Santa Fe New Mexican,* erupted in a spirited attack on Hewett. In describing the envelopes, Dorman declared that their promotional value was such that they would make even the San Diego Exposition's green envelopes turn a shade greener with envy. It is not hard to sympathize with Dorman's predicament. His financially embarrassed Chamber had secured subscriptions from more than a hundred merchants and individuals to pay the cost of this advertising. If those who protested the validity of the claim to the Oldest City title could be discredited, all would not be lost.

One of those teapot tempests that frequently swirled around Hewett now grew to storm proportions. Several factors contributed to the acrimony. When Franz Boas resigned from the Managing Board of the School two years previously, declaring Hewett unfit to serve as Director, several well-established scientists supported his view. Some members of the Board who admired and backed Hewett were nevertheless opposed to his taking on the added duties at San Diego.

Local politics were also involved. Bronson Cutting, who acquired control of the *Santa Fe New Mexican* in 1912, was building the political strength that would ultimately make him a U.S. senator. One of his allies was former governor Miguel A. Otero, who had arranged Hewett's departure from Las Vegas Normal

Edgar Lee Hewett in Palace of the Governors, ca. 1910. Courtesy of the Museum of New Mexico.

Bronson M. Cutting, U.S. senator from New Mexico, 1927-1935. Courtesy of the Museum of New Mexico.

University and continued to be the archenemy of Frank Springer, the Museum's foremost patron. The running skirmishes between Hewett and Prince were notorious, as each sought to defend or enlarge his own sphere of influence. Partisanship, as it lined up in this new argument, was no new thing, although some people like Twitchell did manage to keep friendly with both sides.

Hewett, who had succeeded in getting his own way in most of the arguments, tried to maintain public silence, but he could not resist an occasional sly poke at his opponents. During the summer of 1913 Col. Twitchell was scheduled to lecture under the auspices of the School on some aspects of Indian religion. Hewett, meanwhile, was not only trying to collect the rent from the Chamber of Commerce but was having difficulty finding the money to pay for some book shelving installed in the east end of the Palace for the benefit of the Historical Society, at Prince's request. In writing to Twitchell about the lecture dates he commented, "I note the interesting title you mention *Gods I Have Met* and I am at once moved to the conclusion that you have been seeing things about the east end of the Old Palace."[3]

In a headline asserting that Hewett was attempting to run the Chamber of Commerce in as dictatorial a manner as he controlled the School of American Archaeology-Museum of New Mexico complex, the president of the Chamber of Commerce called for Hewett's replacement as Director of the two institutions. A box on the front page of the paper lauded the Chamber's recent accomplishments (including the distribution of the debatable envelopes) and continued with a listing of WHAT SANTA FE STILL NEEDS:

> A bureau of immigration for which the legislature did not provide.
> A School of Archaeology (recognized as deserving world-wide fame) with a director at its head who is not merely a promoter but who is recognized as an archaeologist in scientific circles and who is able to obtain the endorsement of the leading eastern universities.
> A School of Archaeology which is able to draw students from the most important institutions of the country and not a few dabblers during the summer session.
> A School of Archaeology with a man at the head who is able to devote more than a few weeks of the year to an institution which should be made the greatest in the country.[4]

Another headline in the same issue bragged that Santa Fe as "the oldest city in the United States is well advertised in the automobile blue book."

A few days later, praise previously accorded by the paper to the Museum's Board of Regents turned sour when it was announced that "A bare quorum of the Board of Regents of the New Mexico Museum consisting of Chairman John R. McFie, Judge Napoleon Bonaparte Laughlin, Col. Ralph E. Twitchell and James L. Seligman — after a lengthy session last night voted to oust the Santa Fe Chamber of Commerce from its present quarters in the Old Palace."[5]

In another boxed notice on the front page, Hewett was offered the columns of the *Santa Fe New Mexican* for a reply to the allegations against him — an invitation which he ignored. Quoted in an interview regarding the ouster vote, President Dorman elaborated upon the Chamber's grievances:

> I regard the action as due entirely to Dr. Hewett's attempt to run the chamber of commerce. As soon as he returned from San Diego in August he began to disturb the pleasant relations which had always existed between the school and the chamber of commerce. We were constantly irritated by this man Hewett; he was always intruding and meddling, even dictating to us as to the use of our room. He nailed up one of the doors

and sent word through an understudy that we should keep certain windows closed and the blinds drawn.

All this we submitted to in the interests of harmony; no protest was made for weeks. Finally the "last straw" was when Dr. Hewett tried to tell us what to print on our envelopes. The chamber of commerce ordered 125,000 envelopes printed with the wording "the Oldest City in the United States" at a meeting at which Dr. Hewett was present and said nothing. The next day he came into our office and told us to disregard the action of the chamber of commerce in this matter.[6]

Hewett had not merely told Dorman that it would be unwise to issue the proposed slogan, but had taken the trouble to document his protest in a letter addressed to the president of the Chamber on September 17, in which he advised Dorman that he had referred the question to Bandelier, Lummis, Hodge, and Read for their opinion on his stand. The project could have been abandoned then (or at least postponed until all the evidence was in), because the envelopes were still in the hands of the printer when the charges hit the papers more than two weeks later. While Hewett made no public reply, he was quietly busy behind the scenes, and it is likely that most local history buffs as well as those merchants who had subscribed to the propaganda admitted that the slogan was a mistake. At any rate publicity in support of the envelopes subsided, and a number of local organizations offered to give the Chamber house room so that it could move out of the old Palace.[7]

The basis of attack on Hewett then shifted. Many Santa Feans had grown uneasy lest criticism of the School might result in its removal from their midst. It was rumored that Cutting would like to have its headquarters at his alma mater, Harvard, where he thought the climate would be more scholarly. Others feared that Hewett would be weaned away from New Mexico to the West Coast and take his School with him. No one disputed that he had been largely instrumental in bringing it to Santa Fe in the first place. Now he was building up the San Diego Archaeological Society, and the University of California's distinguished faculty of Americanists might welcome him in their midst.

The first group to raise the question publicly was the Santa Fe Women's Club, which passed a ringing resolution in support of Hewett, the accomplishments of the School, and its importance to Santa Fe. The *Santa Fe New Mexican* balanced this support with statements from four reputable scientists, denouncing Hewett's qualifications. Declaring that they heartily supported the School and had only its best interests at heart, Dorman and his backers presented their scholarly evidence. Boxed on the front page were the accusations:

> *Dixon of Harvard* — Hewett has no standing among scientists in this country or elsewhere, except as a successful promoter.
> *Tozzer of Harvard* — Hewett's methods of work served as a laughing stock to many of us.
> *Boas of Columbia* — I fully agree with Tozzer's opinion of Edgar L. Hewett. I place no confidence in him.

Dorsey of Chicago — Agree entirely with opinion of Boas and Tozzer. In my opinion tremendous mistake Hewett made director.[8]

How many opposing replies to the *Santa Fe New Mexican*'s poll may have been received is not known, but among Hewett's papers is a copy of a letter from G. B. Gordon, a Harvard graduate who was currently director of the University of Pennsylvania Museum and who was more friendly in his judgment. He thought the American Institute of Archaeology was perhaps the best judge of qualifications for the scientists they sponsored, and was willing to leave the choice of Director up to the Managing Board.

Perhaps it was this letter that led the *Santa Fe New Mexican* on to its next step — ridicule of the Managing Board. Hewett's paternalism in referring to the Board of Regents of the Museum as "his" board was already under attack. As a matter of fact, Hewett did have a great deal to do with the choice of Regents. Although appointments were made by the incumbent governor, it was customary for him to be largely influenced by Hewett's suggestions. The practice of minimizing the political value of his office had paid off for the Director.

Governor McDonald's private secretary was the redoubtable Clara Olsen, a maiden lady whose ability and discretion were so valuable that a series of governors retained her regardless of their political affiliations. Miss Olsen was often in contact with the Museum staff, seeking and receiving confidential information — a relationship that was mutually satisfactory to the Governor's Office and the Director of the Museum.

It has been noted that the Regents supported Hewett in his decision to oust the Chamber of Commerce from the old Palace, but they were not necessarily a rubber-stamp group. Hewett made his recommendations carefully, choosing men and women who would be useful to the Museum through their statewide contacts, their influence on legislative appropriations, and their personal benefactions. Several were old friends who had worked with him in building the two institutions housed in the Palace, but they were in no way beholden to Hewett and would exercise their own best judgment. Even when he gave them a hard time because he was too busy to attend to details that he would not delegate to subordinates, however, they were likely to accept his apologies, let him straighten out his problems, and in the long run support his policies.

Now the *Santa Fe New Mexican* turned its attention to the Managing Board of the School, a much larger group chosen from the entire country. The Archaeological Society of New Mexico had come to the support of the Director appointed by its parent organization in a meeting where the bias of Hewett's accusers was proclaimed and a long and vigorous letter from a famous member of the Managing Board, Charles Lummis, was read. Ridiculing Lummis as a "squaw-belted litterateur of Los Angeles," the *Santa Fe New Mexican* denied Lummis' claim that the School was run by people chosen for their fitness to serve on such a managing board by categorizing the thirty-one members as follows:

Competent men engaged in American Archaeology 3

Semitic, Egyptian and classical professors,
    competent and incompetent 6

Zoologists 2

Politicians 2

Lawyers 3

Clergymen 1

Physicians 1

Diplomats 1

Business Men and nondescripts 7

Ladies (including 1 scientist and 1 school teacher) 4

Squaw-belted litterateur . . . . 1[9]

The *Santa Fe New Mexican* also challenged the statement made by Paul A. F. Walter that nearly all of the board members were university men, and demanded proof that even half of them were university graduates. A resolution of support for Hewett was passed by the local archaeological society and two days later the paper published it without comment on an inside page. Listed in the resolution were the members of the Managing Board with their credentials; twenty-three had one or more university degrees from important institutions in the United States, Canada and England. Of those listed without degrees, all were people of distinction who had something special to contribute as patrons. They must have amused themselves in speculation as to which category they had been assigned by the newspaper's classification.

Lummis reacted with characteristic vigor. He had been annoyed by the ridicule the newspaper had given to his first letter in defense of Hewett and declared that he had been quoted out of context. Accordingly he wrote a second epistle which he took the trouble to copyright. With the stipulation that no part of it could be reprinted unless it was used *in full,* he fired it off to Hewett's opponents. Lummis was probably more pleased than bothered to be called a "squaw-belted litterateur of Los Angeles." After all, his rough corduroy suit and the inevitable bandana tied around his head might be called a modified Pueblo costume, he wrote books, and Los Angeles was his headquarters. The description actually bolstered the colorful image he cultivated.

Many of those who had been scornfully dismissed as "summer school dabblers" also rose to Hewett's defense. One of the things he had taught them was that the

Charles F. Lummis, squaw-belted litterateur, in his corduroys and wearing medal conferred by the King of Spain. Courtesy of the Museum of New Mexico.

Science of Man included everybody, and that a knowledge of archaeology and anthropology should not be resticted to scientists. They knew that summer fieldwork often tested the dedication of students and separated those for whom it was a pastime or hobby from those who were willing to endure hot, dusty, unrewarding weeks on a dig because they really wanted to know.

In the meantime the members of the Santa Fe Chamber of Commerce could see that their influence and local popularity were not enhanced by the controversy. On November 15, when Hewett was attending a conference at the Institute in Washington, he received a telegram from Paul A. F. Walter: "The Chamber of Commerce last night on motion of Judge Pope passed the following resolution: That the Santa Fe Chamber of Commerce disclaims any connection with or responsibility for any criticism of the director of the School of American Archaeology at Santa Fe heretofore made in the public papers or otherwise."[10]

Hewett had come a long way in the ten years since the Board of Regents at Las Vegas declined to renew his contract. He could number among his close associates many scientists of international reputation who published his papers in their scholarly journals. While some might belittle the quality of students attracted to the Santa Fe School, leaders in Washington knew that he had helped train and vigorously promote Sylvanus G. Morley, Alfred V. Kidder, Earl H. Morris, John P. Harrington, Neil Judd, Jesse Nusbaum, Kenneth Chapman, and many others. Although it was only six years since he had secured his own doctorate, he was in constant demand as a lecturer, not only across the United States but in Canada and England. The scientists in Washington knew that Hewett did not make a major decision without first consulting them, and while he would press vigorously for his own point of view, when the vote went against him he did not sulk but went cheerfully on to the next project.

He had been instrumental in founding and fostering some of the more widely supported regional and state archaeological societies in the West, and although he could not keep all the people happy all the time, he was willing to give courteous attention to their problems when they could catch up with his whirlwind schedule. He had secured title for the Museum of New Mexico to some of the more important ancient ruins in the state, and entered into agreements with other institutions for joint digs at these sites. Even to those like Clark Wissler who did not like him, he offered the cooperation of "his museum" and the necessary permits for the Museum of Natural History to excavate at "his" sites.

The Santa Fe opponents were quite right in calling Hewett a promoter. He was also a skillful strategist. And so, when Paul Walter warned him that his opponents had not given up the fight to discredit him and that Harry Dorman had gone to New York probably with the intention of making charges against him at the annual meeting of the Institute to be held in Montreal, he made his preparations. Dorman had wired the president of the Institute that as president of the Santa Fe Chamber of Commerce he intended to present a reorganizational plan for the School which had the approval of Roland Dixon, P. E. Goddard and Franz Boas. He had also forwarded to Professor Shipley a letter signed by Dorman and fifteen others asking for a full-time Director for the Santa Fe School, and requesting that a majority of the Managing Board be made up of representatives of the anthropological departments of such universities as California, Chicago, Columbia, Harvard, Yale, and Pennsylvania, whose students would be sent to Santa Fe for special training and fieldwork.

Among those signing the letter were men of political, professional and business importance in Santa Fe whose names will be recognized by students of New Mexico history: Roman L. Baca, J. Wight Giddings, Miguel A. Otero, Frank W. Clancy, José D. Sena, Antonio Lucero, G. G. Van Stone, Richard H. Hanna, Francis C. Wilson, Benigno Muñiz, George W. Pritchard, H. B. Clancy, H. H. Dorman, Hugh H. Williams, H. S. Kaune, and James R. Massie. Even more important, there were attachments asking consideration for the proposal from William C. McDonald, Governor of New Mexico; the Most Rev. J. B. Pitaval, Archbishop of Santa Fe; and former Governor L. Bradford Prince, president of the New Mexico Historical Society.[11]

It was an imposing array of influential names, and Hewett must have winced to find some of his former supporters on the list. But Dorman was no match, as an advocate, for the support Hewett had rallied. Had the opponents known more of the inner workings of the Institute and had they realized that Hewett was the Institute's man from the beginning of the School, they might have realized that the cards would be stacked against them. It seems strange that they did not understand their actions had been insulting to many who may well have agreed with their contention that Hewett was overextended.

Hewett arranged to have full stenographic notes taken of the Institute's meeting, but when he went to pick them up after it was over he found that Dorman had anticipated him, paid the stenographer in full, and made off with the record. Perhaps it is still extant somewhere, but since it could not be found at the time this was written, the results can be summarized by simply stating that the Institute's Managing Board passed a resolution laying the matter on the table.

From the Windsor Hotel, Montreal, Hewett wrote on January 3, 1914 to Judge McFie:

> It would most certainly have afforded you an hour of keen enjoyment if you could have been in the meeting of the Managing Committee when Dr. Kelsey turned his batteries upon poor Dorman. From the experience of past years I know something of Dr. Kelsey's ability under circumstances of this kind, but I feel now that I never really saw the rapid fire-gun in action before.
>
> The coming of Dorman helped our case enormously. Nothing better could have happened if we had planned it ourselves. You can perhaps imagine something of the impression that the collapse of his case made upon these college men. His making away with the notes of the hearing which he came 2,000 miles to have, is a matter so ludicrous in its results

that I hope you will not tell of it about Santa Fe until I have seen you to talk it over in person.

The final action of the committee here was to place these very important documents in your hands which you will receive from the Secretary, Dr. Peabody, and this is done with entire confidence in your discretion as to the use to be made of them. May I ask that you show them to no one at all excepting Mr. Walter until I arrive.[12]

The entire matter was closed as far as Hewett was concerned when, some three years later, Paul Walter forwarded to him a report of action taken by the Museum Board. Hewett replied,

In your account of the Board of Regents meeting I note with entire approval that the Museum Board had generously cancelled the debt of the Santa Fe Chamber of Commerce, notwithstanding the fact that no part of the deficit was paid by the Museum but by the Director in person. I would recommend however that the amount named be stricken out for the reason the guarantee was not $600. It was, as I recollect, $300, and the amount I paid to cover the deficit caused mainly by their default was $325.00.[13]

The fact that Hewett had covered the Chamber's default from his own pocket was known only to a few in the inner circle of his associates, but that was the way he wanted it. He knew that Dorman had gone to Montreal on an errand for Bronson Cutting, whose enmity was so clearly revealed in the columns of the newspaper he owned, and it amused Hewett to have routed his opponent. Hewett wanted and needed the support of the governor, the archbishop and the Historical Society, however. He was pleased that some of his old friends who had signed Dorman's letter were satisfied with the action taken by the Institute, and he quietly set about mending his fences whenever the occasion offered. He wanted the wounds of the controversy healed as quickly as possible, and he had a great many other things on his mind as he urged support for the approaching San Diego Exposition. Yet in spite of his best efforts, bitterness remained to poison many against Hewett in future years.

13

SANTA FE'S ART MUSEUM

With traveling, investigating, reading, teaching and writing, I have never been in the ranks of the unemployed. — ELH

During the years of preparation for the San Diego Exposition several deaths marked milestones in Hewett's life. His mother, Tabitha Stice Hewett, died in 1914. Although he had lived at a distance from her for some years, he tried to see her once or twice a year, and later he wrote of her, "She didn't 'go to Heaven' in her 92nd year. Heaven came to her long before. That 'the kingdom of God is within us' you could never doubt if you knew that saintly soul. As an exemplar of the heroic life she ranks among the peerless pioneers of earth and with the angels in heaven."[1]

To his mother he owed the encouragement that started his education and kept him in school many years longer than his siblings. To her side of the family he owed, perhaps, the healthy longevity that would keep him active as an octogenarian.

Adolph Bandelier died in 1914, also. Through the years as Hewett's fortunes improved, he had often been instrumental in recommending his old friend for commissions that kept the Bandeliers in funds, although finances were always precarious. Bandelier was seventy-four when a bout with pneumonia ended his life in Seville, Spain, where he and his wife had gone to work on a research project on the archival background of the Spanish American colonies. For all his distinguished work and unremitting labor, he died penniless. Hewett sent assistance to his widow, Fanny, and several years later arranged for the School to pay the rental on the *osario* in Seville's Catholic cemetery where his bones were placed. On her

121

return to the United States Fanny Bandelier was forced to take any little job she could find, supporting herself with translation commissions and living in the most humble circumstances. The work that they had begun in Seville was continued several years later by Lansing Bloom, who had married Judge McFie's daughter Maude. She worked with her husband in researching the archives, even as Fanny had worked with Adolph.

One more tie with Hewett's formative years was broken in 1915, when Frederick W. Putnam died at the age of eighty. Putnam, often described as the first systematic excavator in the Southwest, had moved from the Peabody Museum to the faculty of the University of California, where he had retired as an emeritus professor. Hewett owed much to Putnam, who had helped to launch him as Director of the School and remained a staunch supporter.

Although San Diego's Exposition turned into such a success that the sponsors continued it through 1916, Hewett's big contribution was completed when the exhibits were installed. He continued to carry on administrative duties, however, and worked with the Indian groups exhibiting their arts; he also was busy encouraging the growth of the local archaeological society and developing the plans that converted the California Building into a permanent museum, where he was promptly installed as director.

Once this project was assured, he turned his promotional talents to a second museum building for Santa Fe. As soon as the old Palace became a museum Hewett had offered exhibit space to Santa Fe and Taos painters, and small studios on the north side of the patio were offered to out-of-state artists. Usually the visitors were summer people seeking escape from the heat of Eastern cities, stretching their talents in the exhilaration that they found in the sky, mountains and people of the Southwest. Among them were Robert Henri, John Sloan, the Harwoods, Paul Burlin, Gustave Baumann, Warren E. Rollins, Sheldon Parsons, and William Penhallow Henderson. George Bellows worked for a time in Santa Fe but did not find it a sympathetic locale. Kenneth Chapman and Carlos Vierra occupied space for year-round work, and when Carl Lotave was painting his murals he spent many months in the Puyé and Frijoles rooms.

Lighting in the small-windowed rooms and corridors of the old Palace was not adequate for a favorable display of art, however. Furthermore, Hewett and his staff were finding the Palace a tight fit for the many activities centered there. Ex-Governor Prince and his wife finally gave up the fight to expand the headquarters of the Historical Society and moved to their Long Island home, where they were always glad to host visiting friends from New Mexico. Hewett lived up to his promise to allow the Historical Society the use of its traditional space even after the Princes were gone and the burgeoning collection of prehistoric artifacts was crowding the artists out of the building. Obviously, a building devoted exclusively to art was needed. The Museum's lobbying team, headed by Judge McFie and Frank Springer, went to the 1915 Legislature and secured the passage of an act providing for a building "to be devoted to the purpose of an art gallery, free to the public, under proper regulations, and other purposes incidental to the objects of said Museum."[2] The building was to be substantially a replica of the New Mexico Building at San Diego. Of the estimated cost of $60,000, approximately half would be appropriated by the state, and the balance secured from private donors.

The site that Hewett and his associates chose for the new museum, on the corner of Palace Avenue across Lincoln Avenue from the Palace, was occupied by the "Old Barracks Building." The building had once been used for army officers' quarters but now housed private business. The land was owned by the Santa Fe City Schools, and the $1,740 annual rental income was important to the Board of Education. At first the president of the School Board, Col. José D. Sena, vigorously opposed transfer of the property, insisting that the board had no legal right to sell it to the state or anybody else. In a letter to the *Santa Fe New Mexican* he asked some sharp questions: "How many of the children of our city would become artists and derive material benefit from the art gallery? Are you not aware that an exceedingly small percentage of the citizens of this great government of ours can and do dedicate themselves to art, and then those that dedicate themselves to that profession, many of them become subjects of the poorhouse?"[3]

In their usual quiet way, proponents of the site worked behind the scenes until an agreement with Col. Sena and the board was reached. The property would be deeded to the Museum of New Mexico in exchange for $15,000 raised by tax levy, authorized by the Board of County Commissioners. Thus the site became a gift from the property owners of Santa Fe, and since the Board of Education had originally held the property at $25,000, it might be said that the city schools donated $10,000.

Within the year Frank Springer tendered to the Museum a certified check for $30,000, the amount necessary to match the state's appropriation. It was generally understood that the donation was chiefly made by Springer himself. A building committee made up of Springer, James Seligman and Hewett was designated, with I. H. and W. M. Rapp as architects and Jesse Nusbaum in charge of construction. The *Santa Fe New Mexican* reported that the new building would be connected to the old Palace by an underground passage, so that the same officals and staff could readily serve both units. Fortunately this tunnel was unnecessary — the sun-loving Museum staffers have not objected to strolling from one place to the other even in winter weather, and most of the time there have been enough employees to staff both buildings. The Old Barracks Building, a one-story territorial-style adobe with white wood coping, shutters and pillars on the portal that protected pedestrians on the two street facings, was promptly razed to make way for the new.

Money matters continued to plague the hardworking staff through 1916. In November Paul A. F. Walter wrote to Hewett in San Diego regarding the Museum's overdrawn account at the bank and the lack of funds for all projects, including completion of the new museum which was more costly than expected. "We owe to special tradesmen who present their bills with obnoxious regularity and frequency," he complained. "What a tremendous and glorious amount of work we could do if we were not hampered by financial limitations and the Shylocks."[4]

Once again Hewett paused in his commuting between San Diego, Santa Fe and Washington to solicit funds from public-spirited friends. Fortunately, lack of money never slowed his projects for long. Often he paid outstanding accounts from his own pocket — sometimes he was reimbursed when appropriations or donations came in, but many times he simply wrote off the amount, as in the case of the Chamber of Commerce debt.

In the days before income-tax auditing, entrepreneurs like Hewett could move funds freely from one account to another, judging the legitimate needs for themselves and making a proper accounting in their annual reports. Hewett's own personal finances must have been complicated, since he received some income from several of his activities and none from others. The Institute paid him a stipend for his promotional work and for expenses of the lecture tours it sponsored. At this time he charged no fee for lectures, and his income from publications, chiefly in official journals, could not have been large. The San Diego Exposition paid him, as did the San Diego Museum after he became its director, but he received no salary as Director of the Museum of New Mexico.

Real estate records in the Santa Fe County Clerk's office show that he bought and sold property, sometimes in his own name and more often in the name of the School. They do not reveal how much of the money involved was actually handled in behalf of Springer and other patrons. Since Springer was known to be a wealthy man, he felt that the sellers were inclined to increase the price of anything he wanted to buy, and his closely guarded agreements with various Museum officials were considered to be nobody else's business.

Jennie Avery, the Santa Fe real estate dealer (later appointed to the School's Managing Board), handled many of the transactions by which the School acquired property. When the city school board property was acquired for the Art Museum, a warranty deed dated September 1, 1915, covering 123 feet (Lot 1 Block 1, Fort Marcy Map) on Lincoln Avenue, was given to the Museum of New Mexico. The Old Barracks Building was demolished and Jesse Nusbaum placed in charge of new construction. When the building was partially up, Nusbaum found to his dismay that they had encroached about ten feet on the land to the north, which was owned by Cleofas and Venceslao Jaramillo. The Museum's sponsors huddled and came up with a solution. Frank Springer would put up the money to purchase Lot 2 from the Jaramillos, but the deal would be made by Paul A. F. Walter. As soon as Walter acquired Lot 2 (90.5 feet on Lincoln Avenue x 211.25 feet deep), he and his wife conveyed to the Museum a strip 10 by 211 feet to take care of the encroachment. The balance was deeded to Springer, who planned to give it to Hewett. Springer actually executed a deed and arranged for insurance on the building, but Hewett refused to accept the gift, asking instead that the house be deeded to the School, which was done. The remodeled house then became known as the Hewett residence, to be occupied by Hewett for the balance of his life, and for some years afterward by his widow.

Like the larger building on the corner that had been razed to make way for the Art Museum, the Hewett residence was part of the Fort Marcy officers' row. After

Frank Springer, lawyer, paleontologist and Museum patron, at El Rito de los Frijoles, 1912. Courtesy of the Museum of New Mexico.

the federal government no longer needed it for the use of the army, it had housed a series of tenants, among whom were Judge McFie and his family. The Jaramillos, from whom Walter had bought it on behalf of Springer, apparently never lived there but used it for rental property. In remodeling it for the Director's residence, the facade was altered and plastered over to harmonize with the "pueblo" style of the adjacent museum and some changes were made for greater comfort inside, but the principal features of the interior were little altered.

The School acquired the old state armory on Washington Avenue in another involved transaction. Frank Springer bought a tract of land on the southern edge of Santa Fe, as the town then existed. He arranged for Carlos Vierra to design a house at the corner of the Las Vegas Highway and Cordova Road, to be occupied by Vierra during his lifetime. There was also a studio apartment for the use of Springer's daughter Eva, a talented miniaturist. Adjoining land to the south (about eight and three-quarters acres) was held in Hewett's name for a time. He conveyed it to the School of American Research, which in turn traded it to the State of New Mexico

Interior of St. Francis Auditorium, Museum of Fine Arts, during construction, ca. 1917. Courtesy of the Museum of New Mexico.

for the use of the New Mexico National Guard, in exchange for the old armory facing Washington Avenue which was duly remodeled by the School and attached to the old Palace.

As the Art Museum neared completion, invitations to the dedication were issued to important people in scientific, religious, artistic, and political circles. From the Santa Fe Railway, Hewett requested special rates for excursionists who would be lured by the promise that Cardinal O'Connell and possibly Theodore Roosevelt (if not the incumbent President of the United States, Woodrow Wilson) would be among the speakers. He persuaded the New Mexico Educational Association to schedule its annual convention for 1917 in Santa Fe, coinciding with the dedication ceremonies.

Activities for 1917 were complicated by the entry of the United States into World War I. The Santa Fe Museum and its staff were immediately involved in the war effort. Space in the Museum was provided for the hospital and surgical work of the Red Cross and for the Women's Naval Auxiliary, although Hewett's principal contribution to these groups was to referee the continuing altercations between them, a chore he did not relish. He served as chairman of the State Historical Service and also as director of the State Child Welfare Service for the New Mexico Council of Defense (1917-19), sharing his duties with the staff.

Paul Walter was named to the National Young Men's Christian Association War Work Council and assigned the task of raising in New Mexico some $35,000 for work with the armies of the United States and her allies at home and abroad. Many requests were channeled through the Museum, as when George Wharton James sent in an order for slides to be used as illustrations for his lectures to the Boys in Training at Camp Cody.

While the Museum was busy expanding, important changes were taking place in the School as well. During the first ten years of its existence an enlarged concept had been evolving. At the School's inception Hewett was under the necessity of justifying the need for his own fellowship. As acceptance of American archaeology gained ground, his principal concern was building the support of local societies and finding funds for acceptable projects. The success of the San Diego Exposition and its attendant publicity brought Hewett maturity and greater ambition. He envisioned the School as an institution with buildings of its own and a permanent faculty headquartered in Santa Fe, sponsoring fieldwork throughout the Americas and editing its own publications. To accomplish this he wanted to be less dependent on the Archaeological Institute of America, and he needed a corporation so that the School might own real estate. In discussions with members of the managing board a change of name was suggested, so Hewett proposed to Alice Fletcher that the new corporation be called the "Institute of American Archaeology and Art." This title was overruled in favor of something simpler and less likely to be confused with the parent organization. Frank Springer, who was attached to the National Museum in Washington at the time, prepared the incorporation papers, and in January 1917 the School of American Archaeology was replaced by the School of American Research, which was eligible to own the property deeded to it.

In San Diego, those who had participated in the exposition were busy dismantling it after the second year drew to a close. Exhibit materials were transferred to the ownership of the permanent museum or returned to the institutions that had loaned them. Many of the buildings were to remain in Balboa Park, but the temporary structures had to be removed. Furnishings too heavy for shipment or inappropriate for smaller buildings were put up for sale. Then, with the outbreak of the war, the coming of the Naval Training Station and the conversion of many buildings to government use put an end to further salvage. The younger archaeologists, caught up in the draft, sought deferment until they could finish a season's dig or asked for references to help them gain admission to officers' training schools.

The budget for furnishing the Art Museum was tight. Always looking for a bargain that would enhance his museums, Hewett bought the exhibit cases used in the Philippine Building at the San Diego Exposition. Forty-two of these were of the best Philippine mahogany, with plate glass — the price ($1,400) was about the cost of the glass alone. Hewett arranged to have the cases shipped back to Santa Fe in the same railroad freight car that would bring home the New Mexico exhibit. He also bought (for $300) the heavy mission-style furniture used by the Salt Lake Railway Company at the exposition. The canvases that had been prepared for murals remained in Balboa Park. Gerald Cassidy's career had received a nice boost when he was awarded the Grand Prize for his "decoration," which still adorns the walls of rooms in use in the Museum of Man.

With the success of his efforts at San Diego, Hewett had acquired an authoritative style. As replies were received to the hundreds of invitations for the Art Museum's dedication that had been sent to presidents of universities, directors of museums, outstanding scientific leaders, and patrons of art throughout the United States and Canada, the regrets did not disturb him. Every invitation was an item of publicity, and had a substantial number been accepted it would have been an embarrassment to find accommodations and determine precedence. The ceremonies were to take place during Thanksgiving week. Theodore Roosevelt wrote Hewett a warm personal note expressing a desire to attend but explaining that he had promised himself and his family that he would be at home for the holiday. Many others sent regrets because of wartime pressures which placed most of them on limited budgets and expanded duty. The war had caused many problems and was blamed for the overrun in costs, but Hewett and Springer decided that no pall of depression should be allowed to darken the ceremonies. There was no question in their minds that the kaiser would shortly be defeated, life would return to normal, and an unprecedented era of growth would begin for the country at large and the Southwest in particular.

Hewett wrote his friend Col. Collier requesting that he make one of the principal speeches at the dedication and suggesting a topic such as "Education in the New World Democracy." "We are not afraid here of mixing a good deal of sentiment with our business affairs," he wrote, and noted, "The idea is that in the future we shall not look so much to the school for the education of the people but rather to the big experiences and enterprises of the human spirit."[5] (That bold prophecy has waited more than fifty years to develop in the minds of scholastic leaders.)

The Art Museum building was designed as an adaptation of many Southwestern mission features. The church at the pueblo of San Felipe inspired the facade of the auditorium, which was planned to seat 680 people. Features of the church at Acoma were incorporated at the eastern end of the facade. The covered walkway of the interior patio was reminiscent of a cloister. Inside the auditorium, the small balcony at the back might have been a choir loft.

Frank Springer commissioned the murals for the walls to be executed by a young painter, Donald Beauregard, who made a trip to Europe in order to immerse himself in the life of St. Francis of Assisi. He brought back a series of watercolor sketches to his studio at the west end of the Palace, and several well-known Santa Feans were recruited to serve as models. When Beauregard's untimely death left the panels only started, Springer requested that Carlos Vierra and Kenneth Chapman complete the work. The six panels depict the Conversion of St. Francis, the Renunciation of Santa Clara, the Vision of Columbus, Preaching to the Mayas and Aztecs, Building the Missions of New Mexico, and the Apotheosis of St. Francis. Their religious inspiration, together with the lofty, austere nature of the auditorium, led someone to suggest that it be called the Cathedral of the Desert. Since it was neither a cathedral nor located in a desert, the term was soon dropped, however.

Probably only Paul Walter knew how many notables sent valid reasons why they could not journey to Santa Fe for the dedication. There was a goodly collection of dignitaries who could arrange travel to coincide with the opening of the Museum, however, even though the Santa Fe Railroad, busy moving war materiel, did not offer them special rates. In addition to the loyal Santa Fe coterie who could be counted upon to show up at Hewett functions and all the locals who were pleased by a new cultural attraction in the city, there was the statewide crowd attending the Teachers' Convention. Walter had applied considerable pressure on their leadership, and President Frank Robbins was not entirely convinced that the inducements offered them were altruistic. He had been offered the renowned classicist, Dr. Francis Kelsey of Ann Arbor, as a speaker, but then was told by Walter that the teachers could only have Kelsey as part of the dedication celebration in the new St. Francis Auditorium, rather than, as originally planned, for their own session in the Scottish Rite cathedral.

The activities were grandiloquently billed as a Congress of Science, Art and Education. The teachers had their own sessions, and, in addition to the actual evening of dedication, there was a special concert for which tickets must be purchased. The musical artists were friends of Hewett who had been featured in San Diego. It was the first Santa Fe appearance of the famed Indian singer Tsianina and her sponsor Charles Wakefield Cadman, the composer.

The dedication exercises brought together the elements that Hewett liked to synthesize: governors of the Indian pueblos, state and city officials, scientists from

Museum of Fine Arts, Santa Fe, ca. 1920. Photograph by T. Harmon Parkhurst. Courtesy of the Museum of New Mexico.

universities and learned societies, and artists from Taos and Santa Fe, together with all the general public that could crowd into the building. The audience of a thousand or more jamming into St. Francis Auditorium showed their patriotic enthusiasm by singing the "Battle Hymn of the Republic." Maude McFie Bloom, who was given the honor of singing the first solo in the hall, sang the "Marseillaise" in French, accompanied by her sister, Mary McFie Lackey. Their father and the Museum's longtime sponsor, Judge McFie, presided over part of the session.

Hewett spoke first. With tact learned from years of handling jealous controversies among artists, scientists and politicians, he gave credit to no one individual, although some thought he thus slighted Frank Springer. Instead he asked, "Whose conception is this? Who did this remarkable work?," and then answered his own questions.

> Time was [he said] when it existed only in the minds of two or three people, but it quickly became a matter of organization and cooperation of many minds and hands.
>
> All honor to those who endowed it with funds; to legislators and regents and building committees who put the resources of the state back of it; to architects, superintendent of construction and artist, but equal honor to the workmen whose hands produced the result you see here. To do this they had to give up the traditions of their craft, to free themselves from plumb-line and square and level, and work with the boldness of master builders. And how well they did it! They became more than artisans; there are the strokes of their axes, gouges, trowels and brushes. I leave it to you to say if the work is not a master work. On the roll of honor let us inscribe the names of the carpenters, brick-layers, plasterers and painters.
>
> Then, too, the spirit of the contributors who gave the School of American Research the initial sum with which to put up this structure, is built into it. In their donation they say: This fund is contributed by a small group of men and women residents of, or interested in the state who desire in this manner to attest their loyalty to New Mexico, their solicitude for its progress and their appreciation of the benefits which its opportunities have afforded them. If patriotism does not mean gratitude for the opportunities afforded by one's country, it is an empty word.
>
> How fortunate, too, for us that a great institution, the Archaeological Institute of America, gave its sanction to this enterprise. Without it, there would have been nothing of this that we celebrate tonight.[6]

Hewett's facility in commingling the various branches of the Museum with the School of American Research and its parent, the Archaeological Institute of America, seemed to present no problem at the moment. He had scheduled a joint meeting of the managing boards of the Museum and School in order that they might officially inspect and accept the new building prior to its public dedication, and consequently the board members were present in Santa Fe for the gala evening and could receive the congratulations due them.

The Tsianina-Cadman program included "From the Land of the Sky Blue Water" and "The Moon Drops Low," which were from an Omaha Indian theme developed by Alice Fletcher, and "Ho! Ye Warriors on the Warpath," in deference to the Sioux theme developed by Frances Densmore as well as in tribute to the men in the armed forces. Since both Fletcher and Densmore were in the audience, the choice was a graceful bow in their direction.

Frank Springer's hour-long oration was the principal speech, and his tribute to Hewett brought a standing ovation honoring both men. New Mexico's Secretary of

State Antonio Lucero closed the program with a scholarly tribute to the early Franciscans in whose honor the building was dedicated. After the program the galleries were opened with a reception hosted by the Women's Board of the Museum.

During the ensuing week daily programs were given for the benefit of the teachers and other visitors. Indian songs and dances, the second Tsianina-Cadman concert, speeches by dignitaries such as Francis Kelsey representing the Archaeological Institute, and other special features helped to make it a memorable "congress."

Once the Art Museum was safely open, Hewett's next project was to expand the printing facilities of the complex. The building immediately west of the Art Museum was occupied by the *Santa Fe New Mexican* and owned by Bronson Cutting, who was serving in the Army at the time. His sister, Mrs. Cabot Ward, was looking after his affairs. Hewett wrote her, suggesting that the Museum would like to acquire the *Santa Fe New Mexican* building, press and publication. Expressing his admiration for Col. Cutting's abilities and patriotism, he proposed that the enterprise henceforth be known as the Cutting Press, and explained: "It would take the city's newspaper out of political turmoil and prevent its being used as a political organ for any party or faction."[7]

Of course the offer was not accepted. Cutting owned the paper for the express purpose of using it as a political organ. Hewett must have understood this and also must have known that his offer might well be regarded as more opportunistic than altruistic.

Hewett had another hope for improving the plaza area. This was to restore the plaza to its original size, which would require the elimination of the block of businesses between the existing plaza and the cathedral. When the federal government was persuaded to build a new post office in "pueblo" style, facing the cathedral, the plans were sent to Hewett for review. He wrote the Treasury Department that the facade conformed nicely with the effect Santa Feans were striving to achieve, but that the rear of the building was not exactly what he would desire as an approach to the cathedral. His principal worry, however, was that once a permanent federal structure was erected on the site it would become more difficult, if not impossible, to clear the area and restore it to the plaza. From time to time in the fifty-odd years since Hewett's proposal the plan again becomes a subject for local discussion, but the value of the property continues to be an insurmountable obstacle.

The months following the dedication brought both rewards and problems. In a burst of generous enthusiasm, Hewett had enriched the personal invitations sent to many of his scientific colleagues with the request that they present papers during dedication week. If they could not come in person he suggested that they might send along a paper to be included in an anniversary volume that would celebrate the occasion. A number of men who sent regrets for personal non-appearance did forward material for the volume. When Hewett and Walter began to plan the publication, however, they were embarrassed to discover how much it might cost and how difficult it would be to launch such a volume in a country preoccupied with war. The authors began asking to have their work either published or returned. Hewett was able to place some of it in *Art and Archaeology*, and as soon as the war ended *El Palacio* became a weekly publication in the hopes of finding space for as much material as could be accommodated. When all else failed—or if the author had another use for it—the paper was returned. One research report long overdue for publication finally appeared in *El Palacio*; authored jointly by Sylvanus Griswold Morley and Alfred Vincent Kidder, "The Archaeology of McElmo Canyon, Colorado" was a follow-up of their first fieldwork under Hewett.

Hewett received his first honorary doctor's degree in 1918 when, at the invitation of Dr. von Kleinsmid, president of the University of Arizona, he was given an LL.D. degree at the annual commencement. Perhaps, as the two men walked together in the procession, Hewett told his host that he had once applied for his position.

Although most excavations were discontinued during the war, Hewett continued to oversee some summer work at Puyé. He had done his first excavation of the cliff dwellings of the Pajarito Plateau in the summer of 1899 with the help of ten students and several faculty members from Las Vegas who paid their own expenses. Out of recurring summer sessions he had formulated his dream that the entire plateau area be made into a national park. The Lacey Bill had given the conservationists a handle with which to curb vandalism on federal land, but it was difficult to enforce. In 1919 New Mexico's Senator A. A. Jones introduced a bill in Congress to create the National Park of the Cliff Cities and the Pajarito, but like previous attempts it was unsuccessful.

In the meantime, Paul A. F. Walter had been supplementing his Museum salary with free-lance articles for such publications as the *Santa Fe Railroad Magazine,* for which he wrote an account of the new Art Museum. Funding for Museum salaries continued to be a problem, so he finally decided that he must make a change if he was to support and educate his growing family. He accepted an offer to move to the First National Bank of Santa Fe (of which he ultimately became president) but did not relinquish the editorship of *El Palacio*, so his close association with Hewett continued unbroken.

14

ART, ARCHAEOLOGY AND POLITICS

History written for the approval of someone in authority, and art that has had to be authorized by a "jury" before being seen, are worse than futilities to me. They are crimes. — ELH

Because in recent times there has been no close connection between art and archaeology except where artifacts uncovered in excavations exemplify the art of ancient times as distinct from other aspects of vanished civilizations, it may seem strange that Hewett moved with authority in both artistic and scientific circles. In the first third of the twentieth century, however, the two disciplines were comfortably linked. William H. Holmes was curator of the National Museum at the Smithsonian and likewise director of the National Art Gallery. The eminent periodical *Art and Archaeology* was an illustrated vehicle used as much to inform the scientist as to portray the work of creative visual artists, and the Americanists used it in their struggle to surpass the classicists. With Hewett, a natural extension of his scientific School of American Archaeology was the fostering of art and the promotion of American artists.

It has been noted that the walls of the old Palace were first offered for exhibitions by local painters, and the privilege was soon extended to other New Mexico and Southwestern artists. The practice of providing free studio space to visiting Easterners, usually for the summer months when there was no heating problem, brought some famous people from New York and Chicago. One of these was Robert Henri, who has sometimes been called the founder of the Santa Fe art colony although it is hardly fair to give that distinction to any one man. Henri became a member of the managing board of the School, and Hewett shortly found a way to involve him in wider activities.

The simmering feud between classicists and Americanists in the Institute boiled over from time to time, and one of the frequent causes of overheating was control of publications. With colleges and museums competing for funds and recognition, several publications were of special importance. The *American Journal of Anthropology* of the Archaeological Institute of America was a sober scientific periodical devoted to scholarly papers, all properly footnoted. The Annual Reports of the Bureau of Ethnology were quasi-governmental channels for work that had the special sanction of the Smithsonian. They featured beautiful plates, both black and white and colored. In a more popular vein, *Art and Archaeology* was a monthly with lavish illustrations. Hewett contributed to all three, but *Art and Archaeology* had special appeal for him because it was read by the group he most wanted to reach — the lay public, including students, cultivated people and, especially, patrons.

In 1917 the editor-in-chief of *Art and Archaeology* was Dr. David M. Robinson of Johns Hopkins University; William Holmes was art editor, Mitchell Carroll of the Archaeological Institute was managing editor, and the masthead boasted distinguished names from outstanding institutions as associate and contributing editors. The trouble, as Hewett saw it, was that the whole thing was top-heavy and clumsy and the Americanists were not getting the space he thought they should have.

During the summer of 1917, while he was busy installing five rooms of exhibit material left over from the exposition as a permanent collection in San Diego's Museum of Man, Hewett had to rush back to Santa Fe from time to time in order to solicit more funds and urge the completion of the Art Museum. *El Palacio* was now firmly established as a monthly publication devoted chiefly to projects and people of interest in New Mexico, but with some notes of national and international import. In his role as an educator, Hewett had lined up the publication of the state teachers' journal. He decided that it would be possible to use the additional space that would soon become available in the new museum to further expand the press. *Art and Archaeology* was having difficulty with its printers back East, and he thought Paul Walter would be quite capable of taking on the added responsibility of getting it out. To William H. Holmes he wrote:

> I have not considered with Shipley the editorial side of *Art and Archaeology* except to say that its only salvation was wiping the slate clean and putting the magazine in your hands to form its editorial staff and dictate its policy.... In due time, if it becomes necessary, we shall have to assure Shipley that the whole matter of *Art and Archaeology* will have to be made fairly satisfactory to us if we are to continue our relation with the Institute. If we give the classical men the *Journal* and ask for no part in it at all it is only reasonable that the Americanists should have a predominance of influence in *Art and Archaeology*. With everything in the mess

that Robinson has brought about I imagine they may be ready to be reasonable.[1]

The "mess" to which Hewett referred consisted of policy disagreements which had resulted in the resignations of Holmes, Frederick W. Hodge and Mitchell Carroll from the staff. Dr. Robinson was insisting that all copy have the stamp of his approval, and delays in sending it back and forth among the various sub-editors made for great confusion.

Hewett was not complaining of Robinson behind his back. In a blunt letter to the editor-in-chief he stated that in his opinion *Art and Archaeology* had become nothing more than a pictorial supplement to the *Journal*, and that since Robinson could not get along with such men as Holmes, Hodge and Carroll, a change was indicated. Hewett baldly stated his proposal that a new editor-in-chief be secured and the printing be done in Santa Fe. In the concluding paragraph he made a half-hearted conciliatory gesture by admitting that Robinson might have something to say for himself which Hewett, a reasonable man, would be willing to hear.

Robinson tried to placate Hewett, and among other things offered a full issue of *Art and Archaeology* to publicize the dedication of the Santa Fe Art Museum. Hewett accepted; he and Holmes took over the editorship of the entire Santa Fe Anniversary Double Number of *Art and Archaeology* for January-February 1918. They used it to publish a digest of Frank Springer's dedication oration; Kelsey's address to the teachers' association which was entitled "The New Humanism"; Hewett's remarks on "Opening of the New Museum" and "Opening of the Art Galleries"; "The Indians' Part" by Natalie Curtis Burlin; and sundry other items of interest to the Santa Fe School. Nevertheless, when the clouds finally blew over, Robinson was out. Mitchell Carroll became editor of the magazine and ably filled the post until his sudden death in April 1925, when he was succeeded by Arthur Stanley Riggs.

Obviously, on the national scene Hewett was no longer a background figure, working through other people to achieve his purposes. He emerged as a leader of the Institute, sure of his goals. Science was *not* the exclusive province of scholarly men cloistered in the ivy-clad towers of the Eastern Seaboard. It belonged to anybody who could be interested in it. Hewett had sat in many kivas and clasped his knees in front of many campfires listening to the legends of man's emergence on the earth. He was devoutly familiar with the Bible and the Judeo-Christian account of man's long struggle toward a more nearly perfect life. He passionately believed that the facts ferreted out by archaeologists and ethnologists (whatever they chose to call themselves) belonged to all people, and that it was his mission in life to help them get those facts.

When Alice Klauber in San Diego asked him to help her with some material for an article on Robert Henri, he wrote to her, "You will be interested to know that we are preparing to completely organize *Art and Archaeology*, cutting out the old classical stuff and bringing it down to the vital things of the present. Mr. Henri has consented to take the department of Modern Art on the reorganized staff."[2]

Although the magazine was never printed in Santa Fe, Hewett continued to exercise influence on editorial policy and staffing during the rest of its existence.

A great impetus was given to the art movement in New Mexico by the promotion of artists at the San Diego Exposition. The opening of the Art Museum in Santa Fe provided a wider exposure than had been possible previously, and space was in constant demand by the growing group in Santa Fe as well as by the Taos art colony, which had a longer history. The opening exhibit at the Art Museum displayed the work of some forty artists, most of them associated with either Santa Fe or Taos.

It has been said that had it not been for a broken wagon wheel there might never have been an art colony at Taos. The story goes back to two young American artists who met in Paris during the 1890s: I. H. Sharp and Ernest L. Blumenschein. Sharp had made a trip through the Southwest and often described the appeal of the area to Blumenschein. In 1898 "Blumy" and another young artist, Bert Phillips, set out to discover "Mexico" for themselves, leaving Denver by wagon. Neither knew much about horses but they were sure they didn't want to be left afoot on a back road in the Rocky Mountains, so when they camped out they tied their horse to a large tree for the night. In their quest for security they overlooked the necessity for watering the poor beast, and in the morning they found him strangled by the rope in his effort to reach water. In order to continue their journey they were compelled to dip into their slender savings for the purchase of another horse.

Some days later they were approaching Taos when a wagon wheel collapsed. Taking stock, they found that their combined liquid assets were reduced to one silver dollar and a three-dollar gold piece. They flipped the dollar to determine which one should stay with the wreck and which should ride horseback with the broken wheel the twenty miles to Taos. Blumenschein lost and set out for town. There he traded the gold piece for five dollars in paper money, which just covered his overnight expenses and the cost of mending the wheel. Broke, the two travelers decided to settle down in Taos and recoup their fortunes by painting.

Phillips stayed permanently, but after a short sojourn Blumenschein returned to New York City where he always had an illustrator's job. It was 1919 before he came back to establish a home near Phillips. Sharp, too, returned to build a studio. The village where life could be lived simply and inexpensively became a magnet for artistic people, who were drawn also by the wealth of paintable material — the pueblo and its people, Ranchos de Taos and its Spanish-Americans; the towering bulk of the mountains, the infinite expanse of cloud-flecked sky, and the gushing purity of the streams bordered by willow and plum. The colony grew steadily, few of its recruits defecting to the greater convenience of Santa Fe. Although some were at home in either town, most of them developed sharply held loyalties.[3]

Hewett encouraged both schools, often advancing painting materials that a good man might not have been able to acquire otherwise. The *Santa Fe New Mexican* and *El Palacio* gave generous coverage of the series of art exhibitions that were held in the reception room of the old Palace. In December 1915, Walter Ufer (of Taos) hung a week-long show of thirty-five paintings that he called "The Soul of the Southwest." A few weeks later the artistic event of the week was an exhibition by Gerald Cassidy, who was described by a reviewer as "among the few in whose pictures even a layman recognizes the touch of genius."[4] On April 1, 1916 the newspaper noted that "the arrival here of Mr. and Mrs. William Penhallow Henderson, of Chicago and formerly of Boston, has been hailed with delight by local artists and art lovers."[5] Henderson was an etcher and painter in oils; his equally famous wife, Alice Corbin, was a poet who had been one of the founders as well as editor of *Poetry* magazine.

The Hendersons chose a delightful spot for their home on the southeastern edge of town facing the old road that, as a branch of the Santa Fe Trail, had led to the corrals on Canyon Road and was thus known to trail pioneers as the Corral Road. When the telephone line into town followed it the name was changed to Telephone Road, but the Hendersons wanted a more poetic name, and so persuaded the city council to revive El Camino del Monte Sol, which was what the natives called it. This started a fashion of restoring to Santa Fe streets more picturesque names than those used since the American occupation.

Literary figures of note came to visit the Hendersons — Carl Sandburg and John Gould Fletcher among them. It will be remembered that Fletcher was one of the Harvard students in Hewett's first summer field school. In spite of his rough initiation, Fletcher continued to enjoy the Southwest as his interest shifted from archaeology to poetry. Witter Bynner came in 1922, later established his home on Buena Vista Street, and in his turn drew a coterie of distinguished visitors.

During the summer before the Art Museum opened, artists exhibiting in the old Palace included Henri, Vierra, Cassidy, Sheldon Parsons, and his daughter Sara. With the addition of John Sloan and Warren Rollins, who is credited with having had the first one-man exhibition of art in the old Palace about 1893, they came to be known as the old-timers of the Santa Fe art colony. After the new museum opened, they were joined by an ever increasing (and ever changing) procession of aspiring and established painters. Hewett insisted on an open-door policy, leaving it to the viewer to distinguish the good and the bad from the merely indifferent. The artists supported his policy, and half the town was soon judging their offerings. While some meretricious work was given exposure (R. E. Twitchell complained at the end of the first year that the quality of work hung on the Museum walls was far from distinguished), several good results emerged. It was discovered that large numbers of New Mexicans, including schoolchildren, were more interested in art than Col. José D. Sena had suspected when he objected to selling the land for the new building.

Also, collectors came to buy in Santa Fe and Taos; tourists who had never before purchased original art took home pictures as souvenirs. It was still necessary to go back East for wider recognition, and those with established reputations retained their New York or Chicago studios, but many struggling artists kept out of the poorhouse by trading pictures to local merchants and professional men in exchange for goods and services. In time almost every home in Santa Fe displayed original art, and the permanent collection in the Museum grew steadily.

At the end of World War I young men drifted into Santa Fe in search of a healthful climate to restore their bodies and souls. It was at this time that the group which came to be known as *Los Cinco Pintores* joined their friend, Frank Applegate, and others already established in the Camino del Monte Sol area. Fremont Ellis, Will Shuster, and Josef Bakos became permanent residents. Willard Nash and Walter Mruk were drawn to other scenes.

In the postwar release of artistic energy Santa Fe bubbled with yeasty groups allied to the arts; one of these was the fledgling Community Theatre which was dominated for a time by Mary Austin. Mrs. Austin had first come to Hewett's attention just before the Armistice ended the war, when she was planning a trip to Mexico where she would research land tenure and usage of pre-Columbian people for a book. En route she intended to stop over in Santa Fe for two or three weeks. She wrote Hewett (giving him *Who's Who* as a reference in case he had never heard of her), asking for information regarding the "land holdings and workings" among the Pueblo Indians. She was especially interested in anything that might throw light on the "psychology of communism" as practiced by them.[6]

Although it is doubtful that Hewett could assist her in equating the practice of communal landholding among the Pueblos with something she might describe as "communism," he did offer her the facilities of the Museum in her research. Mrs. Austin had become disenchanted with her home in Carmel, California, because she felt the town was being ruined by tourism. She found Santa Fe to be a pleasant small community, as yet unspoiled. Mabel Evans Sterne (at that time the wife of Maurice Sterne) offered her hospitality in Taos, and Mrs. Austin was soon dividing her time between the two New Mexico towns. In Santa Fe the Community Theatre was developing under the sponsorship of the Museum, so she wrote Paul A. F. Walter from Taos suggesting that the Community Theatre production of Granville Barker's *The Dumb Wife* be postponed for a week or two, in the hope that the original producer, Robert Jones, who was soon to visit Mrs. Sterne, might give his personal direction to the Santa Fe show.

She also gave Walter the names of several important people who were expected to visit in Taos in the near future, and then warned him that he must not mention them in the paper yet. She told him that they were all her friends, so she could keep track of them and invite them to lecture at the Museum.[7] One of Walter's many duties was to provide the local press with Museum notes of interest. The two celebrity-loving ladies — Mary Austin and Mabel Sterne — were determined to keep him well supplied with notable names to drop.

Mrs. Austin bought property on the Camino del Monte Sol where she built a delightful home christened *La Casa Querida*, from which she proceeded to enliven the literary scene with her distinguished guests, her outspoken determination to keep the town the way she liked it, and her growing devotion to Indian art.

Early in 1914, shortly after the *Santa Fe New Mexican*'s ill-fated backing of

Harry Dorman and the effort to oust Hewett as Director of the School and the Museum, a new editor came to the newspaper. E. Dana Johnson was a brilliant journalist who spent the next twenty-five years happily running the paper for Cutting, to whom he was always loyal. Editor Johnson had a warm personality that endeared him to the entire town and a wickedly delightful sense of the ridiculous. His staff was constantly embroiled in controversy of the kind that makes legend in the West. Whether he wrote a mock-solemn editorial urging the authorities to bury a dead rooster polluting a street corner or tilted a well-aimed lance in defense of freedom of the press, Johnson was a quotable man.

He had been at the *Santa Fe New Mexican* less than three years when he was indicted for criminal libel, along with Bronson Cutting, ex-Governor M. A. Otero, and two other members of the newspaper staff. The indictment was brought by a Socorro County grand jury and grew out of bitterness over the conduct of the 1917 gubernatorial election when Socorro's son, Holm C. Bursum, was the defeated Republican candidate. Although Johnson was found guilty of contempt of court by Judge Merritt C. Mechem and sentenced to thirty days in jail, the libel case was dismissed on appeal to the state supreme court on October 23, 1919 and the sentence for contempt was cleared away.

In the period following the end of World War I and the concomitant Russian Revolution, a substantial number of intellectuals who sympathized with the Russians in their efforts to reform the world were labeled "parlor pinks" by those who disagreed with them and thought their lofty ideas little more than conversation pieces. Many artists and writers were for a time among the "pinks." Bronson Cutting sought and effectively won the support of the powerful American Legion, an arch-foe of Bolshevism. Although Cutting liked to be known as a liberal, and Dana Johnson usually was tolerant of Santa Fe's Bohemians, an irresistible chance to shaft both Bolshevism and the backers of the Museum of New Mexico led to an editorial in the *Santa Fe New Mexican* for September 29, 1920:

REAL BOLSHEVISTS

The New Mexican has heretofore lightly applied the term "Bolshevistic" to some of the execrable things displayed at the State Museum in the name of Art. It develops that this term was not so far misplaced. It appears that two of the principal exponents of the lunacy which has sought to get in under the term "modernism" are real Bolshevists: one has gone back to Russia to join the soviets and believes that the Lenine-Trotsky [sic] regime is "much-maligned"; the other it is understood is openly preaching here the wild and woolly doctrines of these creatures and slurring the government and governmental institutions of the United States.

We have had a good deal of fun out of the controversy over the alleged "modernism" which has rated in Santa Fe recently. It might be well to become serious for a moment and suggest that Santa Fe nor New Mexico wants any Bolshevism, on canvas or on street corners, in a state institution or out of it. The attempt to make it appear that the

Museum art gallery is principally identified with the violent extreme in art advocated by the "new school" as it loves to call itself will not do the Museum much good in any event; and when we thus call the attention of the museum extremism propagandists to the fact that some of the leading exponents of their pet hobby are openly preaching sovietism, doubtless they will take the hint.

Three fourths of the official publicity put out from the Museum art section has been labored propaganda for art extremism of the most absurd kind. We urge that it will be the part of wisdom to regain a proper balance on this subject and take every precaution to see that the gallery is not regarded as a center of anything remotely connected with Bolshevist ideas in art or otherwise.[8]

The editorial, designed to please ardent patriots and wound the Museum administration, got a violent reaction from an unexpected sector when the entire art colony declared itself insulted. After Paul Walter had resigned his chores as curator of the Art Museum to become a banker, he had been replaced by the eminently respectable painter, Sheldon Parsons. The editorial might have given everybody a good laugh except for the political undertone and the implied threat, as well as the smear on the painters who considered themselves modernists and thought it had nothing to do with their patriotism.

Foremost among the members of the literary and artistic colony who rushed to support the Museum and its policies was Alice Corbin Henderson. Her letter to the newspaper was duly printed and then followed by another Johnson editorial reiterating and elaborating on the editor's original criticism.

Studio and cocktail parties on the Camino and Canyon Road buzzed. At one function, Natalie Curtis Burlin, a specialist in primitive music and wife of the painter H. Paul Burlin, held a spirited discussion with Col. Cutting. When Alice Henderson prepared the draft of a reply to the *Santa Fe New Mexican*'s second editorial, the group decided it would be a good idea for Natalie Burlin to submit it directly to the owner of the paper. Under date of October 11, 1920 Mrs. Henderson had written her lengthy rebuttal, addressed to the editor:

> ... You say in your Sunday editorial that the charge made by The New Mexican that certain artists in Santa Fe have openly advocated Bolshevism as a political doctrine and have slurred the government and governmental institutions is not denied. Naturally I did not deny the charge, as I have no evidence for or against the statement, either from hearsay or from direct knowledge. The burden of proof in this case rests with the New Mexican, and until it furnishes evidence, naturally no defense is possible.
>
> Nor did I say that the charge of advocating sovietism constituted an insult — although it apparently does so to the writer of the editorial in question. But to accuse a citizen of "slurring the government and governmental institutions of the United States" is definitely an insult,

which, if unsustained by the evidence, becomes libel. In refraining from publishing the names of the two artists so accused, the New Mexican is doubtless safe, so far as a suit for libel is concerned. But on account of the anonymous nature of the attack, every artist in Santa Fe is subject to the accusation, and will so remain until the Santa Fe New Mexican gives the names of the artists accused and furnishes evidence in support of its statements.

... Furthermore it is as little the concern of an Art Museum to enquire into a painter's political views as it would be to enquire into his religion, his bank account, or his domestic affairs. Nor can an Art Museum arrogate to itself the right to deal with political misdemeanors. If the Santa Fe New Mexican has a real complaint to make in this direction, it should take it to the proper department of government, and not attempt to lay it at the door of a Museum whose sole function is to foster art.

As regards the artistic policy of the Museum, the editorial in question did suggest that the Museum curtail the exhibition privileges of certain unnamed artists, and so, by implication, advocate "state-controlled" art...

Apropos of possible action by the state legislature, let us quote from the New Mexican of September 28th, the day before the first editorial appeared:

"As a friend of the Museum and of Santa Fe we would intimate that one of these days a bunch of low-brow legislators are going to get up in meeting, exhibit some of these specimens [of art] and read some of that propaganda and raise a howl that will be heard clear over to Apache Canyon. This is a perfectly good tip."

Just as a perfectly good tip, one would like to know if calling our statesmen a "bunch of low-brow legislators" is a "slur against our government and governmental institutions?" And does the paper mean to infer that the only paintings to be shown at the Museum must be such as would receive the approbation of the least qualified (by his own statement) to judge? ...

The Santa Fe New Mexican has indeed been unique among newspapers in treating art as news, equal in importance to other public events and enterprises. This has been moreover a far-sighted policy of manifest financial advantage to the city and the paper. If the New Mexican wishes to retain its prestige in this respect, it can of course assign the work formerly done by the Museum staff to a member of its own staff and be assured of criticism and point of view directly amenable to its own censorship. But that the Museum refuses to accept this censorship, real or implied, is hardly to be wondered at. Every paper, of course, has a right to its own point of view, but not the right to coerce another paper or institution or individual to accept it.

Yours truly,

Alice Corbin Henderson

Col. Cutting returned the draft to Mrs. Burlin with a note scribbled on the last page where the words *of manifest financial advantage* had been underlined and emphasized by a couple of exclamation marks. The note read: "Please excuse marginal comment, but would Mrs. Henderson be willing to specify? For years we have been printing Museum publications at a loss; and for a long time have begged the Museum to install a printing-press of their own. At the present price of paper what does the author of the above think the space devoted to Museum news has cost us and what has been the return?"[10]

Mrs. Henderson's careful reasoning was not destined to take up any of that valuable space in the *Santa Fe New Mexican*. It was less than two weeks until the 1920 election, and although Col. Cutting usually let his editor speak for him, on this occasion he was sufficiently moved by his talk with Mrs. Burlin, by Mrs. Henderson's arguments, and by the uproar that was influencing voters in Santa Fe, to write a long statement of his personal beliefs on several subjects. On the letterhead of his Santa Fe home, *Los Siete Burros*, he chided Mrs. Burlin for taking their little discussion too seriously; it had been his impression that they were talking more to make conversation than to settle the complex problems of Bolshevism and free speech. He assured her that he did not dictate the policy of the *Santa Fe New Mexican*'s art editorials and that having read them after they were in print, he could see nothing in them to justify the almost hysterical excitement they stirred up. He pointed out that the newspaper had promised to print the artists' protest and suggested that those who agreed with Mrs. Henderson might sign her letter (provided they could think of nothing more to say), but it was his belief that if Editor Johnson printed the letter it would be only with a guarantee from all members of the artistic colony that it would be the last article submitted on the subject.

He took issue with Mrs. Henderson's point that legislators would consider it a slur to be called "low-brow." Asserting that no one who adopted a superior attitude could accomplish much in this country, he questioned that low-brow legislators would be less qualified to judge works of art than high-brow cliques. "Surely all art that has endured the test of centuries was popular in its own time," the Harvard-educated politician wrote. "It did not require diagrams and commentaries. Its only critics were the professional art-critics, who it is fair to assume are usually wrong."[11]

Cutting went on to say that Mrs. Henderson was mistaken in speaking of the Museum of New Mexico as an art museum. He ignored the legislative action in appropriating money for the specific purpose of building an art museum, quoting instead from the laws of 1915, ch.19 that the purposes for which the Museum was owned and managed by the state were the excavation and study of ancient ruins, the preservation of archaeological sites, and the publication of investigations. He continued, "While I do not for a moment object to the Museum's generosity in going outside of the letter of the law to exhibit works of art, this is not its primary purpose, and it cannot in fairness be treated as though it had been created for the encouragement of exhibitions of works of art, like the Metropolitan or other institutions of that class."[12]

Editor Johnson had not suggested that the Museum should be guided by political standards in *hanging pictures*, but rather was protesting the encouragement given to the *men* in question, Cutting declared. While he personally was not prepared to affirm or deny the nature of the political activities of the artists in question, he argued that the pictures of an artist suspected of criminal acts might be hung on the walls of the Museum, but the man himself should be reported to the police.

The letter covered several tangential points that he and Mrs. Burlin had discussed in their party conversation — points which had to do with the upcoming election, with Cutting's stand in favor of free speech and a free press, and with his insistence that the artists should be more concerned with local politics than with idle conversation over Bolshevik ideology. The owner of the *Santa Fe New Mexican* proposed that Mrs. Henderson's letter be modified to meet "the point at issue" and repeated his decision that whatever the artists decided to offer for publication, it would be the *end* of the discussion. He granted that there might be much more to be said, but the opposing sides would not convince each other. He concluded with the statement, "So let us say no more about it, except in so far as any publication — after the election — may seem advisable."[13]

If the members of the artistic colony were confused by the arguments in Cutting's letter and were not sure just what he considered "the point at issue," several points were quite clear: they could not attempt to curtail the rights of free speech by guaranteeing that everybody on their side would refrain from writing further to the newspaper about the controversy over the two unnamed artists; the newspaper could not be persuaded to name the offending painters; the owner of the *Santa Fe New Mexican* would not permit more than one more article in support of their protest before the impending election. They could only voice their indignation to one another.

The presidential election of 1920 was a sweeping national victory for Warren G. Harding. Cutting, although nominally a Republican, supported the Democratic state ticket in New Mexico and a Santa Fe County coalition calling itself the Independent Fusion Party ticket which was dedicated to throwing the Republican Old Guard stalwarts out of the County Courthouse. It was Friday following Tuesday's election before the *Santa Fe New Mexican* conceded that the Republican candidate for governor, Merritt C. Mechem, had been carried into office by the national sweep, but that it was pleased some of the Independent Fusion candidates had won in Santa Fe County.

Hewett received copies of Mrs. Henderson's unpublished letter and Col. Cutting's communication to Natalie Curtis Burlin, and filed them for future reference. He asked the Art Museum staff to prepare for publication the long list of eminent painters whose work had been shown by the Museum to date. He also quietly began preparations for assuring that the next meeting of the Legislature would vote sufficient funds to support the complex dedicated to art and archaeology which he directed.

He must have been pleased by the Christmas letter he received from Robert Henri telling of artists who returned to New York from New Mexico with the report that the Santa Fe newspaper had blundered into calling for an art censor at the Museum of New Mexico. Henri praised the open door policy from which many artists, including himself, had benefitted, and urged that it should have the devoted support of the *New Mexican*, as well as the citizens and artists who profited by it.[14]

In his Annual Report for 1920, Hewett made a statement of his philosophy to the management of the School which was reprinted in *El Palacio* for February 5, 1921 under the title, "Art Policy of Museum and School." It was his oblique way of having the last word in print, even though the columns of the local newspaper were closed to the defenders of the Museum.

After explaining his reasons for thinking it doubtful that any other part of America afforded a parallel to the art activity of New Mexico at that time, he continued:

> ... The Museum extends its privileges to all who are working with a serious purpose in art. It endeavors to meet their needs for a place of exhibition and as far as possible offers studio facilities, as tables are furnished to visiting writers, laboratories to scientists and the library to readers and investigators. The artist is the judge of the fitness of his work for presentation to the public to the same extent that the speaker is who occupies our platform. Both are conceded perfect freedom of expression within the limits of common propriety.
>
> The Museum seeks to reflect what is passing in the minds of the artists who are working in this environment.... If Modernism, Ultra-Modernism, Impressionism, Post Impressionism, Expressionism, or any other phase of esthetic endeavor appears to predominate in the exhibitions at any given time it is merely an evidence of the exuberance which no one will condemn, but on the contrary will sincerely welcome. Whether it lasts or not probably will depend upon its spiritual soundness. The casual likes and dislikes and prejudices of individuals affect the matter but little. Out of this strong flow of impressions, emotions, striving, of men and women who are painting and writing in New Mexico there will come the pictures, poems and dramas that will immortalize the strength, beauty and life of our Southwest. It is a noble service ...
>
> Santa Fe is beginning to enjoy preeminence in some enviable ways. It is sometimes spoken of as the intellectual capital of the Southwest — to its region what Alexandria was to its age. This is high distinction, which to maintain calls for toleration and generosity and genuine friendly interest in all the efforts that are contributing to this good fortune.[15]

While some might sneer at this grandiloquence, no Santa Fean could fault Hewett for underestimating the little city he loved.

15

HEWETT AND THE SANTA FE FIESTA

From the depths of the dripping cave to the pinnacles of civilization, man has fought for physical, intellectual, spiritual freedom. The race has, from its lowest levels, seemed to realize that only in an atmosphere of freedom can man live. — ELH

Hewett hated the First World War as a backward step in man's progress, even though it was a necessary battle for the freedom he prized so highly. He did not believe that war is inevitable in man's culture, and writing on "The Conquest of War" many years later he observed, "Three good men sitting down together in a spirit of good will in July, 1914, and seeing eye to eye, could have prevented the first World War. Crises hinge upon the wisdom or unwisdom, the courage, the character of a few men."[1]

He was deeply distressed to find many of his German friends numbered among his country's enemies, but tried to take the long view that this, too, would pass. He was too old for the Armed Forces and he had no sons to send; his contribution must be in building morale. He must do what he could to soften the tragic interruption to so many lives and so many projects. Through the museums and many organizations to which he belonged he planned patriotic celebrations, and he gave space for bandage rolling and other activities contributing to the war effort. Hewett accepted appointments to boards and commissions working for the Allied cause and was especially interested in the White Cross Society, which, under the leadership of Madame Montessori, endeavored to ease the trauma of war among European children.

Many of Hewett's protégés were subject to the draft. He wrote letters recommending his young men for their chosen branches of officers' training

147

schools, then tried to get them deferred until they could finish the projects on which they were currently engaged. He needed Nusbaum to complete the Art Museum; he thought the Armed Forces could wait for Earl Morris until the end of the season's excavations in Central America on which Morris was currently engaged. In San Diego, Hewett cooperated in turning the museum to wartime uses and helped to arrange the encampment of Marine and Naval forces in Balboa Park. He mourned the former students who were war casualties and, like all decent men, prayed for the end of hostilities.

The actual involvement of the United States in the shooting war lasted only a little over eighteen months. After it was over Hewett had great hopes for the progress of mankind through the League of Nations and the World Court. Business as usual might be restored. In San Diego the museum, the archaeological society, and a teaching job at San Diego State College occupied his winter months. He and Doni made an ever widening circle of friends as they returned year after year. In Santa Fe the Museum complex and the School marched forward, with summer digs at Chaco Canyon and in the Pajarito. But Hewett needed a good promotional project on the home front — he found it in the Santa Fe Fiesta.

There is a tradition that the annual Santa Fe Fiesta as decreed by De Vargas in 1692 has been continued without interruption to the present day. It is true that the beginnings of an annual celebration of the reconquest following the Pueblo Revolt of 1680 have been traced to 1712 and even earlier. The custom of carrying the statue of La Conquistadora in solemn ecclesiastical procession through the streets of Santa Fe may have occurred every year since De Vargas, grateful for her assistance in his military success, vowed to honor her with a chapel. But the secular demonstration is based on a proclamation by the Marquis de Peñuela in 1712 and must have lapsed many times through the centuries. The record of Spanish and Mexican days is incomplete, and after the coming of the American regime in 1846 the governing authorities had scant interest in continuing customs based on a culture alien to them.

By the time Edgar Hewett first visited Santa Fe in the 1890s, the concerts played by the military band in the plaza bandstand were the most widely attended civic celebrations. Ruth Seligman, wife of plaza merchant James Seligman, in an interview with the author gave her recollections of how the revivial of a civic celebration honoring the reconquest came about in the years after 1896 when she arrived in Santa Fe:

> I remember the Women's Board of Trade held a plaza fete every year to raise money for charity and for the library; we had a small library in the back of the barracks building. The first year the fete was a great success, so we decided to hold it again. Miss Bertha Staab [of the old Staab family who lived in the brick house where La Posada is now] said, "I don't think we should call it a *Fete*. I think we should call it a Plaza Fiesta."
>
> So, for some years we had a booth and sold things. We served ice cream and cake all afternoon and evening. The band would play. One year we had

Sheldon Parsons in fiesta costume, ca. 1932.
urtesy of the Museum of New Mexico.

Alice Corbin Henderson and William Penhallow
ıderson in fiesta costume,1932.Photograph by Will
ınell. Courtesy of the Museum of New Mexico.

Ina Sizer Cassidy and Gerald Cassidy in fiesta costume,1932. Photograph by Will Connell. Courtesy of
the Museum of New Mexico.

a platform that Mr. Rapp, the architect, donated. Everybody danced on that platform, and we had music all night. There were lights, too — I don't remember what kind but they weren't Japanese lanterns as some people have suggested. It was always quite a success but they finally gave it up because the Women's Board president for that year thought it was too much trouble.

But the real idea of a town fiesta came from the Episcopal minister named James Mythen — a very brilliant young man who preached the most marvelous sermons. I forget how long he was here, but he decided to go back east. A day or two before he was leaving my husband and I were going out to dinner at Jaffa's, and we stopped in the old Santa Fe Club. At that time the Club was on Lincoln Avenue right next door to where the Hewetts later lived — in a house that Dr. Knapp built. Mr. Mythen got to talking to us and he said, "You know, I don't see why Santa Fe doesn't have some yearly historical event as they do in New Orleans at Mardi Gras. Santa Fe is so full of history."

So Jim and I were very much interested, and a few days after Mr. Mythen left, Jim asked a few men to come up to the house. We sat around our dining table, and Jim suggested that one of the best things to start with would be the reconquest by De Vargas.

The men fell for it right away. There was Sam Cartwright. I think he was president of the Chamber of Commerce, but it might have still been called the Men's Board of Trade. I'm very sure Celso Lopez was mayor at the time. We had the mayor, anyway, and four or five other men Jim thought might be interested.

That's how the De Vargas pageant got started. We didn't call it that; we called it the Reconquest . . . or really, we didn't call it much of anything. I think that was in 1910, though I'm not quite sure. We got Jesse Nusbaum interested. He was always a help with everything. Jesse got all the Indians to come in, and George Armijo was the first De Vargas. Of course they didn't know what sort of costumes they should wear, and his costume was too elaborate, with feathers — a plume — and all that. Soldiers having been on the road for months wouldn't be dressed like that, you know.

That's the way it started, right there in our house. In those days all the little towns had fiestas. They used to have cock fights in Agua Fria and things like that, but in Santa Fe they had had only a small religious remembrance each year. For a few years we just had the De Vargas parade. It was in September because we thought the rains would be over then. They knew De Vargas had taken a vow, as in the religious processions, but they never combined the two — the religious and the military conquest in those days. De Vargas and his soldiers started at Rosario Cemetery where they gathered. They marched into Santa Fe and down Lincoln Avenue, into the plaza. They erected a cross at the east end of the plaza — that was before the plaza was made over. The De Vargas men came in on their horses, with Indians. Then the Indians accepted the cross. It was very impressive in a simple way. George Armijo read the proclamation as De

Vargas returning after being driven out.

It was Jimmy Mythen's idea to have some historical event and Jim Seligman's idea to have De Vargas. After a few years it was Mr. Twitchell's idea to have a fiesta — they called it the 300th or whatever year it was, but in all the years I'd lived here we'd never before had one. It had probably been dropped in the early days.

Then Dr. Hewett got interested in it and Mr. Twitchell. They decided to have a candlelight procession. It had nothing to do with the De Vargas parade which we had several years all by itself.[2]

Thus, as an old woman, Mrs. Seligman recalled how it had been. James Mythen served at Holy Faith Episcopal Church from September, 1910 to April, 1911, so the revival Mrs. Seligman remembered probably began in 1911.

The *Santa Fe New Mexican* for July 4, 1912 carried an article describing the De Vargas Pageant and Plaza Fiesta to be held the following day. Events in the plaza started with a rummage sale, and included refreshment stalls on the east side of the plaza and games on the west side. Booths were described as selling homemade candy, cigars, and "fragrant nosegays and boutonniers . . . the wearing of which will be the badge of honor and local patriotism for the day." Mention was made of a Mexican booth and an Indian booth. The band played part of the day; in the pagoda a lunch counter was set up to serve sandwiches, wieners, doughnuts, and delicious coffee. The *Santa Fe New Mexican* boasted that such a success was expected that it would be hard to excel in years to come.[3]

In the years between 1912 and 1918 bits and pieces were added or dropped from the celebration. The San Diego Exposition had featured historical pageants and parades, with a large amphitheater for concerts. Many Santa Feans and a goodly number of Indians from nearby pueblos who had participated in the exposition came home with the experience fresh in their minds. The whole West had become tourist conscious, and San Diego had shown what the publicity provided by a civic spectacle could do to encourage tourism. The war slowed things down as the populace was busy elsewhere, but once the armistice was signed, Santa Fe's energies could be turned to entertainment and the courting of tourists once again.

Col. R. E. Twitchell was the official director of the 1919 Fiesta, and the staff of the School of American Research was given almost complete responsibility for the activities. For comic relief a group of young businessmen staged a mock bullfight which, to their delight, gained national attention. Artist Will Shuster produced a papier maché bull, animated by two men inside. Martin Gardesky, owner of the Capital Pharmacy, was the toreador, and at the proper moment punctured a bag filled with colored water which drenched the bull in gore. Editor Johnson described the fight in the *Santa Fe New Mexican* as if it had been a real one and the news got on the wire services. It caused a flood of protests from animal lovers across the country, and chuckles in Santa Fe for years afterward.

Paul A. F. Walter was chosen to direct the 1920 Santa Fe Fiesta. A journalist by profession, Walter had been a close associate of Hewett through the formative years of the School and Museum. After he and his brothers-in-law, John K. and Charles Stauffer, were forced to sell the *Santa Fe New Mexican* to Bronson Cutting in 1912, Walter became editor of the newly founded *El Palacio*. Although he used many articles by other writers, much of the unsigned material that made up *El Palacio* for the next forty-five years was written by Walter.

Carrying the title of Associate Director of the Museum, Walter performed many duties for Hewett. In the absence of the Director he kept Hewett informed about political hazards threatening the budget, and received visiting dignitaries. He scheduled exhibitions in the Art Museum and wrote publicity for them, including free-lance articles for national magazines. He supervised many tasks in behalf of the artists, including such homely chores as arranging for the framing of pictures and their shipment to exhibitions around the country. Handling pictures eventually grew into a full-time job for which he hired a Museum staffer, and thus Sam Huddleson became known to three generations of artists for his expertise in storing, crating and shipping their work. It was Walter who carried out Hewett's instuctions to buy the first tentative efforts of many Indian artists destined to become famous, such as Maria Martinez, Tonita Peña and Velino Shijo. All this labor Walter performed for a stipend which scarcely supported his wife and growing family of five children.

Then, in 1920, Walter decided to change his profession from journalist to banker. Offered a position in the First National Bank of Santa Fe, he resigned as director of the Fiesta and suggested that Hewett be appointed to succeed him. Hewett wanted to keep the show under the watchful auspices of the School, and since there didn't seem to be a better man available, he accepted the appointment when the Fiesta committee offered it. He had been actively involved anyway, and he could rally the entire Museum staff to carry out his plans. For him there must be an educational spin-off to justify the expenditure of time and money, so the historical aspects of the Fiesta, as well as the chance to inform visitors about Indians, appealed to him.

Hewett kept in mind that San Diego had provided something for everybody, highbrow and lowbrow — a happy commingling of a street carnival with the best cultural features of a Chautauqua, a form of entertainment that was at the height of its popularity during the years the Exposition promoters were planning their show. Chautauquas took their name from the town in New York State where they originated. In the early years of the twentieth century the Chautauqua movement brought cultural recreation to hundreds of American communities where people could not otherwise see good theater, listen to good music, or hear outstanding lecturers. The programs were especially popular in the Midwest. During the summer lull between haying and harvest, farm families could drive into town every day to join their city friends in a week-long cultural binge usually held under a big canvas tent in the town park. Morning activities kept vacationing schoolchildren busy; in the afternoons and evenings thousands of Americans saw their first Shakespearean plays enacted by the Ben Greet Players, heard William Jennings

Bryan thunder his "Cross of Gold" speech, and tapped their feet to the ringing marches of John Phillip Sousa's band. Chautauqua was big business for entertainers until World War I interrupted it and the postwar development of radio made it unprofitable. As developed by Twitchell, Nusbaum, Walter, and Hewett, the Santa Fe Fiesta carried out a similar concept, with emphasis on the special features of the Southwestern community.

Although Col. R. E. Twitchell was officially listed as director of the 1921 Santa Fe Fiesta, the four-day program bears the unmistakable stamp of Hewett's ideas and philosophy. A large temporary grandstand in the plaza faced Palace Avenue, where the *portal* of the old Palace and the street itself became the stage. The first day, Aboriginal American Day, began at nine o'clock in the morning; most of the two thousand spectators were already seated in the grandstand. Indians from San Ildefonso, Cochiti, Jemez, Santa Clara, and Tesuque who had appeared in previous years were featured, with the addition of a new group from Zuni. According to the *Santa Fe New Mexican,* the Indians were "clad in their gayest and most precious finery, with brilliant blankets and headdresses, jingling silver accouterments, plumes and foxtails, bracelets and beadwork." They seemed "to live over again the days when their ancestors greeted the men in golden mail from across the seas."[4]

After time out for lunch, the afternoon offered Indian dances and songs by Tsianina, "The Indian princess and famous prima donna."[5] A brief respite was allowed for dinner, but at seven o'clock the band struck up once again, with more songs by Tsianina and the Santa Fe Fiesta Chorus, ending in a grand finale of Indians marching by at nine o'clock. After that people who were tired might go home to bed, but many celebrants went on to the grand baile at the Armory, which was under the auspices of the Fiesta management and the Santa Fe Cavalry troop.

The second day began with the entry of De Vargas. This procession had lapsed from 1912 to 1916, when it was revived by the Chamber of Commerce. As Ruth Seligman pointed out, it was probably not historically correct for the long-suffering Spanish leaders to arrive wearing their beautiful velvet costumes and plumes, but the aristocrats among them *could* have dressed in finery saved for special occasions, and their impressive appearance made a very good show. After the procession came Spanish songs sung by the chorus, local soloists and the indefatigable Tsianina, and more Indian dances. The *Santa Fe New Mexican* reporter was especially taken by a visiting chief who gave a speech "probably in Zuni."[6] Of the several locals who attempted to translate his dignified address, the most popular was Col. José D. Sena (as usual an officiating mayor domo), when he declared that the Zuni chief said, "After this, boys, I'll have to set up the drinks, and it will cost me seven dollars and a half."[7] Hewett must have winced at this putdown as well as the playful descriptions of the Indian ceremonial dances reported in the newspaper by writers who made coy copy of something they didn't understand, but the paper obviously considered it more interesting than the Museum public-relations handouts.

The evening pageantry included the "Reconquest of New Mexico" and ended with a playlet called "An Evening at the Governor's Palace in the 18th Century," after which the second day ended with *two* grand bailes, one at the Armory for which anybody could buy tickets and an invitational affair held at the Scottish Rite Cathedral under the auspices of the Knights of Pythias.

On the third day, which was Spanish-American Day, the flag of Spain was replaced on the flagstaff by the Mexican banner, amid huzzas from the crowd. A special afternoon event was a ceremonial race by Zuni runners, who covered the seven and a half miles around Circle Drive north of town in fifty minutes, kicking the stick as they went. Hewett explained to the audience, "It is run by the Zunis only in the spring, the racing season being of two months' duration . . . on their home course they often run ten or twenty, or even as many as thirty-five miles."[8]

The *Santa Fe New Mexican* account says ten runners, five on a side, used little sticks painted red for easy recognition. The runners wore turquoise earrings and only one moccasin, which was on the left foot. The big toe was wrapped on the bare right foot. The stick had to be kicked the entire distance, untouched by hand, or carried between the toes. Two horsemen rode ahead to clear the track, carrying extra moccasins in case a runner should lose his foot protection or develop a blister. The winning team received several prizes, including a watermelon and $100 donated by the Fiesta management.

On the fourth day the theme centered on the Santa Fe Trail; the pageant, the "Commerce of the Prairies," included Kit Carson, Dr. Josiah Gregg and General Kearny with his Army of the West. The floats showed the coming of the railroad, then brought things up to date in a section covering 1880-1921 which included automobiles carrying old-timers who had crossed the Great Plains in wagon or stagecoach and ended with a modern airplane. In the evening there were more songs, a classical Castilian ballet performed by the Fiesta Dancers, and the climax of the Fiesta — the Grand Baile in the Armory.

The performances, which had taken weeks of preparation and rehearsal under the general chairmanship of Hewett, were directed by Col. Twitchell with a different associate director for each day. Everyone who could be persuaded to perform was recruited for some part in the festivities, and while the names were predominantly Anglo, there was a goodly sprinkling of Spanish-surnamed social and political leaders of the community. A role had been found for anyone who offered to sing, dance or otherwise display his or her talents.

The format, with some modification, was followed for several years. Gate receipts for the grandstand ran between four and five thousand dollars (sufficient to cover the cost of the show), with a special fee sometimes charged for Indian dances shown in the Palace patio, to defray their cost. As the fame of the celebration spread the crowds grew too large for the plaza grandstand and the activities were dispersed. The First Annual Southwest Indian Fair was held in connection with the 1922 Fiesta in the National Guard Armory facing Washington Avenue at the northeast corner of the old Palace, a building which later became part of the Museum complex. The Fair was reported to be "the most remarkable, complete, varied and beautiful collection of the products of the Indians' skill ever held in this country."[9]

A local businessman, Carl A. Bishop, was director for the 1923 Fiesta. He convinced the plaza merchants that the annual show had grown to proportions that made it worth their money to keep it going, and collected about three thousand dollars from them as seed money for the following year. Two months before the 1924 celebration was scheduled to begin, however, little had been planned — the financial backers began to panic. Through their civic organizations they begged the School of American Research to take charge, and for the first time the sole responsibility for the character of the celebration was accepted by Hewett.

El Palacio devoted most of one issue to its report on the overwhelming success of that effort. It was emphasized that the Museum, in spite of its close relationship with the School, was not involved except in offering the facilities of a public institution, and that staff who participated volunteered "vacation time," but it is hard to see that any real distinction was made between the two institutions. The names of the entire Museum staff are to be found among the leading participants.

For several years members of the artistic colony had been grumbling that the spectacles were planned for the affluent tourist; the poor local citizen could not afford the prices charged and had to be content with glimpses gained from the periphery. Hewett, who was aware of their feelings, set out to make this Fiesta the property of the entire community. With his limited budget, he needed the voluntary help of everybody. His first step was to name a Fiesta Council of nineteen members and seek their assistance in naming fourteen sub-committees. Henceforth the responsibility for the annual celebration would rest with a Fiesta Council.

Participation of artists and writers was assured by giving them important roles. Witter Bynner was named director of the merrymaking activities, "El Pasatiempo," with Mrs. John Sloan and Mrs. Randall Davey as committee members. Dramatics were placed under Earl W. Scott and his wife Marian Gallager Scott, who were Chautauqua veterans. Prior to World War I they had headed a troop of professional actors traveling the circuits. After Scott was mustered out of the Army the couple bought a home on Acequia Madre in Santa Fe, contributed their talents to civic affairs, and built a reputation as detective-story writers for the pulps.

The dramatic productions for 1924 were comprehensive. The two downtown theaters were leased and their combined seating capacity of 1,500 was supplemented by using St. Francis Auditorium in the Museum for overflow audiences. Four plays were offered on different days. "Tonita of the Holy Faith" by Maude McFie Bloom was based on the legend of the Spanish natives; "Kaw-Eh," a musical play with an Indian theme, was written and staged by Elizabeth Willis DeHuff, wife of the superintendent of the U.S. Indian School. The other two plays were traditional. A Spanish-speaking troop that usually gave "Los Pastores" at Christmastime managed to compress it into a one-hour version, and "Los Matachines," a pantomime presented for several previous years by a group of

Cochiteños, was also on the program. A fee was charged to defray the cost of the theaters, but all pageantry and fun features were free.

Great care was taken by the emissaries sent to enlist the cooperation of the Pueblo people. *El Palacio* says:

> It was impressed on the Indians that it was desired that their ceremonies be staged in their primitive beauty, in accordance with their own traditions and their religious significance. They were instructed and informed as to the character of exhibits desired for the Indian Fair which was to present the highest achievement in their racial handicrafts.... In more than one instance it took considerable persuasion and renewed assurances of good faith on the part of Santa Fe representatives, before the governing body in the pueblo would give its consent. But the result made it all worth while, for the Indians came imbued with the thought that this was "their" Fiesta, just as much as it was that of Santa Fe's heterogeneous population.[10]

The popular Tsianina was back and a Mohawk singer, Oskenonton, made his first Fiesta appearance.

Gertrude Espinosa of Albuquerque, in charge of the Spanish dancing, trained a group of young people of both Spanish and Anglo backgrounds in traditional dances that have been popular at civic celebrations ever since. There was also a Spanish Chorus under the direction of José D. Sena and a group called the Troubadours who were recruited from among the local Spanish-American musicians accustomed to playing guitar, violin and mandolin at the dances held by the native people.

In the best Hewett tradition several conventions were held preceding the Fiesta. Although three new hotels had opened since the Fiesta of 1923, the town's housing facilities were so overtaxed that the Chamber of Commerce made a canvass of private homes willing to accept visitors in addition to their friends and relatives. The dormitories of St. Michael's College, the U.S. Indian School and the School for the Deaf were made available; campgrounds were thronged, as many who came in their cars brought their own camping equipment. Churches and civic organizations supplemented hotels and restaurants by serving meals in food booths, empty stores or their own facilities. "As a consequence," according to the *El Palacio* account, "there was no real congestion at any place at any time, and there prevailed an orderliness and a law abiding spirit which were as characteristic of Santa Fe as they were admirable."[11] The Santa Fe Fiesta had become a nationally known celebration.

But the outpouring of total community participation was not destined to last. Although for several ensuing Fiestas many of the same people continued loyal participation, the volunteering of so much effort began to pall. The Historical Parade grew shorter, and the Hysterical Parade which parodied and lampooned local events grew more baudy each year until the archbishop made a formal protest that this event had become unworthy of Santa Fe and her people. After that there was an informal censorship of entries, until only a few tried to be funny and the rest were patriotic or strictly commercial. Once the celebration lost its educational flavor, Hewett and the Museum staff quietly dropped back to encouraging Indian participation in dances and craft fairs and the staging of the art exhibitions in the Museum.

Hewett was actively engaged in promoting the Fiesta program for about ten years. Paul Walter withdrew to the dignity of a bank vice-president; Col. Ralph Emerson Twitchell died in 1925. Tsianina, whose friendship with the Hewetts began in San Diego, dropped out of the changing Fiesta format but continued to keep in touch. Because she outlived most of the other participants in the Hewett story and continued as an active friend in their lives, some further account of her should be given.

Charles Wakefield Cadman was probably America's most popular composer in the years between World War I and the Depression, and surely the most famous white musician to use Indian themes at a time when the American Indian was becoming a source of such inspiration. It was easy to sell tickets to any lecture or concert that shed more light on these fascinating people. In 1908 Cadman was touring the United States, lecturing on Indian music and using white singers to demonstrate his songs, when Tsianina, a precocious sixteen-year-old girl of Cherokee-Creek parentage, was brought to his attention by her Denver voice teacher, John C. Wilcox.

Within six months she was touring the country with him (his mother went along as chaperone), presenting concerts featuring his songs. For their appearance Tsianina wore a fringed buckskin dress which came to her ankles, with beaded moccasins. Her hair, bound with a beaded headband around her forehead, fell in two long braids over her shoulders. Throughout her career she made small variation in this costume — it came to be her trademark. Cadman at the piano wore the traditional white tie and tails of a concert artiste.

Tsianina's first meeting with Edgar Hewett came some eight years after her association with Cadman began. It was "Cadman and Tsianina Day" at the San Diego Exposition. The young Indian woman was assigned the task of judging a contest of white children wearing Indian dress. Later she told of that day:

> After the awards were made, an unassuming, slow-moving distinguished looking man came up to me and invited me to see his exhibit. He was that great "maker of archaeologists" Edgar L. Hewett. In showing me around and explaining his purpose and interest in the exhibit he said, "My mother made me promise her that when I grew to manhood, I would give all my efforts towards doing something for the American Indian that would let the world see him as he is, and not as wild west shows, cheap fiction, and moving pictures present him. The best we can do is to save what we can of the priceless heritage and make every effort to comprehend it. Then the archaeological heritage from the unknown American of two or three millenia becomes an authentic history of the Indian people.[12]

Tsianina knew little about archaeology, but she was to remember the day and Hewett vividly because of a peculiar request he made of her. She noticed that as he showed her the skulls of ancient people on display in his Museum of Man he paid particular attention to her own head. Presently he said, "You have made so much out of your life in so short a time and your head is so beautifully shaped, I would consider it a great contribution to the history of your people and archaeology if you would let us have your head when you depart for the Happy Hunting Ground."

Tsianina made no reply but inside she didn't feel so good. She later wrote, "He frightened me, and I had a secret fear of having my skull on display for all to see. Imagine my relief when my beloved friend left for his Happy Hunting Ground before me!"[13]

When she came to sing at the dedication of Santa Fe's Art Museum in 1917 she found that New Mexico Indians loved and trusted Hewett, speaking of him fondly as "Him, old ruin."[14] She described the dedication ceremony in words written long afterward, perhaps dramatized but quite different from the contemporary newspaper accounts:

> This great humanitarian moved with a new spring in his step when, the day of the Fine Arts Museum's solemn opening on November 24, 1917, he saw the streets of Santa Fe lined with people from all over the state and dotted with colorful Indian costumes. It made this a highlight of his life in Santa Fe. The Museum's new auditorium, beautifully executed in Pueblo design, was packed to overflowing—a scene long to be remembered by all Santa Feans. As Dr. Hewett stepped upon the stage to open his heart to the people and reveal his purpose, the applause was overwhelming. For fully five minutes they cheered him and then came his words of thanks to the people of Santa Fe for their friendship, their loyalty to his dream, to the Indian for his inspiration and faith in him. In such a manner was the stage set for Mr. Cadman and me to open our program.
>
> Many Indians from the different pueblos came to the concert in their colorful costumes, making a bright splash in the auditorium. Not only did they come to hear Dr. Cadman and me, but also to pay tribute to Dr. Hewett, out of love and respect for him and his noble kinship with them. It was revealing to observe how they received Mr. Cadman's music, based on melodies from their own people. They nodded their heads approvingly after each number. In this great southwest country, Mr. Cadman was truly inspired with the opportunity to present his music to the Indian himself.[15]

Tsianina noted that Alice Cunningham Fletcher had stirred in Cadman his first interest in Indian music. Confined to her bed for several weeks after an automobile accident on the Omaha Reservation, Fletcher had lain where she could hear music and the throb of the tom-tom. At first she found it monotonous, then she came to feel the heartbeat of the underlying rhythm. She communicated her excitement about it to Cadman, and later Tsianina commented, "In Cadman's music I could feel this kinship with the heartbeat of the Indian. He composed many other great pieces of non-Indian music and rose to great heights in this field, but his Indian compositions opened the door to his wide accomplishments. The music

Tsianina Blackstone, famed Cherokee-Creek singer, 1924. Courtesy of the Museum of New Mexico.

critics and the press paid me the gracious compliment of considering me a very important part in this stage of his development."[16] She felt that Hewett also was opening the door for the American Indian to develop a rare art that would give him a good income and lift up his own sense of self-respect. For Tsianina, Hewett's promotion of Indian art and ceremonials and Cadman's use of native song and rhythm were proof that some white men could begin to understand the Indian.

The 1922 Santa Fe Fiesta was the last ever attended by Alice Fletcher. Hewett usually tried to schedule a meeting of the Managing Board of the School during Fiesta week. It was a time of pleasant weather in Santa Fe, members of university faculties were on vacation between summer schools and the fall term, and the Fiesta activities offered a demonstration of the School's integration with community life. At the sessions and social functions, the gentle old woman who had been so largely responsible for founding the School in Santa Fe sat and waited for friends to greet her. She had recovered remarkably well from a stroke suffered a few years previously, but she was very frail. Hewett later recalled "how cogently and how prophetically" she spoke to a gathering in St. Francis Auditorium of the Art Museum the summer before her death. "She realized this was to be the last of her visits to Santa Fe. She spoke in a way that aroused apprehension in the minds of all of us of her approaching passing off the scene."[17]

She died in Washington on April 6, 1923, at the age of eighty-five. She had lived long enough to know that her pioneering effort to make farmers of the Indians had been a failure. They had signed over their surplus land, which had increased enormously in value during the fifty-year interim; the allotments they received and the implements hopefully acquired had long been squandered. The Indian problem was not to be solved in a generation, no matter how good the intentions; but some Indians *had* become self supporting, some had been absorbed into the general population, and Alice Fletcher was not held responsible for the failures. Her Indian friends knew she liked them, tried to understand them, and made no personal profit from her attempts to help them.

In Santa Fe a memorial service was attended by many of those who had been with her when the School was incubating. Judge McFie told of her courage and endurance as she limped up and down the trail at El Rito de los Frijoles, scarcely considering it a hardship in her eagerness to see and know more of the Pueblo people. Hewett recalled that he would not have had his chance with the Institute had it not been for Alice Fletcher. Paul Walter read a brief biography of her outstanding achievements, and Mrs. N. B. Laughlin recalled how much she had done to encourage the Women's Board of the Museum.

After consultation with Alice Fletcher's friends in Washington, it was decided to place her ashes in a niche in the patio wall of the Art Museum, with a suitable bronze plaque. The sculptor Bush Brown, commissioned for the piece, had difficulty in achieving a likeness of her that satisfied both Hewett and Springer. Finally a youthful photograph was used for a bas-relief profile. Hewett prepared the inscription—a quotation from Fletcher about the inspiration she had found in her life with the Indians, which was approved by the Institute leadership. The base of the plaque supports a blanketed Indian on either side of the central panel and is inscribed to Alice Cunningham Fletcher, Chairman of the Managing Board, School of American Research, 1907-1912.

Charles F. Lummis, who had been among her admirers since the founding days of the School, wrote an eloquent tribute that was published in *Art and Archaeology* and read at the Santa Fe memorial service. In summing up her life he wrote, "We shall not look upon her like again. We shall know other splendid women; but there will never be another Alice Fletcher—dear, noble, beloved, revered Alice Fletcher!"[18]

16

WRECKED IN THE DESERT

The desert at its worst is fiendish; at its best it is paradise. By its charm, its mystery, its majesty, the spirit is raised to its loftiest imaginings. No matter what the punishment, one goes back to it over and over again. No wonder that the great religions of the world have emerged from the desert! — ELH

One of the problems never solved to Hewett's satisfaction was the matter of salaries for well qualified men in the museums and universities. Some were fortunate enough to have independent means to supplement the meager pay; some were so passionate about their work that they were willing to make any sacrifice for it; but a more substantial number could not ignore the hardships on their families and had to seek other employment. Hewett encouraged those who worked with him to augment their pay with outside activities and made every effort to place their publications. Such vehicles as *El Palacio* in Santa Fe and its counterpart *El Museo* in San Diego made no payment for contributions to their pages, however, and the popular journals were not interested in the sort of material most scientists wrote.

The School of American Research and the Museum of New Mexico were quite firmly rooted in Santa Fe before they had to endure the buffeting of World War I. The museum in San Diego was established under wartime pressure, and Hewett found it difficult to keep supporters and staff enthusiastic about its future. He had reached an age where he believed a slow and steady growth to be desirable, however, so he was content to keep the project in the minds of the people without undue pressure. As early as 1919 he wrote a San Diego staff member from Washington, apologizing for the low stipend offered him and explaining, "I have not been quite able to inspire my associates out there with the determination to keep things steadily going without me. If it should come about that my work should be such after this year that I could not give personal attention to San Diego, the museum might sag to such a degree that would make any connection with it uninviting to the ambitious and able man."[1]

He was also concerned that he had so little time for his own scientific writings and for the travel and exploration that had enriched his earlier years. In 1922 he was able to retrace part of the journey he had taken during his 1906 fellowship year; once more he visited the plaza of Nueva Casas Grandes in Mexico. Life in the state of Chihuahua had not changed much during the sixteen years he had been busy elsewhere, and in the home of the *jefe politico* he was remembered and recognized. When they talked of the healer, Francis Schlatter, Hewett was told that the huge saddle had worn out and no trace remained of the Bible. But the copper rod, which was more durable, was still treasured in a back room. When they brought it out to show him, Hewett tried to keep his keen interest within the bounds required by Mexican politeness. Before he left the plaza he made a contribution to the fund the village was raising to pay a schoolteacher from the city of Chihuahua, and once again he rode away.

The village leaders did not forget his generosity. Some months later in Santa Fe he received a heavy express package, bundled in gunnysacks and tied with scraps of rope. When it was opened, the copper rod was revealed. Hewett donated this last tangible link with the healer to the Museum of New Mexico.

By 1923 Hewett had reached the high plateau of his active life as an archaeologist. He had continued brief field trips in the Southwest, escaping from the complexities of "civilization" to the more primitive scenes of his youth, but he recognized the need for a longer change of scene and decided to take a leave of absence from his several jobs, to be spent in foreign travel. In San Diego, Santa Fe and Washington younger associates had assumed some direction — or at least a holding action — of his many duties. Accepted as a force in the American scientific world, Hewett planned to use his credentials in a leisurely visit to the sites of Old World archaeology, where he could broaden his base by acquiring credentials in the Oriental School.

The first half of 1923 was spent in preparation. Before he could take off on the journey, he was involved in helping to defeat the infamous Bursum Bill that threatened to strip much Reservation land from the Indians. John C. Collier and Francis C. Wilson, two men who were to be noted for their defense of Indian land titles, conferred with him during this outbreak in the chronic fight to keep white entrepreneurs from grabbing the last strongholds of Indian ownership. Collier held jobs in government and with privately funded societies; Wilson was a Santa Fe attorney retained by some pueblos and eventually by Collier as the fight progressed. The Bursum Bill was ultimately defeated; the men and women who had led the opposition to it continued to work on behalf of the Indians, although they could not always agree among themselves as to the most advisable way to help.

In public lectures and private conversation Hewett was still promoting his dream of turning the Pajarito Plateau and adjacent Jemez Mountains area into a national park. At this time the focal points were the region around the valley of the Rito de Los Frijoles, where his excavations had followed Bandelier's earlier discoveries, and Baca Location Number One, part of a private land grant in the Valle Grande, an extinct volcano crater in the Jemez Mountains. He found both

Donizetta and Edgar Lee Hewett, travelers, ca. 1924. Courtesy of the Museum of New Mexico.

enthusiastic supporters and rivals for his plan. The supporters were largely among the members of women's clubs in New Mexico; the opponents were private landowners and people working for parks in other locations. The chief problems lay in the cost of purchasing private land and the jurisdictional rivalries among government agencies. The Forest Service did not want to lose any territory to the Department of the Interior; backers of Los Alamos Ranch School loved their wilderness site and did not want to relinquish it.

During the summer of 1923 Hewett's longtime associates were busy in and around Santa Fe. Paul Walter could always be trusted to find time from his bank duties for editorial work and special confidential projects. Lansing Bloom looked after the many activities centered in the Museum, where Kenneth Chapman was still available as he continued his quiet studies of Indian design. Wesley Bradfield was supervising work sponsored by the Museum on the Cameron Creek site in southwestern New Mexico near the mining community of Hurley, which he was finding to be a rich source of Mimbres pottery. Even as he coordinated the work of these men, Hewett was busy arranging an itinerary for R. V. D. Magoffin, president of the Archaeological Institute of America, who had agreed to make an extensive lecture tour through "Hewett territory" on behalf of the Institute's plans for reorganization, which would include broadening its popular base.

In the meantime, plans went forward for the Hewetts' extended travel abroad. Hewett made reservations for Doni and himself to sail from Montreal on August 3; the ocean journey might take from ten to twelve days, which could be devoted to rest and preparation for the commitments ahead. After a brief sojourn in London and a visit with friends in England and Scotland, they would proceed to Geneva where Hewett kept up associations made in his days as a doctoral candidate; thence to Roman and Greek classical archaeological sites, and on to Constantinople for a side trip to the Trojan plain. After that came the ultimate purpose of the journey — a survey of Near East sites, with headquarters at the School of Oriental Research in Jerusalem.

Companions for the Asiatic portion of the trip were to be Albert T. Clay, director of Yale's Oriental Museum, and Mrs. Clay. Dr. Clay proposed that they purchase two Ford cars in Jerusalem for the trek across the Syrian desert, along the Euphrates, ending in Baghdad where the cars could undoubtedly be sold for a sum close to the original purchase price. It sounded like a good idea.

The itinerary called for the Hewetts to be in Palestine by October first, when Hewett and Dr. Clay would be under the auspices of the Yale Babylonian Expedition for their travel through the Euphrates region. Since Hewett had no experience with the rigors of the Arabian desert, he wrote to an old friend, Lewis Bayles Paton at Hartford Theological Seminary, seeking advice on dress and supplies appropriate for the desert area where the Paton family had resided for some years as missionaries.

Paton's reply was long and reassuring. He suggested that desert life in the Near East required equipment similar to that used in the American Southwest. He recommended sleeping bags supplemented with down quilts, and regulation desert water bottles.

"As to dress, it is well to wear pure wool underwear at all seasons of the year," he wrote. "A woolen band over the bowels is a great protection against digestive disorders. Dr. Sterrett of Cornell advised me to get ten yards of flannel, cut it into two long strips, wind one around the waist and let the other hang down the back as a protection against the actinic rays of the sun."[2]

A pith helmet supplemented by a scarf to protect the back of the neck and a small net of fine mesh to put over the head and shoulders against malarial mosquitoes were also recommended. How much of this sartorial counsel the Hewetts followed is not known. No photos have been found showing them in full desert regalia, which is a pity because the flannel waistbands would certainly have rounded out their customary silhouettes.

Oriental School party in Syria,1923. School of American Research Collection in the Museum of New Mexico.

Paton recommended typhoid inoculation and, as a protection against cholera, the boiling of all water used for drinking and for washing food. They were to eat no fresh vegetables such as lettuce and no fresh fruit which had been washed in doubtful water. Hewett was warned to supervise the water boiling personally, since it could not be trusted to the natives. If these *simple precautions* were followed, Paton assured his friend that he and Mrs. Hewett should enjoy the trip in fine health.

The misadventures that befell the Hewetts in the Arabian desert could hardly have been anticipated, and were not the result of failure to take advance precautions. Arrived in Jerusalem, the expedition found it inadvisable to buy, equip and man their own cars, and turned instead to a local transportation company offering cars with drivers and guides familiar with the terrain. The party, which set out in three automobiles, was made up of the Hewetts, Dr. Clay (for some reason

Mrs. Clay did not accompany them), a French Intelligence officer, two students named Carroll and Childs, and four Arabians to serve as drivers, guides and camp helpers. The Arabs were supplied by the Kittaneh Transportation Company and came well recommended.

Hewett wrote of some of the happenings of that journey in a chapter in *Campfire and Trail* entitled "Arabia Deserta." He relates that the party was lost in the desert west of the Euphrates and that one car had broken down, when they were met by a small band of Arabs whose sheik offered hospitality. Taken into the sheik's large camel's-hair tent, the American party was given food and entertainment lasting far into the night. After about three hours' sleep they resumed their journey before dawn, breakfasting as usual on cups of tea. They left the disabled car behind to be picked up later.

On the morning of the accident, Mrs. Hewett exchanged seats in the car with a venerable Bedouin who had guided many camel caravans over the trackless desert and knew the elusive landmarks. The two serviceable cars started out briskly with their party of ten, sometimes traveling tandem, sometimes parallel. It must have been a heady pace for the guide. Forty miles an hour would cover the journey so much more quickly than the swiftest of camels. Probably he leaned back, awed, but enjoying the experience. At this speed it was hard to know exactly where they were.

Suddenly the two cars shot over the brink of a vertical cliff and plunged forty feet to crash on the floor of a dry waddy.

Hewett was thrown clear of the wreckage. Stunned but not unconscious he staggered to his feet and took off his shattered cork helmet. He must have landed on his head and shoulder. Other men were getting up — where was Doni?

Some of the party were pinned under one car. As the men struggled to free them they found the Bedouin guide dead, Donizetta Hewett unconscious. Edgar gathered her in his arms and carried her to the shade of a nearby boulder, where he propped her up and began to feel for wounds. He kept calling softly, "Doni, Doni, can't you hear me?"

The other men searched among the scattered food and water bottles. They found the first-aid supplies and moistened a cloth with a little of the precious, salvaged water, and Hewett bathed his wife's face. Her pulse was good; after a time she opened her eyes.

Hewett never afterward remembered the sequence of events during the next hours. They made Doni as comfortable as they could, administering sips of water. He even tried to make a little joke, asking her, "When you consented to spend your life tagging an archaeologist, you didn't know just where antiquity was to be looked for, did you?"

Doni struggled to draw a deep breath and winced with the pain. "When are we going on to Palmyra?" she asked.

At the moment the prospect seemed dubious. Hewett was sure she must have some broken ribs, if not more serious injuries. There was nothing to do but make the best of their plight. In the following days Hewett, Clay and the two students set up the best camp possible with such supplies as they could save; the drivers pieced together a vehicle which eventually carried their search for help fifty miles farther into the desert before it collapsed once more. The two men left it and continued their struggle on foot. The French army officer and a second man whom Hewett describes as a Jewish rabbi (but who had not previously been mentioned in the account of the trip and who does not appear in subsequent newspaper accounts) decided to follow the waddy eastward. They figured that the watercourse should drain into the Euphrates. The drivers from the abandoned car walked until they intersected the old Damascus Trail, where they were picked up. The second team

Wreck of automobiles in Arabian Desert waddy, 1923. School of American Research Collection in the Museum of New Mexico.

following the waddy reached an Arab village where the tribesmen promptly sent out a camel-borne rescue party with supplies. Hewett says this group intercepted a Ford car on the Baghdad Trail, which helped to evacuate the wounded party to the village of Abou Kemal on the Euphrates.

For some days the solicitous people of the village gave them care, until a Red Cross ambulance attached to the French Foreign Legion at Deir es Zor arrived and carried the party back to their field hospital. There they recuperated sufficiently to proceed. Dr. Clay and one student, together with the surviving Arabs, went on to Damascus. But Doni Hewett's first thought had been for the objective that was "the most cherished place" of all the Mesopotamian tour — the ruins of Queen Zenobia's capital, ancient Palmyra, known as Tadmur of the Wilderness. She did not want to miss it, and convinced Hewett she was well enough to go there. The Hewetts and the student W. D. Carroll arranged transportation to Tadmur where Edgar wrote, "as guests of old Abdullah, Grand Sheik of Palmyra, we were able to explore the, to me, most beautiful ruined city of the Ancient World."[3]

Hewett's essay on that visit is included in *Campfire and Trail*. It is perhaps the most poetic of his writing, with a lyrical quality reminiscent of the "Songs of Solomon." Probably Hewett wrote his notes on the spot, while he was under the influence of Oriental phraseology, and later transcribed them with only a little polishing.

That Edgar and Donizetta Hewett could continue their planned itinerary was testimony to the triumph of spirit and willpower over physical pain. Both had been severely injured; Doni had difficulty taking a deep breath and suffered agony when she coughed; Edgar carried his right arm in a sling to support a broken hand. Yet from Palmyra they went to Damascus, and on to Jerusalem via Haifa. They visited Jericho and the Dead Sea. Hewett gave his scheduled lectures at the School of Oriental Research in Baghdad. They checked into the American University Hospital where a Dr. Ward gave them interim care, then completed their planned visit to Egypt. There they received anxious inquiries from friends who had read newspaper bulletins on the expedition's fatal accident in the desert. Hewett sent a cable to Paul Walter in which he stated that the three cars had reached Damascus safely (which may have been true, if one were not concerned with *when* or *how*) and that he and Mrs. Hewett were in good health (which was certainly inaccurate, to say the least). Whether this cheery misinformation was designed to reassure their friends, or whether it was the normal reaction of a man who rarely acknowledged any infirmity, it was duly published as fact in *El Palacio*. Having fired off this piece of understatement the Hewetts returned to Naples, where Mrs. Hewett and her seven fractured ribs were placed under the care of a nurse and Hewett began to assess his ailments. It was not until they reached San Diego (eight months to the day from their departure and exactly according to schedule) that Edgar finally had diagnosed the full extent of his injuries. He says succinctly, "An inventory of my injuries made some weeks later disclosed a shattered arm, a bunch of broken ribs, a ruptured ear drum, a smashed knee, and a neck apparently driven down between my shoulder blades."[4] That probably *was* an exaggeration.

In March 1924 Hewett wrote Dr. Clay, who by that time was back in New Haven, that the only injury which deeply concerned him was his broken right hand, which was not yet functioning. Surgery was recommended for the removal of a displaced bone which might have been salvaged with proper attention right after the accident but was by now beyond repair.[5] In April Hewett entered a California hospital and had the semilunar bone taken out of his wrist. In response to solicitous inquiry he wrote Holmes that Charley Lummis recommended he have some bone removed from his head at the same time, since it was obviously not functioning properly when he allowed himself to get into such a predicament. Hewett had scarcely recovered from the anesthetic when he returned to teach his anthropology class at State Teachers College in San Diego.

The entire economy of the country underwent a recession during 1923-24, and life was especially difficult in the Southwest. Drought conditions brought bankruptcy to overextended cattlemen, which in turn closed many banks. Tax collections were slow, and in New Mexico the state treasury failed to deliver Museum appropriations when due. Hewett's salary from San Diego (about $3,000 a year) kept coming, enabling him to stay afloat financially, but he was forced to much scrounging to keep good men on his staff.

The Western tour Hewett had arranged for Magoffin on behalf of the American Institute of Archaeology had not been an unqualified success. Magoffin was critical of the decline in membership and support from the groups in Hewett's territory. With considerable asperity he wrote, "I hope you will not mind my expressing my admiration for the way you are able to bring forward so many good reasons for not doing any of the things I suggest.... Los Angeles has gone entirely to pieces, San Diego has practically dropped away to nothing, and the Santa Fe society you rather like to hold as your personal property."[6]

There was disagreement among the leadership as to the disposition of funds to which the Institute had access. The more conservative wanted to build up endowments; the rest thought the money should be spent as fast as it was received. Hewett favored approaching individual donors for contributions; Magoffin thought financial salvation lay in wooing various foundations for endowment support.

Alice Fletcher had left a bequest of ten thousand dollars to the School of American Research. Magoffin thought this sum should be added to the Institute's endowment. Hewett had plans to spend it, and of course he could dictate its disposition. The loss of Miss Fletcher's balanced, mature judgement was felt by all of them.

Many things were changing. As Hewett's earlier students moved into positions of importance he continued to encourage young men and women who sought his counsel on their academic training, came to the summer field schools, and turned to the Director for jobs when they were ready.

Hewett constantly sought to replace the members who had left the Managing Board of the School with new patrons. Among the longtime regents was a valued friend, Dr. R. C. Corwin of the Colorado Fuel and Iron Company in Pueblo. It was Corwin who introduced John D. Rockefeller, Jr., to Hewett; Rockefeller and his sons made several trips to the Southwest for which Hewett arranged hospitality, including visits to cliff dwellings, Indian villages, and various scenic wonders for the members of the Rockefeller family.

It has been said that John D. Rockefeller, Jr., considered Santa Fe as his choice for a city to be restored to its early colonial appearance, and that Hewett's opposition to the plan influenced him to turn ultimately to Williamsburg, Virginia instead. Some of Hewett's associates say there is no truth in this tale; however, if Hewett's advice was ever sought in the matter it seems likely that he would have been against turning the whole ancient city into a museum — he was always too deeply interested in its life and growth as a living, modern entity. Also, he had plans

"J.D.R." (identified as John D. Rockefeller, Jr.) and Edgar Lee Hewett, ca. 1928. Courtesy of the Museum of New Mexico.

of his own for the future of New Mexico's capital city. This led to the purchase, on behalf of the School of American Research, of a tract of about three hundred acres adjoining the Allison-James School property on the northern edge of the town. The land was to be the site of a greatly enlarged School, with an amphitheater for future Fiesta spectacles, an Indian Fairgrounds with temporary living quarters for visiting Indians (who always had trouble finding proper accommodations in the town), and facilities for expanding summer schools. In Hewett's opinion the time for such expansion had arrived, and he needed sponsors to help him realize his dream. He therefore was glad to discuss it with representatives of the Federation of Women's Clubs of the Southwest who were seeking an appropriate site for a proposed summer colony. Their quest brought about the next big civic uproar in Santa Fe.

17

SANTA FE FIGHTS
THE CULTURAL COLONY

*A host of men and women in our time have determined
to possess themselves of a full measure of the world's
culture; have acquired a taste for learning; have found a
world apart from the commonplace in which lie
possibilities of infinite happiness; a realm in which
there are joys of the spirit that transcend the amuse-
ments and sensations of the passing moment.* — ELH

In the mid 1920s some leaders of the Federation of Women's Clubs in the
Southwest conceived a project to establish a summer colony where members could
bring their families for recreation, education and cultural growth. They were
invited by the New Mexico Federation to choose a mountain location within the
state that could be developed into an organized vacation resort. Civic leaders,
including the chambers of commerce of Santa Fe and Las Vegas, were approached
and all welcomed the idea. Committees of clubwomen visited both cities to study
proposed sites.

From its inception one of the principal functions of the Museum of New Mexico
had been to welcome visitors and assist them in learning about the Southwest in
general and New Mexico in particular. Whenever the Hewetts were in residence
they entertained a procession of special visitors. The federated women from Texas
arranged a conference with Hewett at which he briefed them on his plans for
developing a university for adult education under the auspices of the School,
beginning with an enlarged summer session in Santa Fe. The proposed program
appealed to the women; they invited Hewett to visit Dallas and later attend their
annual convention in Austin, where he could explain to the Texas Federation the
special attractions offered by Santa Fe.

When the Santa Fe Chamber of Commerce learned that Hewett was going to
Austin, he was appointed an official representative to plead Santa Fe's cause. A

delegation from Las Vegas also attended the convention to present the attractions of that city, but when it became evident that a majority of the women favored Santa Fe, the Las Vegas people withdrew. The Santa Fe City Council, briefed on the needs of the summer colony, voted to donate a piece of land on the southern boundary of the city as an inducement. So far, so good. All was sweetness and light, with no premonition that anyone was unhappy with the plan.

The tract that the city fathers voted to give to the Federation adjoined land owned by Sunmount Sanitorium, which specialized in the treatment of tuberculosis patients. At the time, the accepted cure was bed rest, wholesome food and great doses of clean, fresh air, even in the bitter cold of winter. It was believed that the high, semiarid climate of Santa Fe, like Saranac, New York, was especially beneficial. A specialist in lung disease, Dr. Frank Mera, had built an attractive main building for the sanitorium, with offices, kitchen, dining room, and a recreation area centered around a large living-room fireplace. Surrounding the main building were small frame shacks with canvas walls, to provide individual airy bedrooms for the patients. The customary routine was for a patient to spend most of his time in bed in his private quarters. In summer the canvas walls could be rolled up, allowing cool mountain breezes to keep the room comfortable. In winter the curtains were buttoned down, extra covers piled on the beds, and wood fires lighted in small iron stoves to heat the area when the patient was out of bed. All patients who were ambulatory went up to the main building for some meals. Dinner at night had an especially social atmosphere, with family and other guests invited on occasion.

Many invalids who came to Sunmount to die recovered under the watchful care of Dr. and Mrs. Frank Mera. Among them were artists, writers and socialites. Young veterans, seeking a healthful climate to recuperate from war-induced lung ailments, found new friends at Sunmount. Many of those who were cured chose to remain in Santa Fe, where the peaceful pace of life and the crisp mountain air helped them to keep their improved health.

There was another group of new residents in the ancient city, who came first as guests at one of the dude ranches in the vicinity. Among those establishments were The Bishop's Lodge, developed on the site some four miles north of the city where Santa Fe's first archbishop, Jean Baptiste Lamy, had sought a rural retreat, for which he had built a small lodge and a chapel; San Gabriel at Alcalde, some thirty miles north of Santa Fe near San Juan Pueblo in Rio Arriba County; and Valley Ranch on the Pecos River, where Hewett had once owned a summer ranch. Some of the newcomers had independent means and chose to live where they enjoyed life; many more found a place in the professional, business or government circles of the city. In their social life the newcomers gravitated toward the artistic colony rather than toward the old-timers who had been Hewett's friends and supporters for more than twenty years. Earlier social leadership of the little city had centered on state officials, lawyers and successful businessmen whose wives belonged to the Santa Fe Women's Club and Library Association, and to the more exclusive Fifteen Club. That "ruling class" was a small hard-core group including some descendants of wealthy Spanish landowners and political leaders, but largely made up of non-Spanish families. It was not easy for a new resident to break into it. The long-established Spanish families tended to lead a social life of their own, closely holding to their homes, their large family connections, and their church with its confraternities. They liked their own *sociedades;* a newcomer almost had to marry into the clan to be admitted to their inner circles, yet they mingled easily in community life.

It has been noted that Hewett found his most dependable local backing among the Republican Old Guard — Frank Springer, Judge McFie, Judge N. B. Laughlin, Roman L. Baca, Paul A. F. Walter, and their friends. The older, first-established artists formed a bridge between this group and the colony that developed around the Camino del Monte Sol, which expanded rapidly after World War I in spite of the artists' desire to keep the town small.

A third clique of Spanish Americans and non-Spanish grew up around the followers of Bronson Cutting, with their strongest social bond in the American Legion. These people tended to lean toward the new art colony. Cutting himself, as has been related, was Hewett's most implacable opponent.

Quite suddenly, when the civic leaders thought the whole town was behind them in their encouragement of the growth promised by a substantial colony of federated clubwomen and their families, rumblings of opposition began to reverberate through the town. It seemed to come from three sources: the Sunmount set, including Drs. Mera and Massie and their friends in the medical community as well as some of their more active patients; painters and artists surrounding Mary Austin, who promptly became their loudspeaker; and the backers of Los Alamos Ranch School, who had opposed Hewett's proposals for converting the Pajarito Plateau into a national park and now opted against this Southwest culture group that they believed to be sponsored by him. At first Cutting's *Santa Fe New Mexican* seemed to be neutral, evidently in the belief that since the civic leadership and business community were favorable, the proposal must have merit and wide support.

Nobody among the leaders of the opposition seems to have taken the trouble to sit down with the Federation women and learn exactly what they proposed to do. None of the opposition seems to have discovered that the Federation women hoped to build substantial, permanent summer homes in the approved Santa Fe style. Instead, somebody learned that one woman among their leadership was a professional promoter of Chautauquas, and immediately deduced that the summer colony would be a jerry-built conglomeration of tacky cottages and shacks around a tent auditorium. E. Dana Johnson, the *Santa Fe New Mexican*'s editor, was a close friend of many artists and writers. He was soon persuaded that the most important people in town were against the new development, and newspaper editorials began to stress that the whole idea was much too controversial to be acceptable.

A protest meeting was called by the opponents, and there the Old Santa Fe Association, dedicated to keeping the traditional character of the city, unblemished by "group development," was born. The story of the founding of the Old Santa Fe Association which attributes its parentage to the group that fought the "culture colony" has been told many times by people who were there, and by reference to the accounts published in the *Santa Fe New Mexican*. In the Hewett file at the Museum of New Mexico are fragments of the other side of the story, from which one can piece together a somewhat different picture.

A reporter for the United Press and the *Albuquerque Tribune* was present by invitation at the meeting of what he called "The Old Santa Fe Protective Association, otherwise known as Mary Austin, Inc." He was muzzled by a decision of his hosts that the discussion was off-the-record and was thus limited to writing his report in a personal letter to a journalist friend who was a member of the Texas Federation. (Evidently the off-the-record rule did not apply to the representatives of the *Santa Fe New Mexican*.)

In his letter the Albuquerque reporter described the women's plan as he understood it — "*not* a chautauqua, but something really worth while." He saw a program that would attract national visitors to the town and provide New Mexico, Texas and Oklahoma people with a cool place readily accessible for them to spend the summer and at the same time enjoy some profitable adult education. He named the Santa Fe leaders who backed the proposal as Mrs. Frank W. Parker, wife of the chief justice of the state supreme court; Mrs. George W. Pritchard, wife of a former state attorney general; Dr. Edgar L. Hewett, Director of the Museum of New Mexico and School of American Research; and Col. Paul A. F. Walter, vice-president of the First National Bank of Santa Fe, former owner and editor of the *Santa Fe New Mexican,* president of the New Mexico Historical Society, and associate of the School of American Research. He also identified the prime movers of the Old Santa Fe Protective Association. He noted that fear for the peace and quiet of Sunmount led the doctors and other property owners in the area to support the Association.[1]

The whole controversy became one of the prime examples in Santa Fe history of the failure to communicate reasonably. The organizers of the protective association were informed that only a small handful of Texas clubwomen was determined to come to Santa Fe, and that one of them had come to the conclusion that Las Vegas would be preferable. Mrs. Austin was quoted as saying, "We would be glad if she would take the chautauqua to Las Vegas. I think it appropriate that it should go there. We then would have all the advantages without the ferris wheels, merry-go-round, hot-dog stands, etc. They would drive over to Santa Fe to see the sights, spend their money here and if they wanted Santa Fe artists and writers to come over there to lecture to them, they would pay for it."[2]

Nobody could convince Mrs. Austin that she was confusing the Chautauqua idea with a circus or a carnival. She was before her time in recommending that for city planning, "Bigger is not necessarily better." Determined that she would not let Santa Fe be spoiled as Monterey and Carmel had been for her, she fought with bitter tongue and trenchant pen to defend the small-town quality of her adopted city.

That the women's club leaders were mostly college graduates from upper

Mary Austin, writer and patron of the Indian Arts Fund, ca.1932. Photograph by Will Connell. Courtesy of the Museum of New Mexico.

middle-class backgrounds was of no importance to her. They respected her ability and reputation as a writer, and were hurt and resentful of her scorn. They attempted to explain that their dignified program would injure no one, but nobody seemed to be listening. Bolstered by the faith that the Santa Fe city fathers wanted them to come, they decided to ignore the noisy opposition. The pro-Federation citizens of Santa Fe (and they were many) could not believe that anything would come of the opposition. They even felt that the uproar might serve to advertise the project.

While the attack accelerated during the autumn of 1926 Hewett was in Syria, working on an archaeological site for which he had made a preliminary survey during his ill-fated journey in 1923. It seems unlikely that, even had he been in Santa Fe, he could have averted the serio-comic warfare of which many writers throughout the land were making good copy as they were fed material by their Santa Fe friends.

The New York *World* for Sunday, June 27, 1926 carried a feature article by Kyle S. Crichton of Albuquerque, who was identified as a man of scrupulous impartiality with friends on both sides of the controversy. The opening paragraphs set the tone:

> The great battle of Santa Fe, New Mexico, now raging is a deadly combat between two philosophies, between the Philistine and the Artist, between Progress and Atmosphere.
> On the one side are artists and writers such as Mary Austin, John Sloan and Witter Bynner. On the other are the Chamber of Commerce and the business interests of Santa Fe. The artists want to keep it OLD Santa Fe. The merchants want a NEW Santa Fe and some profits...[3]

Of the fifteen-year growth of the art colony he comments:

> The artists came because Santa Fe was unique and paintable and they brought their friends and were followed by the same prosperous followers who always seem to follow artistic pilgrimages. Things were lovely in Santa Fe aside from the one fact that Democrats came into power in the State in 1922 and took over the State Capitol, much to the sorrow of divers Santa Fe residents who had spent their days for years calmly resting their feet on a desk in the State House. But this is not a political article.[4]

The article continues with a lighthearted account of the plans of the federated women's clubs of Colorado, Texas, Oklahoma, Kansas, Arizona, Arkansas, Missouri, Louisiana, and New Mexico (the incorporators of the Culture Colony of the Southwest), as set out in an announcement appearing in Dallas newspapers that described a Chautauqua to be laid out in the unique city of Santa Fe on the plan of the original at Chautauqua, New York. "There were to be lectures and concerts and jolly outings in the artistic atmosphere of Santa Fe," Crichton says. The Dallas account led E. Dana Johnson to utter an editorial caution, "We wish to extend a welcome to the estimable ladies from Dallas but not if their intention is to establish a chautauqua in our midst."[5]

According to Crichton, it was when the City Council offered the land close to Sunmount Sanatorium for the use of the cultural colony that the roof blew off:

Mary Austin, who had been desperately ill for weeks, arose from her bed and issued a clarion blast that hasn't fully come to earth to date. It has reverberated up and down this land of freedom and has brought editorial comment from gentlemen who were always formerly of the opinion that Santa Fe was simply the roundhouse connection of the railroad.

"A chautauqua, a cultural colony!" said Mrs. Austin. "Do you want to ruin Santa Fe! Do you want to spoil everything that makes it what it is!"

There was a mass meeting of the artists. There was later a mass meeting of the artists and the supporters of the cultural colony. "Certainly we want a culture colony," said Charles E. Doll, President of the Chamber of Commerce. "It will bring 3,000 people here every summer. They are the best people in Texas. Why shouldn't they come?"

"Because," said the bitter opponents, "if they come they'll ruin Santa Fe. A chautauqua in Santa Fe! It isn't possible. They'll put up a flock of tent houses and have prayer meetings."

"Nothing of the sort," said the Chamber of Commerce. "They'll put up homes that will be a credit in Santa Fe and they'll spend their money here."

Mary Austin made a speech in which she referred to the club women as "these yearners." Mr. Doll made a speech in which he referred to the entire high-brow colony in words which created burning indignation in every artistic breast that ever daubed a canvas or made scratchings on a sheet of white paper. It was a rousing meeting which "split Santa Fe wide open," according to the *New Mexican*. The issue of slavery never did more to separate families than did the battle of culture which fulminated in the crowded rooms of the Santa Fe Chamber of Commerce.

"Who are these artists who shall tell everybody else that they can't come to Santa Fe?" demanded the culture colony advocates. "The colony has been invited and it is coming. The artists are comparative newcomers. What right have they to try to influence the future of Santa Fe? What did the artists and writers ever do for the town anyhow—except neglect to pay their grocery bills?

"The colony would be a fine thing for business and heaven knows we need some business. What city can afford to turn away 3,000 summer visitors? We can't live on what the artists spend here. We haven't any industry and very little agriculture. The artists were tickled to death to have the Indian Detours but they kick at the Cultural Colony. How come?"

Whereupon the artists arose up and shouted in unison, "Nobody objects to these people coming as individuals. We object to an incorporated army. It's simply a lot selling proposition. They get the land and sell the lots to people back in Texas. They'll put up fine homes! Yes they will! California bungalows and tent houses more likely."[6]

The article proceeded to list more than thirty artists and writers of national renown who owned homes in Santa Fe and claimed that they made a substantial contribution to the city's economy, since they made their money elsewhere and spent a goodly portion of it in Santa Fe. The artists opined that Santa Fe was on the verge of becoming like any other Main Street town when they came and rescued it by keeping the old charm. To all this the pro-colony residents retorted:

> "We are as sensitive as the next one ... of the charms of Santa Fe. So much so that we settled here years before the artists ever thought of it. We love the old Governor's Palace, and the old homes and the mixture of the Indian, Spanish, Mexican and American regimes. But it is ridiculous to think that a cultural colony is going to spoil any of this. It is because of this that the cultural colony is coming."[7]

Crichton notes that the artists had all the best of it — publicly — because they were articulate and had access to channels of publicity. The Chamber of Commerce was sitting tight, in the belief that the whole controversy would simmer down and ultimately be forgotten. The city had survived the arrival of the artists and would undoubtedly survive the arrival of the federated women. Significantly the author continues:

> The strangest silence of all comes from the Federated Club Women of Dallas. They have uttered no public word since the uproar began, and an outsider is moved to wonder whether or not they intend to carry out their plan ...
>
> So stands the matter on the lap of the gods, who will make the decision amply prompted by Mary Austin and every other forceful pen wielder. It is a battle between Art and Progress, with Art putting up a wonderful scrap.[8]

Crichton understood New Mexico well enough to imply some of the underlying prejudices that helped align the battle lines. He noted that two Spanish-American groups, *La Union Protectiva* and *El Centro de Cultura,* had come out against the proposal, which caused the culturists to mutter, "That's all politics. They're simply afraid of bringing 3,000 Democratic voters from Texas into this country." Although the leaders of the group came from Texas, there were nine other states, including the New Mexico Federation, involved in the corporation formed to own the colony. By playing up the Texas emphasis, however, opponents could count on prejudicing the Spanish Americans who had hated Texans ever since the ill-fated Texas-Santa Fe Expedition of 1841, when the Lone Star State dreamed of annexing New Mexico.

Not all the artists were members of the Old Santa Fe Association, which some scornfully dubbed a "cuckoo organization." Many saw the development as Hewett envisioned it — centered on a summer university with speakers of importance drawn from many disciplines. As the Albuquerque reporter who was barred from public comment by the off-the-record rule mentioned to his Dallas clubwoman friend, the influx of a large number of summer residents interested in culture might well result in more picture sales at the museum gallery and in the sale of more books written by Witter Bynner, Mary Austin and others. He asked to be kept informed of the progress made by the Federation.[9]

In reply the Dallas journalist said that when she had gone to Santa Fe with the clubwomen's committee seeking an appropriate site for the colony, they were welcomed by "practically everybody worth while." Although some of these later joined the opposition, promoters from both Santa Fe and Las Vegas remained eager for their business. In outlining the kind of colony they planned, she stressed their desire to build permanently and beautifully; their architecture would be in harmony with the best Santa Fe buildings. It was her opinion that Mrs. Austin and others of the opposition were probably doing a service to the Federation with the nationwide publicity. She seemed quite sure of the ultimate success of the culture center in Santa Fe.[10]

The proud promoters of the colony underestimated the vigor of the newly formed Old Santa Fe Association, however. The Association sent two well-known Santa Fe women as its representatives to a meeting of the Texas Federation held in Dallas in November, 1926. They brought a three-and-a-half page typewritten, single-spaced document entitled, "An Open Letter to the Federated Club Women of Texas." The letter states that Santa Fe's protest was made in all courtesy and should not be considered an affront to the clubwomen. It asserts that the action of the Chamber of Commerce and the City Council was taken by a small group which was not representative of the city's residents, and that the city fathers had no legal right to dispose of the land they had offered to the women. It states flatly that any attempt to thus dispose of the city land would be opposed in the courts, and notes the difficulty the city would encounter in furnishing water to a colony of several thousand people on that site.

Alleging that the Old Santa Fe Association, organized to fight the coming of the colony, has a membership of over six hundred, including businessmen, lawyers, architects, clubwomen, laborers, educators, craftsmen, writers, sculptors, painters, and "those agencies which have brought Santa Fe her recent and most substantial development," the letter goes on to clarify the position of the Association in opposing an incongruous development thrust upon the local scene, and suggests that there are other towns which could offer landscapes, tonic climate and an undivided welcome. Stating that the newly created Old Santa Fe Association is the recognized community agency for preserving old Santa Fe and keeping its future in character, the missive declares, "Its successful activities include reviving of old Spanish arts and crafts; development of the architecture, and management of El Pasatiempo, the Latin Fiesta in which the entire population takes part."[11] The letter concludes:

> It is plain that you would be placed in an untenable position before the country if you persisted in coming in search of culture to a community whose citizens are organized to resist what they regard as an invasion. To

precipitate such a fight would bring only discredit on women's clubs in general and invite ridicule in the press of the country which already has shown a nationwide sympathetic interest in Santa Fe's fight.

The extent and determination of the opposition here may be easily verified and we will gladly demonstrate the truth of all our statements to any representative of your body who may care to come here.

We are sure if you can be made to realize the actual situation here, you will immediately drop the plan to locate the Colony in this vicinity.[12]

This remarkable document was signed for the Old Santa Fe Association by J. A. Massie, president, and E. Dana Johnson, secretary. The Federation members understood the message, even though the arguments in its support bewildered them. Many of them knew that Hewett, Walter and the Chamber of Commerce in Santa Fe had been promoting arts and crafts, indigenous architecture and community fiestas for years. One club member who knew Santa Fe remarked that Dr. Massie owned and lived in a two-story brick building in the best Main Street tradition. Another woman was so confused by the letter that she thought the two Santa Fe women representing the Old Santa Fe Association had been sent by the Chamber of Commerce and the School of American Research to lobby *for* the Federation scheme. She felt that the two elderly women were not well posted on what the movement was about.

One factor in the battle over the future expansion of Santa Fe involved the development of open land. Aligned with the Old Santa Fe Association were several landowners on the south side of the city who saw its future in low density residential planning and did not want the clustered housing the culture center might bring. Ownership of the tract being offered to the Federation was unclear. The best the city could offer was a quitclaim deed to the land, a dubious title if ownership was to be challenged by the Old Santa Fe Association. On the north side of the city, Hewett had arranged for the purchase of large tracts by the School of American Research as sites for his proposed university and Indian center.

In an effort to solve the dispute, one of Hewett's friends suggested the purchase of Bishop's Lodge by the Federation women. He knew it was currently on the market, and proposed that the existing building could form the nucleus of the culture center and "tents could be put up along the Bishop's Creek out of sight of the main building and auditorium."[13] Whether the price was too high or the women rejected the idea of "second hand buildings" and wanted to do their own designing, nothing came of this effort.

Nevertheless, the two women from Santa Fe who presented the open letter to the Texas convention received a courteous reply addressed to them at the Baker Hotel, Dallas. The letter states that as far as the Texas Federation of Women's Clubs is concerned the matter is closed, and explains, "The offer made as you state 'by the City Council was made in good faith' and this offer was legally submitted and closed by your Honorable Mayor and Council, and we feel as above stated is closed. We must, therefore, ask that you please desist from any further negotiations with us as a committee, or with the Texas Federation of Women's Clubs on the subject."[14] It is signed for the clubs by Mrs. J. B. Fields, president; Mrs. J. C. Nagle, vice president; Mrs. A. H. Bailey, chairman of fine arts; and Mrs. W. C. Martin, chairman of incorporation papers, Culture Center.

As they learned the full extent of the opposition, however, enthusiasm for Santa Fe waned among the colony's promoters. Santa Fe had seemed an ideal site because, in addition to its natural charms, it had the appeal of a warm civic welcome and the offer of a cheap, desirable location. The Chamber of Commerce, the Santa Fe Railroad (eager to promote travel in the Southwest), the City Council, and the local clubwomen had assisted them. Now, as they were ridiculed in the press, dissention arose in their own ranks. Their leaders had no desire to push the project into a court fight over the land and could not muster financial support for an expensive site. Those interested in a Chautauqua turned to Las Vegas hospitality, and for several summers sponsored a cultural program there.

The Santa Fe Railroad drew back in the face of the local row, and the School of American Research and the Museum people saw no point in further jeopardizing their own interests. Paul A. F. Walter had tried to work out a compromise site, as he kept Hewett (absent in San Diego and abroad) informed. Hewett had envisioned a large enrollment of intelligent, well-to-do women in a summer university in Santa Fe, but he could not subject prospective students to its hostility. Even some of his own staff leaned toward the opposition. Paul Walter wryly commented that the whole plot would make a good musical comedy.[15]

The opponents of the culture colony lobbied against Hewett personally. Witter Bynner ran for the legislature in an unsuccessful campaign to have Hewett ousted as Director of the Museum. Members of the School's Board of Regents received communications seeking to influence them against him. Since most were his close friends, they merely turned to him for an explanation. Hewett replied that the trouble with Santa Fe was that it was still a very small town, and a single controversy, like the culture colony argument, or a single incident involving a nearby pueblo, could become an all-engrossing fight with everybody choosing sides. He contrasted it with San Diego, where half a dozen battles were being fought simultaneously — concerning harbor improvements, the changes in Balboa Park, the location of the college where he taught, and other pressing civic matters. "I am accustomed to dealing with so many large matters at once in San Diego," he told them, "that the Santa Fe battle over the culture colony does not deeply worry me. It has upset our plans for a larger summer school, but we have adjusted to that. Otherwise, the outcome will not affect the School of American Research in any way."[16]

Members of the Old Santa Fe Association could claim credit for changing the course history might have taken in their small city. The School of American Research eventually sold off its land holdings and a residential development grew up on the north side of Santa Fe, with no facilities for Indians and no amphitheater of a permanent nature to supplement the limited space of St. Francis Auditorium.

Other entrepreneurs like Mike Kirk developed the Gallup Inter-Tribal Indian Ceremonial to the point where that city claimed title as The Indian Capital of the Southwest. Mrs. Austin gleefully reported that she had been invited to lecture before some of the women's clubs at a nice fee. In Santa Fe bitterness over the defeat of the plan lingered among members of the business community for many years. The Old Santa Fe Association was accused of being against anything that made for progress, and a long period of careful policy development and constructive action was required before it earned the prestige it early claimed for itself as the guardian of Santa Fe's heritage.

Oliver La Farge, in his book *Santa Fe, The Autobiography of a Southwestern Town,* which was drawn from the files of the *New Mexican,* gives an account of the controversy as viewed by one group of participants. The Hewett files help to balance the picture. Somewhere, no doubt, there are old accounts written by members of the Federation that would shed additional light on the brouhaha. In any case, both the women's group and Hewett probably would have agreed with La Farge's assessment: "There seems to have been no final decision, properly speaking; the project simply died away in the face of the hostilities it was arousing."[17]

18

OPENING UP
THE INDIAN COUNTRY

*And so, as we go among people everywhere, near
neighbors or so-called savages, we find what we take to
them. You find suspicion, distrust, treachery, if that is
what you take with you. If you go with sincere trust,
giving of what you have with no concern about return,
your problem will be how to match the generous
kindness with which you are met.* —ELH

In 1926 the Fred Harvey Company took over the modest Koshare tours operated
out of Albuquerque by Erna Fergusson, and established headquarters for a larger
enterprise known as The Indian Detours at La Fonda in Santa Fe. La Fonda had
existed as a hotel since early Santa Fe Trail days, but by 1920 the building then in
existence was badly run down. A group of local businessmen organized to build a
new hotel on the site, but their ambitions were greater than their financial
resources. The venture was at the point of bankruptcy when it was bought by the
Fred Harvey Company, which had Santa Fe Railway connections. A subsidiary
transportation company was formed under the direction of R. Hunter Clarkson, a
Scotsman who was the son-in-law of a railroad official. The company purchased
comfortable buses and luxury touring cars to take travelers on sight-seeing trips
over the back roads of New Mexico and to remote sights throughout the Southwest
that could not otherwise be reached from the railroad.

Miss Fergusson was retained to train, supervise and schedule a group of young
women familiar with the country, who served as hostesses-cum-guides for the trips
and were known as couriers. Drivers were cowboy-type young men, preferably born
in the area, who dressed in broad-brimmed hats, colorful shirts, whipcord britches,
and boots to carry out the image. Both couriers and drivers soon acquired wardrobes
of bright velveteen shirts such as those worn by the Navajos and collected choice
handwrought silver jewelry to wear with them.

187

Before he took off for his season's work in Syria, Hewett was asked to have the Museum staff assist in training Indian Detour personnel and providing evening lectures for the enlightenment of the tourists. In the long run, the Detours probably had greater impact on the future of Santa Fe, the Pueblo Indians and the entire Southwestern area than the clubwomen's colony would ever have brought. Kyle Crichton in his New York *World* article mentions the Detours' ready acceptance by the townspeople. Even as the *Santa Fe New Mexican* was inveighing against

Harvey-cars on the Indian Detour, at the ruins of Pecos Pueblo church. Dorothy Woodward Collection, State Records Center and Archives.

bringing three thousand clubwomen to reside part of the year in Santa Fe, the editor bragged that the Detours would bring more than five thousand visitors annually. This discrepancy led some cynics to suggest that the real point at issue was not *whether* the city should grow, but *who would profit most* from the new developments.

The regular Detour was a three-day excursion. Westbound guests were taken from the crack Santa Fe trains at Las Vegas where the Detour headquartered in the Harvey Hotel, La Casteñeda. The first day they were escorted on a tour of Pecos ruins, lunched at Valley Ranch on the Pecos River, and then were driven to La Fonda, where they checked in by early afternoon. They were encouraged to visit Santa Fe museums, artists' studios and shops; a free lecture with slides enlarged their knowledge of the area and its people.

The second day they went to the cliff ruins at Puyé, where the Harvey Company built a rest house for shelter. There, after a stiff climb to inspect the cliff dwellings and a stroll around the small museum, they ate box lunches. For a time one of Hewett's protégés, Odd Halseth, was resident curator of this hospitality house and lectured informally on the archaeology of the area, chatting with the guests and

Maria and Julian Martinez at work in their San Ildefonso home, ca. 1930. Photograph by T. Harmon Parkhurst. Courtesy of the Museum of New Mexico.

answering their questions. Several Indians from Santa Clara Pueblo, who claimed Puyé as the home of their ancestors, were employed at the site and added to the interest. The afternoon trip back to Santa Fe included a stopover at either Santa Clara or San Ildefonso pueblo, where arrangements had been made with some of the Indian families to show the interior of their homes and the potters were given a chance to display and sell their polished black ware to the visitors. Maria Martinez was among the women who enhanced a growing reputation by welcoming guests to their homes; fortunate visitors could see Julian Martinez tracing freehand designs with a yucca brush on the ceramics his wife formed.

On the third day the party was driven to Albuquerque, where the Alvarado Hotel was headquarters. They sometimes stopped off at Santo Domingo Pueblo en route, but the Indians there were suspicious and inclined to be hostile, so this visit was often omitted. They went instead to the pueblo of Isleta a few miles out of Albuquerque, where they were shown the church with the legend of the early Franciscan padre who would not stay buried at the foot of the altar steps. The Detour ended when the travellers were put back on the train at Albuquerque to continue their journey. Eastbound travellers were not so numerous, but they could be scheduled for the three-day detour in reverse.

For guests who wanted something more venturesome (and more expensive), *land cruises* could be arranged by private car to Mesa Verde or Carlsbad Caverns, to the Gallup Inter-Tribal Indian Ceremonial or a Hopi Snake Dance. One-day special trips included visits to the headquarters of the Pecos River, to the mountain villages in the Sangre de Cristo range where only Spanish was spoken, or to the town of Taos and its neighboring pueblo. The Detour management made all arrangements for transportation, meals, lodging at hotels or at the trading posts that accepted guests, as well as entry into national parks and monuments, old mission churches, and a hospitable welcome at the Indian and Spanish villages. The Detour couriers and drivers made friends with the traders, the Indians and the mountain people, whose cooperation was essential to give the visitor a feeling of really being an insider.

The travellers had money to spend. They bought pottery, blankets, silver jewelry, and wood carvings. From the artists in Taos and Santa Fe whose studios were opened to them, they bought paintings and sculpture. In the towns where they stayed overnight, they helped to keep the hotels busy and purchased books and other souvenirs. Hewett, Nusbaum and Erna Fergusson were among the resource people who, knowing the country and its people, made important contacts and opened doors.

Visitors from around the world found the Detour a wonderful way to learn about parts of the United States that otherwise would have been inaccessible. Transcontinental travellers, accustomed to speeding across New Mexico and Arizona immersed in reading, conversation or card playing to relieve the tedium of the uninteresting terrain visible from the train, suddenly discovered a whole new world of mountain and desert scenery and were intrigued by what they learned of Indian and Spanish-American culture. Their coming brought needed cash and a widening view of the outside world to the isolated people of the reservations and the backcountry villages.

For the well-heeled Easterner, the Harvey land cruises became a status symbol. Knowledge of New Mexico and Arizona was offered to tourists just as knowledge of California had been offered at the San Diego and San Francisco expositions ten years earlier. On a smaller scale, the results were similar. Many people, seeking a new environment, returned to live in these sparsely settled states, bringing their families and followed by their friends.

In the 1920s the federal Indian Bureau was marked by a condescending paternalism that Hewett tried to combat. Some of his most tactful energy was spent in mediating between the emerging expectations of his Indian friends and the blundering bureaucracy responsible for their guardianship. He had arranged to take Indians to San Diego, and helped develop some of the first markets for their arts and crafts. The 1922 Fiesta featured an Indian market, under the sponsorship of the School and the Museum. Teams of dancers had been scheduled even before 1922, and they were encouraged to go on to the Gallup Inter-Tribal Indian Ceremonial

Santiago Naranjo, five-times governor of Santa Clara Pueblo, ca. 1932. Photograph by T. Harmon Parkhurst. Courtesy of the Museum of New Mexico.

where trader Mike Kirk was building a good market for them. The Indian Detours provided another channel for the growing confidence of the younger Indians by encouraging interest in their way of life and their handicrafts.

Much of this effort was viewed with a jaundiced eye by the representatives of the Great White Father. Indians were supposed to become self-supporting farmers, and these dancing jaunts and the concentration on handicrafts interfered with the proper tilling of the fields and the time of harvest. The superintendent of the Indian Bureau for the New Mexico area actually "advised" the governors of the pueblos which ceremonials their people were permitted to attend away from home. And when the Cochiti Indians observed that they were free American citizens with a right to go where they pleased, C. J. Crandall, Superintendent of the Indian Field Service, told Hewett he had informed the council that should the Indians disobey his request in the matter he would have them arrested and brought back to the pueblo. He said that a copy of these instructions was also sent to Mike Kirk in Gallup.[1]

Hewett had no stomach for fighting the Indian Bureau. He thought he knew better than they what was good for "his Indians," but he knew the Indians still needed many things that only the federal government could supply. He had to be content with trying to influence individual Indian Service employees, reasoning with the higher-ups in Washington, and doing all in his power to help his individual Indian friends. He had joined John Collier in opposing the Bursum Bill, which would have confirmed title to non-Indians living on Indian lands; later, when he felt that Collier was wrong in some of the "protective" measures he was sponsoring, Hewett opposed him.

An Indian Service ex-employee who still frequently appealed to Hewett for assistance was Clara D. True, the doughty woman who was a battling Carrie Nation in her efforts to rid the Indian reservations of booze and bootleggers. Clara True had been a teacher at Santa Clara Pueblo before she was appointed to the superintendency of the Mission Creek and Twenty-Nine Palms reservations near Banning, California in 1908. She believed it is easier to defend an accomplished fact than to defend a proposed plan, so her actions were direct, forceful and often unexpected. As Indian agent in California she had the backing of most of the tribesmen as she emptied illicit liquor into the irrigation ditches, ran the bootleggers out of her territory, drove off trespassing cattle and turned Indian cattle into their own pastures, built a good jail and kept it clean, and instituted Sunday afternoon horse racing to keep her charges out of nearby city temptations.

After her dismissal from federal service (Indian Commissioner Leupp said he was sorry but she really had done a lot of things that were difficult to justify legally), she went back to New Mexico where her efforts to solve the alcoholism problems of her Indian friends earned her the nickname "The Devil of the Rio Grande."

Not all Indians appreciated Miss True's efforts to save them from booze and otherwise improve their morals. Anthony Lujan of Taos Pueblo was one. Tony had been introduced to John D. Rockefeller, Jr., on one of the financier's New Mexico visits and was later the recipient of some gifts for himself and his family. In writing to express his thanks, Lujan complained to Rockefeller that Miss True was interfering with the rights of the Indians to carry on their religious ceremonials and other old customs. Rockefeller sent the complaint on to Hewett, asking that he look into the matter. The record does not show what steps Hewett took to influence Miss True, but she often asked him to help her in her efforts to curb alcoholism in the pueblos.

Hewett's relationship with Rockefeller has long been the subject of much speculation, and the exact story is difficult to unravel. In 1924, on the occasion of Rockefeller's first visit to the School and the Museum, Hewett was absent from Santa Fe and asked Kenneth Chapman to substitute for him as host and guide. Two years later, when Rockefeller returned to the Southwest, he showed sufficient interest in its archaeology and ethnology for Hewett and his associates to hope he might become the patron they had long been seeking to provide the needed endowment for the School.

Accordingly Hewett wrote to Dr. R. V. C. Magoffin, president of the Archaeological Institute, proposing that Magoffin try to arrange an appointment with the financier in New York, where Magoffin was currently a professor at New York University. The suggestion was that a committee composed of Magoffin, Rockefeller's friend Dr. Corwin, New York attorney Percy Jackson, and financier Willard King join with Hewett in presenting the plans of the Managing Board to Rockefeller and asking his support. Hewett could be in New York any time in the week preceding his departure for Europe on September 5, 1926. Magoffin tried to set up the meeting through Rockefeller's New York office, but was told that the financier would not be in the New York area until after the final date beyond which Hewett could not postpone his sailing. The proposed meeting did not take place.[2] In the light of subsequent events one wonders whether Rockefeller had already made up his mind to finance an institution independent of the School of American Research, or whether succeeding events in Santa Fe might have been different had he been available to meet with the friends of the School as Hewett had requested.

After Hewett passed his sixtieth year his increased participation in scientific research in Africa and the Near East reinforced his credentials as an archaeologist, but those who carried the burden of administering his directors' jobs in his absence were left more and more to their own devices. Wesley Bradfield was transferred from Santa Fe to San Diego as associate director of the museum, with the responsibility of acting for Hewett. In Santa Fe, Kenneth Chapman held seniority. He had been on the staff of the Museum and the School since their founding; he participated in the excavations at Frijoles and elsewhere and had become an authority on Indian ceramics. The revival of excellence in Indian pottery-making was due in large measure to his steady, knowledgeable influence. His first major publication, *Evolution of the Bird in Decorative Art,* had appeared in 1916, and was followed by other publications featuring Indian design. Chapman helped found the Pueblo Pottery Fund, which later became the Indian Arts Fund, and he spent as much time as he could in the basement of the Art Museum where the pottery was housed. He was primarily an artist, and was content to leave administration to the group of younger protégés who moved into the various Museum departments.

During most of 1926 the opposition to those who had favored the cultural colony in Santa Fe grew in strength and vociferousness. Leaders in this group were among the artists and writers who were close friends of Kenneth and Kate Chapman. Many of them were influential in the Old Santa Fe Association, with its avowed desire to keep the town small and unchanged. But the Indian Detours were bringing hundreds of tourists every month; real estate developments were expanding (the Santa Fe Holding Company was organized to subdivide a thousand acres in the southern part of the city); and the *Santa Fe New Mexican* was bragging that Santa Fe was the fastest growing city in the state.

When Hewett returned from his season in Syria, it was obvious that his dream for the future growth of Santa Fe was outdated. The pressures of fighting losing battles had begun to weigh heavily on him. He decided to withdraw from the activities which no longer seemed to require his supervision.

19

SHIFTING LOYALTIES

*...when we contemplate the everlasting mess that the
"advanced" peoples are making of their newly acquired
"civilization" we have some acute misgivings about
what they are trying to bestow upon the "backward"
races.* — ELH

After his sixty-first birthday in 1926, Hewett began to concentrate his energies in
the New Mexico area, cutting down on the travel required to meet his obligations.
His plan had been to schedule about six months headquartered in San Diego and six
months in Santa Fe, but these periods were still interrupted by trips to Washington,
speaking engagements across the country, and foreign research. In San Diego,
Wesley Bradfield continued to act for the director, with William E. Pate accepting
increased responsibility. In Santa Fe, Kenneth Chapman, Lansing Bloom and Paul
Walter made decisions for Hewett during his absences, each in his own special field.

From 1922 to 1927 Hewett continued to carry a teaching load at San Diego State
Teachers' College, where he offered courses in archaeology and anthropology
which gave him a changing group of new students. He arranged for museum
experience as part of the training, and several students went on to become
professional anthropologists, Arthur J. O. Anderson among them. One of Hewett's
proposals — the combination of the Museum of Man with the college — was typical
of his urge to meld the institutions with which he was affiliated. He was not
successful in San Diego as he had been in Santa Fe. About the time that the culture
colony dispute was splitting Santa Fe, the San Diego situation was summed up by
Hewett's old friend and longtime supporter, George W. Marston, when he wrote:
"What with election days, Grand Jury investigations and indictments, Aimee
McPherson's scandals and our usual city squabbles over water, college site and
harbor improvements, we have had a lively summer."[1]

Although his zeal for hard work and zest for learning did not diminish, Hewett found that the problems proliferating in the two areas allowed him no time for the serious writing to which he wanted to devote his later years. He suggested to the San Diego Museum board a gradual withdrawal from his responsibilities there. Wesley Bradfield wanted to go back to New Mexico, so Hewett found a place to which he could return. In 1927 he arranged an exchange between his Santa Fe secretary, Janie Janowitz, and his San Diego assistant, Charlotte Arnold. This was helpful because both women knew the personnel in both institutions as well as having an understanding of Hewett's working methods. They were delighted with the move, because Janowitz found the sea level in California improved her health and Arnold realized her desire to live in New Mexico.

Hewett sloughed off other burdens. The 1926 Santa Fe Fiesta — the last for which he carried any responsibility — had seen Charles Wakefield Cadman conduct "Shanewis" and "The Sunset Trail" in the open-air theatre constructed by the School on the northern outskirts of the city. Soloists included Hispanic Metropolitan Opera tenor Rafaelo Diaz, Cherokee soprano Tsianina, Mohawk singer Oskenonton, and two Anglo tenors of national reputation, J. Allen Grubb and Lewis Mehan. The chorus was made up of local talent who gladly served in exchange for the enrichment of their musical experience. No similar opportunity would come to Santa Fe in the next three decades. Once Hewett's pioneering outdoor concerts were allowed to lapse, Santa Fe had to be content with indoor music until entrepreneur John Crosby came along and in 1957 established the Santa Fe Opera in the hills north of the city, bringing artists of national significance once more to sing under the stars.

Under a reorganization of the Fiesta sponsored by the Santa Fe Chamber of Commerce in 1927 Hewett was elected a member of the newly formed corporation, which had a governing group of sixteen members chosen for staggered terms of from one to four years. The four-year terms were assigned to Hewett, José D. Sena, Gustave Baumann, E. Dana Johnson, and Witter Bynner. Sena was a leader in civic and church affairs who had worked with Hewett for several years on Fiesta programs; Gus Baumann was an artist who bridged the gap between the older group and the newcomers to the colony. Poet Witter Bynner had openly campaigned for Hewett's removal from the Museum directorship when he ran for the state legislature the previous year, and Johnson, as editor of the *Santa Fe New Mexican,* was hostile to Hewett's administration. The Chamber was evidently trying to bring together the various factions, but Hewett declined the appointment. He gave lack of time and pressure of business as his reasons. Privately he told his friends that it was impossible to get Santa Fe people to work together.

The Chamber asked him to reconsider. Hewett knew that the dramatist Thomas Wood Stevens had been hired to direct a Fiesta pageant and the Indian Detour's management was in charge of local arrangements. It looked to him as if his appointment was a courtesy only, and he stood by his refusal. But he could not resist the temptation to remind the Fiesta Council that the Museum and School were leaving a good legacy, so he included specifics in his formal letter: "When the Fiesta became soundly established, a good permanent equipment, including outdoor theater built and paid for, free of debt and some funds in the bank, and with a reputation from one coast to another that assured as large an attendance as the two could accommodate, we felt justified in asking that the burden be taken over by someone else."[2]

Lansing Bloom came upon him one day at his desk, with a list in front of him of more than fifty organizations to which he belonged. He was using his red pencil to eliminate the ones he no longer considered essential. He had worked through organizations all his life; now he wanted to be independent of them.[3]

Hewett's withdrawal was consistent with his philosophy that once a project became a going concern and others were willing to take over, he should turn to other interests. (The directorships of the Museum and the School in Santa Fe were the two exceptions. They were his life; he was not convinced that anyone else could cope with those two jobs as well as he.) Hewett was not merely making excuses when he pleaded lack of time, for President Zimmerman had asked him to head the Department of Archaeology and Anthropology at the University of New Mexico, and the two were deep in arrangements.

Hewett terminated his teaching assignment with San Diego State College in 1927, and the following year resigned as director of the San Diego Museum. One more chapter was closed, though he kept in touch with many old friends and for some years he and Mrs. Hewett spent part of the winter in California. One of the San Diego associates, Col. D. C. Collier, had also moved on to other things. Out of his experience as general manager, then president of the Panama-Pacific Exposition, Collier had gone on to a career in world's fair planning. He was appointed commissioner-general for the United States at the Brazilian Centennial Exposition, and served as director-general of the Philadelphia Sesqui-Centennial during its formative stages. Hewett had him appointed to the Managing Board of the School, and in 1927 Collier asked Hewett's opinion about serving on a committee to choose and set up scientific exhibits for the World's Fair that Chicago planned for 1933. The Colliers were living in Chicago, where the colonel was assisting in preliminary planning. Hewett replied freely to his old friend:

> I have had occasional intimations that advice on World's Fair matters would be greatly appreciated, but as yet have nothing tangible to advise about. I did go so far as to say that I might be counted on to act in an advisory way only, but have had some regrets over going that far.
>
> As you doubtless know, the plan has been to have all the scientific exhibits handled by the National Research Council which, as you also probably know, is a holdover from the World War. Now, I sat with that body of petrified pundits and foresaw that the war would be ended long before they could decide what road to take. They did not, however, overlook the opportunity at the close to get an endowment from the

Carnegie Foundation to enable them to continue their activities [!] in times of peace. As it is pretty largely the same bunch that is to work out and execute the plans for the Chicago World's Fair in 1933, I rather expect them to have a few suggestions ready with reference to continuing themselves in some remunerative capacity about ten years after the Fair closes..."[4]

Hewett was narrowing his own activities as much as possible to the New Mexico area and to academic courses that could be tied to the practical work of the Museum and the School. He had failed to establish a university in Santa Fe, but Albuquerque was offering him a welcome alternative.

It will be remembered that when Hewett first sought to establish the American School in Santa Fe, President Tight of the University of New Mexico made a farsighted attempt to bring the School to his university, with the inducement that Hewett should head his own academic department. At that time Hewett did not consider Albuquerque and its struggling little state university so desirable a headquarters as Santa Fe's old Palace. In the intervening years, however, Albuquerque had grown. As the state's most important railway junction it had a central location, and it was on the way to becoming a metropolitan center. The university had grown under President Zimmerman until it became the dominant force in New Mexico education. Now Hewett and Zimmerman were determined to develop a social science department that would rank high in the nation.

Although it was currently fashionable for each academic department to insist on its existence as a separate entity, Hewett stressed their interdependence. All through his career he had preached that the "sciences of man" could not be encapsulated. He offered to the university all the resources of the School and the Museum of New Mexico to be used in history, archaelogy and art, and was especially interested in enlarging available library and museum material. At the same time the resources of the state university—in federal grants, scholarship funds and legislative support—became available to him and the institutions he directed. The scholarly press he had hoped to build in the basement of the Art Museum now became a part of the university press. Politicians who hesitated to give financial support for Museum projects that were intermingled with a private corporation like the School of American Research willingly voted appropriations to the state university in which they found a source of growing pride.

Hewett's new department at the university was immediately popular. His classes were filled, and he set about recruiting additional faculty. One of the big attractions was the summer field schools that supplemented classroom work and could be offered for college credit.

Their continuing concern over the destruction of ancient sites by pothunters and others who vandalized them without regard for scientific value or future preservation led Hewett and Zimmerman into further planning. Hewett recommended that in conjunction with the state Museum the university proceed to acquire by gift, purchase and exchange as many sites of prehistoric, historic and scientific interest as possible, and that Congress be asked to grant an additional allotment of unappropriated public domain to the state university, to be used for scientific purposes. Hewett estimated that thirty to fifty thousand acres should be adequate and should have a fair chance of passage by Congress.

In order that they might work more closely together, Zimmerman was invited to become a member of the Managing Board of the School of American Research, an appointment that he gladly accepted. Hewett's ability to enlist the enthusiastic interest of outstanding men and women and persuade them to join the boards of the School and the Museum continued to provide him with influential backers.

Most of the board members developed a lifelong loyalty and devotion to Hewett and his projects. Staff members often found themselves and their families challenged by the enmities toward Hewett that continued in some important groups in Santa Fe, however.

One year when Bradfield and Chapman lobbied more successfully than usual for the Museum's appropriation from the State Legislature, they were elated to secure approval for the largest budget that had ever been passed. They believed that the Director would be pleased and were astonished and dismayed when Hewett, on his return to Santa Fe, asked that the budget be reduced. Since both the School and the Museum were always hard pressed to pay salaries, those suffering most from a reduced budget were the staff members, whose pay raises were not so great as they deserved. Hewett had convinced the lawmakers that the School provided great benefit to the State Museum and the two organizations working together accomplished more than could be done separately. Some of his staff suspected that his chief concern was to conceal how much the State Museum carried the expense of the School, however.

The School's board members had spent considerable time in wooing the interest of John D. Rockefeller, Jr., and the Director was hopeful of their success. When Rockefeller decided to fund a museum in Santa Fe, however, it was to establish a new Laboratory of Anthropology, entirely separate from the Museum of New Mexico and the School of American Research and thus independent of Hewett's control. It must have been a bitter blow for Hewett that the man claiming credit for the coup was Kenneth Chapman, who moved to the staff of the new institution.

Many years later Chapman, aware that he had been accused of disloyalty by Hewett's supporters, explained his close association with the Rockefellers. In Hewett's absence from Santa Fe, it had been Chapman's responsibility to show the financier and his wife around the Museum of New Mexico. On one of their visits, Mrs. Rockefeller asked to be shown the pottery collection housed in the basement of the Art Museum, of which she had heard great praise. Naturally Chapman was eager to display the material and explain its valuable features. Mrs. Rockefeller was much interested, and commented at the time that the collection deserved a depository of its own better suited to its importance than the dusty basement shelves of the Art Museum.

Jesse Nusbaum, whose career had been sponsored by Hewett from the time of the excavations at Quirigua through the remodeling of the old Palace, his tenure in Washington at the National Museum, the building of the Art Museum, and his subsequent appointment as Superintendent of Mesa Verde National Park, became the director of the new Laboratory. Working under him, Kenneth Chapman held the title of Curator of the Indian Arts Fund. Once again the pottery collection, now greatly enlarged, was housed in the basement, but this time it was well displayed on specially designed shelves, with wide aisles permitting easy access for viewing and study.

John Gaw Meem, the Santa Fe architect who was famous for his skill in designing buildings in the historic tradition of the Southwest, had been retained to plan and supervise construction of the Laboratory building, and his quiet taste made it an outstanding example of the style.

One of the associates at the Laboratory was Dr. Harry Mera, who had long sought a professional outlet for his amateur interest in archaeology — particularly in ancient pottery, but whose aspirations had never been taken seriously by Hewett. Mera spent several years as a district health officer with offices in the Santa Fe County Courthouse. His duties were not onerous, and after checking into his office for an hour or two each morning he was free to pursue his study of Indian ceramics, which gradually crowded out completely his interest in medicine.

The new Laboratory of Anthropology opened its doors in 1931 and became immediately known as the depository for the Indian Arts Fund, which proceeded to acquire important collections of textiles and silver purchased by funds raised by Chapman, artist Frank Applegate, Mary Austin, and their associates. Hewett found himself confronted by a rival organization competing for patrons and museum material.

However severe his chagrin and disappointment, Hewett took no public notice of the defection. Instead, he concentrated intently on building up his university department and the summer fieldwork sponsored jointly by the university and School. A new generation of students became his associates as he moved them into staff positions, and most of them remained his loyal admirers for the rest of his life. It was always a comfort, too, that Paul Walter remained shoulder to shoulder with him in all his undertakings. As Walter rose to the presidency of the First National Bank of Santa Fe and took on increasing business prestige, he still found time to edit *El Palacio,* to serve as a liaison in seeking out new Board leadership, and to influence important backers.

With his resignation from the San Diego Museum and the faculty of San Diego State College, Hewett had freed himself from the necessity for dividing his time and attention. In order to keep open his California contacts, however, he accepted an offer from the University of Southern California at Los Angeles to head the Department of Archaeology and Anthropology, *without remuneration.* This post simply meant that he would have a voice in the choice of faculty members who actually carried the teaching load and that he would assist in departmental

Edgar Lee Hewett, San Diego, California, 1932. Photograph by Jack Adams. Courtesy of the Museum of New
xico.

planning. His protégé A. O. Bowden (once president of New Mexico's small teachers' college at Silver City) actually directed the department. The prestige of Hewett's name and his consultation on curricula and graduate programs were his principal contributions. He read Master's theses and gave advice on doctoral programs, but he was not often able to squeeze a trip to California into his taut schedule, even to be present at doctoral examinations of the students he sponsored. He continued to find fellowships, scholarships or teaching assistant positions for a stream of students who sought his help in furthering their careers. Eventually credentials from USC held as much or more prestige than those at San Diego or Albuquerque.

In New Mexico Hewett helped to finance young men and women seeking careers in archaeology and related fields by appointing them to part-time positions funded by the university, the state Museum complex and the School of American Research. Some salaries were paid by a rotating system of checks drawn against funds of the three institutions. Wayne L. Mauzy became secretary and business manager of the School and the Museum. It was his task to keep the financial juggling act from crashing.

Mauzy had come to Santa Fe as a patient at Sunmount Sanatorium, where Dr. Frank Mera helped to restore his health. He knew the important people in the various cliques, moving easily and unobtrusively among them. His bent was perhaps more scholarly than financial, but he had unswerving principles and a flair for detail. Hewett left in his hands the day-to-day administrative routine that had once been carried by Walter and Chapman.

As the reputation of Hewett's field schools grew, students came from many institutions. For a time the University of Southern California cooperated under a jointly sponsored program with the University of New Mexico and the Museum, but the alliance was not altogether successful and friction led to its termination.

Hewett was more and more inclined to postpone unpleasant decisions and leave dilemmas unresolved while he traveled off to inspect and give brief supervision to fieldwork in Peru, Mexico, Guatemala, or one of the Near East sites that interested him. With advancing age he acquired an aloofness based on the belief that, given time, many problems would solve themselves. He felt also that complete detachment from local conditions for a period of time helped to clear his mind and make his decisions more objective. His associates and subordinates, unable to escape, were left to cope with situations that might have cleared up quickly with a prompt decision, but unresolved, festered into resentment between staff members and the rival institutions.

Hewett's genuine concern for people and his ability to find scholarships, jobs and loans (often actual gifts out of his own pocket) endeared him to the younger group that now filled his classes and moved into museum posts, however. Among those who studied under him at the University of New Mexico were men and women who would make notable contributions to American archaeology: Bertha Dutton, Edwin N. Ferdon, Marjorie Fergusson Lambert, Arthur J. O. Anderson,

Paul Reiter, Marion Hollenbach, and Reginald Fisher. Among the faculty members serving summer field schools such as the one at Chaco Canyon were Hartley Burr Alexander, Mamie R. Tanquist, Florence Hawley, and Clyde Kluckhohn.

Charlotte Arnold, who came from San Diego to Santa Fe in 1927 and changed her name to Carlotta Warfield, was secretary to the Director and carried many administrative responsibilities for seven years. Reginald Fisher became assistant director in Santa Fe, while Paul A. F. Walter still held the title of vice-director. Others who served on the Santa Fe staff over a period of years included Mary R. Van Stone, curator of art; Hester Jones, curator of history; Lansing B. Bloom, custodian of archives; Helen Dorman and Ruth Rambo, librarians; and Dorothy Walter, museum assistant.

On the financial side, Wayne Mauzy and Albert Ely looked after business details and managed to get the bills paid for field schools, curatorships at a growing number of state monuments on important archaeological sites, and the daily operations of the two institutions. Promising students were given travelling fellowships, became supervisors at summer field schools, and moved into faculty or museum positions. Dr. A. O. Bowden continued as director of the school in California, combining that title with the chairmanship of the Department of Archaeology and Anthropology at the University of Southern California. The list of those who felt affection and gratitude for Hewett's teaching and moral support through the years grew with each new class at the institutions he served.

In 1937 the rival Laboratory of Anthropology on the south side of Santa Fe was joined by another privately supported institution on a nearby site, when the Museum of Navajo Art was built as a repository for the important collection relating to Navajo sand paintings and other ceremonial material collected by Mary Cabot Wheelwright. Since both institutions required staffing, some Hewett-trained scientists sought and eventually found jobs there. Hewett would have preferred to keep them in his own institutions, but further expansion was slow to develop. There were some, too, who felt that they had outgrown his teaching and preferred to move on to wider horizons.

At the Laboratory of Anthropology the collections of pottery, hand-wrought silver and textiles became the inspiration for a growing renaissance in Indian handicrafts and an outstanding resource for students from many lands. The Rockefeller grant that had built the Laboratory provided for diminished operational funds over a period of ten years, on the theory that the seed money thus offered should be supplemented by other gifts and the Laboratory grow independent of Rockefeller support. The museums in Santa Fe all needed wealthy patrons, and when the flow of contributions dwindled during the Depression years, the scope of operations had to be cut accordingly. Thus the Laboratory tended to become a research center with a small staff that worked quietly, undisturbed by the general public; the Navajo ceremonial collections in their huge octagonal hogan were available for only limited scrutiny; and acquisitions in all three institutions were stored until funds for new exhibitions might become available.

Meanwhile, Hewett maintained surface friendly relations with the rival groups. The animosity of Cutting and his newspaper did not lessen, but Hewett tried to sidestep confrontations. Cutting pretty well controlled state politics by this time, although Frank Springer's brother Charley still battled him, especially for control of the huge job-dispensing state highway department. Cutting was appointed to the U.S. Senate on the death of A. A. Jones in December 1927, and the following year ran for election to the office, defeating Democratic candidate J. S. Vaught. In 1932 he campaigned for Franklin D. Roosevelt, outraging the Republicans, even though he shortly broke with FDR's policies. In 1934 he ran for reelection, narrowly defeating Democratic Congressman Dennis Chavez in an election that was still being contested in May 1935 when Cutting, en route to Washington after a brief visit at home, was killed in a plane crash in Missouri. Chavez was appointed to his vacant seat.

Before Cutting's death Hewett continued to be attacked not only in the press but by letters written to officers of the American Institute of Archaeology and members of the Managing Board of the School. In reply to an inquiry about such a letter that he received from an old friend, Hewett ruefully wrote that Santa Fe no longer had a place for an old-timer like himself and continued:

> Of all the evils however that have come upon New Mexico, I do not refer to Santa Fe alone, nothing else can compare with that which came with a personally owned press, a press acquired solely for personal ends, devoid of any feeling of responsibility in the community and used with an unscrupulous mendacity to suppress and distort and pervert truth to an extent that becomes a blight upon the whole community. The extent to which this view concerning several of our New Mexican newspapers is shared throughout New Mexico convinces me that this is not merely one of my personal prejudices.[5]

After Cutting's death the *Santa Fe New Mexican* passed into other hands. Dana Johnson stayed on for two years, but failing health and the change of ownership led to his resignation in June 1937, and he died six months later in California, where he had gone in search of better health. After his departure the tone of the newspaper changed drastically. It was the policy of the chain owning it not to get into controversies, and, as one reporter commented, the editorials were the kind that pointed with pride rather than viewing with alarm. The long, unremitting pressure was off Hewett at last, but since he reached his seventy-second birthday a few weeks before Johnson's death, it no longer mattered very much anyway. Hewett had become the grand old man, destined to outlive his most formidable opponents or gradually to receive their respectful homage. In 1935 San Diego put on another exposition, but it lacked the glamour of the 1915 spectacle. As one writer described it, "The second exposition was like warmed over toast or a relit cigar, but then, we were all twenty years older."[6]

20

EMPHASIS ON WRITING

We shall not be able to ignore many things that are spurious, many that are ignoble in man's history; but with the stress always upon the genuine, manly traits, with veneration of the godlike achievements which have carried man so far up in his world, archaeology may take and hold the highest place among the humanities.—ELH

Frequent mention has been made of the activities of the Archaeological Institute of America as they affected the lives of Hewett and his friends. Prior to 1920 the pulling and tugging between the Classicists and the Americanists was continuous. The San Diego Exposition helped to improve the prestige of the American school, however, and after World War I the battle in the Institute became a struggle between the elitists, who felt that the organization belonged to and existed for the scholars, and men like Magoffin and Hewett, who believed that learning for its own sake was not enough but that knowledge should be diffused throughout the nonacademic community.

Magoffin had labored diligently to build up the local scientific societies through which the Institute could increase the support of interested laymen. His scolding of Hewett over the decline in membership of the Southwest groups reflected his concern. One local society, however, threatened to become more prestigious than the national organization. In Washington, D.C., a distinguished group had the backing of the Smithsonian and its Bureau of Ethnology as well as the patronage of wealthy sponsors who opened their grand homes for its functions. Indeed, the Washington Society wielded such substantial influence that many of its members saw no reason for being subordinate.

In the years after the San Diego Exposition, Hewett was a popular speaker before the Washington Society. He often appeared at one of the society's winter meetings, where he brought out an audience representing intellectual and social Washington at its best. A group of two or three hundred cognoscenti did not intimidate the self-made scholar who had built himself into an international authority. Rather it afforded him some of the more stimulating experiences of his lecturing life. He spoke with charm and authority, drawing on anecdotes from his own experience as well as his wide reading.

For a time Mitchell Carroll was both director of the Archaeological Society of Washington and general secretary of the Archaeological Institute of America, which helped to keep the two groups in balance. On his sudden death in 1925, however, the leadership was thrown into a battle for control. Robert Lansing, who had been Secretary of State in Woodrow Wilson's cabinet, became president of the Washington Society and brought in Arthur Stanley Riggs to succeed Dr. Carroll. One of Carroll's responsibilities had been the editorship of the magazine *Art and Archaeology* for the Institute; the need to find a good replacement in that post called for a determination of the future policies of the magazine. Largely at Hewett's urging, Professor H. R. Fairclough of Stanford University agreed to go east and edit *Art and Archaeology* until a permanent successor could be found. Riggs was next selected to take over the magazine, and served for the following ten years during the struggle for supremacy that built up between the Institute and the Washington Society. Because Hewett had no ambitions for any position that had not already been achieved, he came to be trusted by the contending factions. Magoffin and Riggs both consulted him. He defended each man to the other, understanding their goals and believing that cooperation was more important than the supremacy of either group.

Riggs always credited Hewett with being one of his staunchest helpers during his years of editing *Art and Archaeology*. Much of Hewett's writing appeared first as papers of the School of American Research, but he responded to Rigg's pleas for material with contributions of his own as well as from his colleagues and students. It was Riggs who recommended to his book publisher, Bobbs-Merrill of Indianapolis, that Hewett was the best man to write a popular archaeological study of early Americans. Free of his San Diego responsibilities, Hewett accepted the assignment; the result was *Ancient Life in the American Southwest*, published in 1930.

He wasted no time worrying over the success of the book. The reviews were generally favorable and the publisher was pleased. Riggs, who felt that he had godfathered the book, seems to have been more concerned about its acceptance than the author. Shortly after the book appeared he wrote Hewett, teasing him about his unspoiled innocence in regard to critics. Riggs told of his own experience in being misunderstood, and warned that the breed of critics was a mean one; once they had put their hooks in a few times, the writer wouldn't worry about whether he was right or wrong, but would be willing to murder anybody who looked like a critic. He wished Hewett better luck than he had experienced.[1]

To this friendly counsel Hewett replied that any kind of reading matter

Donizetta and Edgar Lee Hewett at ruins of Xochimicalco, Mexico, ca. 1936. Courtesy of the School of American Research.

concerning himself failed to interest him, and that he rarely saved newspaper clippings.[2] Hewett's lack of regard for biographical details concerning himself has made it difficult to document many periods in his life, but it underscores his lack of concern for petty details. He infuriated those scientists who derived significance from minor deviations in pottery shards, by shrugging off such niceties as unimportant. The length and width of a ruin might be dutifully measured and become the subject for study by a student, but unless such measurements could be shown to have a bearing on the inhabitants or the way they lived, Hewett would waste little time on them.

For nearly fifty years he had been developing four or five articles a year for publication. Many of these were reprints of speeches he had delivered, accounts of recent excavations on which he must make reports, or simply the usual annual reports of the institutions he directed. He drew on these in structuring his first full-length book, which established him as an author as well as an educator and builder. It was still difficult to find time to schedule his writing, but the favorable reception of the book persuaded him to undertake the second book commissioned by Bobbs-Merrill, *Ancient Life in Mexico and Central America*, which was published in 1936.

Even in the later years of his career, Hewett's promotional abilities were formidable. His wide contacts, cultivated for a long lifetime, continued to bring important backers onto his governing boards, and while the School slowly diminished in influence and activity, the Museum of New Mexico and the department under his direction at the university gained in prestige. Even with the curtailed budgets of the Depression years, there was no longer any substantial agitation to replace Hewett as the director of the two institutions he had brought through so many years.

For a time it looked as though the Laboratory of Anthropology would succeed as an independent institution, but as the Rockefeller support diminished it became apparent that the Laboratory's backers had not succeeded in attracting a director with outstanding fund-raising skill, and activities there slowly diminished. As some of the prime sponsors of the Indian Arts Fund died or drifted to other interests the burden of funding fell each year on a smaller group, until there began to be whispers that it would be better off if it were combined with the state Museum complex. Kenneth Chapman took on the directorship in 1936, showing a firm faith in the institution which by then had lost much of its local backing.

By the mid-1930s Hewett, too, had lost many of his longtime sponsors and close associates. Alice Fletcher had died in 1923, and there was never another who took her place as a backer of the School. Each time Hewett walked through the patio of the Art Museum he passed the niche where her ashes rested behind their bronze plaque. Often, he must have paused to remember all she had done for him and the School.

J. Walter Fewkes died in 1930 at the ripe age of eighty. Known as the first systematic excavator in the Southwest, Fewkes had been a friend since the Washington days when Edgar and Cora spent their last months together.

Charley Wallace, the high-school friend with whom he had kept in touch all through the years, died of cancer in Wichita Falls, Texas, in 1932. Wallace had built a reputation as a Shakespearean scholar through the research he undertook in England after he earned his doctorate at the University of Freiberg in 1906, and had published a series of studies that were well received at the time, though his scholarship was later superseded. His wife Hulda had aided him in his London research period and kept pace with him when they moved to Texas as he turned his attention to his other prime interest — oil geology. Together they achieved substantial wealth. In the *Dictionary of American Biography* listing on Wallace no mention is made of his poetry, but it was as a poet that Hewett thought of him. Edgar wrote a moving tribute to his old friend Charley in *Campfire and Trail*. Remembering how events in their lives had paralleled, Hewett was reminded that death was the last great adventure they would share. He recalled Wallace's line about morning on the hills, and wrote, "And never doubt, old comrade, that I am coming and that as surely as we rode the boyhood trail together, we will together face the 'Morning, morning on the Hills.'"[3]

William H. Holmes was ninety-three when he died in 1933; Hewett regarded his death as the passing of his last old chief. Edgar had been a schoolboy in Illinois when Holmes made the first thoroughly scientific study of Southwestern archaeology in the Hayden survey of 1874-75 which laid the basis for the U.S. Geological Survey. Throughout the years when Holmes headed the Bureau of Ethnology at the Smithsonian Hewett worked with him in many undertakings, and he could always count on Holmes' helpful counsel in his own decision making. He considered Holmes and Bandelier the outstanding figures in Southwestern archaeology.

Frank Springer's death in 1927 marked the end of a long and fruitful collaboration and left a void that could not be filled. Beginning in the days before Springer's influence brought Hewett to the presidency of Las Vegas Normal University (later Highlands University), the two men worked with mutual esteem — Springer usually behind the scenes, with Hewett as the front man. In their prime Frank Springer, Paul A. F. Walter and Edgar Lee Hewett had formed an almost unbeatable triumvirate.

Bronson Cutting's death in 1935 brought an era in New Mexico politics to an end. New loyalties would be formed as leaders emerged, but Edgar Hewett had reached an age when he was more interested in his personal philosophy than in political activity. His generation was moving off the scene. He reached his seventieth birthday a few months after Cutting's death. It was time to make way for newcomers.

The occasion of Hewett's seventieth birthday was celebrated by his associates and admiring former students with a memorial volume dedicated to him. A distinguished body of backers was enlisted to make the publication possible. Among the financial contributors were longtime board members and regents such as the educator Lydia Trowbridge of Winnetka, Illinois; New York lawyer Percy Jackson whose advice had often been sought and sometimes followed when Hewett needed legal counsel; financier Willard V. King; fellow scientists H. R. Fairclough of Stanford and R. V. Magoffin of New York University; and college administrators such as W. K. Moorhead of Phillips Academy, Frank C. Spencer of Adams State Teachers College and W. W. Postlethwaite of Colorado College. They were joined by two New Mexico philanthropists who gave generously to Hewett projects — Ruth Hanna McCormick Simms and Leonora S. Curtin. John P. Harrington, by now comfortably employed at the Bureau of American Ethnology in Washington, and Frederick W. Hodge, who had moved west to head the Southwest Museum in Los Angeles, joined in the tribute.

The memorial volume, sponsored jointly by the University of New Mexico and the School of American Research, was entitled *So Live the Works of Men*. It did not actually come off the press until 1939 (which surprised no one familiar with the time lag in scientific publication). It included biographical details and tributes from men who had worked loyally with Hewett: J. F. Zimmerman, Paul A. F. Walter, Lansing B. Bloom, and Arthur Stanley Riggs. The table of contents listed scholarly contributions ranging over many fields that had been touched by Hewett, from "The Empire of the Incas" by Julio C. Tello to "Mongolian Epic" by Nicholas Roerich. Some of the writers — like Ales Hrdlicka — had in times past been bitterly critical. Others, such as A. V. Kidder and Sylvanus G. Morley, had remained friendly though they often differed vigorously from Hewett in field methods. All joined in respect for Hewett's integrity and constructive idealism, and all had reason to be grateful for his support given at some time in their careers. The volume was edited by Donald B. Brand and Fred E. Harvey.

Hewett now turned more and more of his time to writing that had been long postponed. In 1936 the University of New Mexico Press brought out *Chaco Canyon and Its Ancient Monuments*, distilled by Hewett from many years of summer fieldwork. It was followed in 1937 by *Indians of the Rio Grande Valley*, coauthored by Adolph Bandelier. This volume combined Hewett's description of the Rio Grande pueblos as he had learned about them throughout his career with Bandelier's hitherto unpublished documentary history of the people of the valley. (Although Fanny Bandelier had undertaken to finish some of her husband's work, much material for which a publisher had not yet been found remained in the Museum's custody.)

The two volumes were the first of a series which Hewett called nontechnical handbooks of archaeology of the Southwest. In the third volume of the series, *Pajarito Plateau and Its Ancient People*, Hewett prepared a foreword paying tribute to his Indian informants and to the two cronies who were associated in his mind with the Pajarito more than any others: Adolph Bandelier and Charles F. Lummis. The opening paragraphs set the mood for this compilation of notes and reminiscences which was forty years in the making:

If you want to feel the power and pathos of time, roll up in your blankets some night on any one of a hundred mesas, or in any one of a hundred canyons of the old abandoned land of the Pajaritans....

Across the centuries, soft voices rippled in unison with the *ritos* and the gentle winds that stir the cornfields. The shadowy beings that till the fields, climb the cliffs, and chant the rituals that dramatize their simple faith and trustful life seek only to share the ineffable harmony that is all about...[4]

The third and last Bobbs-Merrill volume, *Ancient Andean Life*, came out in 1939. Hewett had visited many South American sites and had sponsored students there. He had made several journeys to Peru and had supervised field schools there while this volume was in preparation, but in the view of specialists he was hardly qualified as an outstanding authority on the subject. The book was not so well reviewed as the two previous Ancient Life books; henceforth, his book publication would be undertaken entirely by the press at the University of New Mexico.

Hewett gave the prestige of his name to several volumes coauthored by the young associates he sponsored in Santa Fe: *The Pueblo Indian World* with Bertha Dutton, *Landmarks of New Mexico* with Wayne Mauzy, and *Mission Monuments of New Mexico* with Reginald Fisher. Several other volumes were projected but not carried out.

Hewett used the writings of this phase of his life to put into print some of the speeches he had prepared for special occasions. The chapter entitled "The Utility of Beauty" in *Man and Culture* gave publication to the dedication address he had made at the opening of the Arsuna School of Fine Arts in the Mary Austin house in Santa Fe in 1937. In it he alluded to Santa Fe's long battle for historic preservation and to some of the incidents in the culture-colony battle.

He used his writings to answer critics on some other subjects, also. One researcher who had carefully authenticated the background of the Pueblo "filth societies" never forgave Hewett for refusing to print his study. The "filth societies" were a degeneration of the power of some ceremonial healers. It was reported that a person must be almost *in extremis* before he would resort to their aid, because he must agree that when he recovered he would allow himself to be initiated into a group whose rites included eating of excrement and other abominations.) It may have been with this incident in mind that Hewett set out his philosophy regarding the publication of sordid aspects of Indian culture in the opening chapter of *Indians of the Rio Grande Valley:*

Irreparable injustice has been done to the Pueblos by writers who have apparently sought out and published the degenerate phases of their culture, failing utterly to discover and make known the normal, wholesome life that is still the rule in spite of the mutilation that it has undergone at the hand of a strong, dominating, "superior" race.... It is the special duty of ethnologists to counteract the false picture of Pueblo life that has been produced in the name of scientific research. Vulgarity there is, to be sure, in the Indian society, and sordid immorality, as in the white race, the black, the yellow — in all humanity. But I do not want the pictures of my race that goes into history to be made up from the social sewage that can be found and wallowed in almost everywhere that observers of that bent of mind look for it...[5]

Hewett was accused of romanticizing his Indians and of refusing to print all the truth about them. For him it was a matter of emphasis. He simply rejected the sordid as a distortion of the true nobility he wanted to exist in all mankind.

21

LOOKING BACK FOR THE RECORD

These are old, old trails over which we have walked in the Southwest in order to bring the experiences of the past into the life of today. Nature is our surest teacher, and Man's place and part are fairly clear. —ELH

In 1938 a young couple of Hewett's acquaintance approached him for permission to write his biography. He consented and prepared some suggestions summing up his philosophy of life which are worth quoting at some length:

> It seems to me that the best biography that could be written of a man whose life has been devoted to scholarly pursuits would be one that would present a picture of the development of his mind and character — in other words, the story of his intellectual life. The rest is not of much consequence ...
>
> Now trying to know one's world is a large undertaking. A good many years must be devoted to exploratory work before worthwhile judgments are possible. Then whatever comes through the crucible of public opinion still prized by thinking people may be worth putting into the permanent record.
>
> The scientist engaged in research must of course put down his observations from day to day and occasionally publish them for the information of others who may thus be saved from blundering over the same ground, sterile or otherwise; but he should be chary of premature conclusions, published or not ...
>
> So to come to the point about this matter, building or helping to build institutions leaves a fairly obvious record. Administrative work is not as barren of permanent results as it sometimes appears to be. Then as to

one's teaching: when a good many thousand students have had their say about that, and have in one way or another worked the results into their own conscious or unconscious procedure, one's ideas about humanity, nature, or whatever his subject is, will be established for what they are worth.

Whatever one has done in the way of scientific research will be found in reports that are read as much as they deserve to be. These, with three or four books written for laymen as well as scholars to read if they want to, form a part of the record. Then there are the hundreds of scientific projects initiated, being carried forward by young people who soon are teaching their teachers. Starting something at the right time in the right way is quite as important as keeping it going. Vision is as essential as action.

So in one way or another the activities of the man in public work are prolonged to infinity. I have often had the awesome feeling of Wuarin, from his university chair in Geneva, teaching students in the University of New Mexico or Southern California, six or seven thousand miles away. The years are long since I was privileged to walk with Cheney, Bowman, Marshall, Suyder, Naville, Powell, Fletcher, Holmes, but I am keenly aware that without any one of them something vital would be missing from my own teaching today. So every one who earns it attains his immortality...

The lectures, addresses, talks, formal and informal, that are called for constitute a large increase of one's load. In fact, here is where the man in public life sums up his philosophy. Most of my utterances of this kind were never written down, few ever reduced to notes. But there have been occasions that called for the most careful statement, for the formulation of mature convictions. Some of these talks have been written; some, if provocative of discussion, put into print.

Looking over these utterances of the last fifteen years, I find that a small number — a dozen or so — assembled so as to be read in relation to one another, will adequately represent my philosophy and practice in science, education, and human relations. The subjects most thought about through life: human aspirations, achievements, responsibilities, cultural values, are touched upon with more or less of final conclusion. I am told that there are noticeable inconsistencies if one goes through the whole. I hope so. One should change his mind once in a while...

So with me, learning became exploration, adventuring into the unknown, and what we call teaching for lack of a better term, a matter of scouting, inviting young people to go along if they feel like it; watching those who are not afraid of the hard road; helping to find the opportunity that youth needs to try its muscles on. The field for that kind of education I have found not only in college classrooms but in the open spaces — the wholesome camp life in mountains and deserts with nature as chief guide and authority. It has been a life of widening horizons, of adventuring in many fields of thought and action, of happy association with those who cared to go along, not so much as pupils as companions in the fascinating business of getting acquainted with our world...[1]

The letter, dated May 11, 1938, is addressed to Mr. and Mrs. Miller. Who were they? Was the biography ever started — or finished? There is nothing in the Hewett file to answer these questions, but perhaps having set down his idea of a biography sent Hewett to his notebooks and led him to think back over events that would help to tell his life story. Out of this contemplation came five small volumes that were brought out by the University of New Mexico Press.

Campfire and Trail and *From Cave Dwelling to Mount Olympus* were published in 1943. The first is a collection of anecdotes about people and places, gathered in his wide travel; the second, subtitled *Man in the Pageant of the Ages*, includes much material Hewett had brought to audiences in his public speaking.

Man and Culture and *Man and the State*, published in 1944, continue the *Pageant of the Ages* series.

A final small volume of reminiscences published in 1945, *Two Score Years*, goes all the way back to his childhood. Hewett was now in his eighty-first year, and as so often happens with old people, his mind returned to the early events that had shaped him, fondly recalling parents, siblings and other relatives as well as schoolmates and teachers who had been quietly waiting in his memory to be brought back once more.

It was well that he had his writing to keep him occupied, for his personal life grew very difficult. It became apparent that Donizetta, his companion for thirty-five years, was failing in competence. As she grew erratic and forgetful Edgar tried to cover for her, but at length he had to admit to close friends that Doni was childish, and often not responsible for her actions. Ruth Elvin, who had looked after their Santa Fe home for many years, helped care for her, but Doni sometimes eluded them and, wandering away from home, got lost.

World War II was another cause of sadness for Hewett. Like so many Americans of his generation, he truly believed in the slogans that proclaimed America's destiny to make the world safe for democracy. He had many friends and honored associates in Europe — men who sat in scientific sessions and joined his expeditions. The plight of these friends horrified him as the Nazis took over and Hitler (whom Hewett called the "super criminal of Germany") drove his people on their obscene conquests. Hewett asked, "What is war?" In his dialectic style he then answered himself:

> War is a phenomenon of civilization. Man-to-man fighting in the pre-civilized ages was not altogether abhorrent. "Civilized warfare" (machine gun and bomb manipulated by "experts" against defenseless women and children, the aged, sick, helpless) has no prototype in culture history. War is not inevitable. Nothing in human relations is inevitable if strong, determined men so will.[2]

Remembering all the people throughout the world who had been kind to him, Hewett made a plea for understanding:

> I should like to have the means to start a new kind of university — one

without students (the dream of professors), without professors (the dream of the student body), one devoted to the study of humanity — that could maintain a thousand level-headed young people out among the peoples of the world; living with them; speaking their languages; sharing their hopes, ambitions, strivings; understanding their culture, thinking their thoughts. Since bayonets and battleships and fighting are failing, we might next try dispelling ignorance of one another.[3]

Edgar Hewett did not live to see the Peace Corps implemented; he would have put great faith in the idealistic young people who joined in that experiment, and he would not have been discouraged when it turned out to be too simplistic for mankind at that particular stage of civilization. He would only have said that man must keep trying, striving, for a more nearly perfect state.

Between 1943 and 1946 Hewett's fine physique gradually diminished under the strain of the years. In 1943 Donizetta underwent a second mastoid operation, and her "memory malady" — attributed to iodine deficiency — was placed under medical treatment. Edgar, too, had some surgery performed in Los Angeles. During the winter of 1943 they found the West Coast in wartime to be a dreary and unfriendly atmosphere, so they went to Albuquerque where they took up residence for the winter at the Presbyterian Sanatorium. There Doni could have supervision and Edgar could devote more time to his work. He wrote John Harrington, urging his old associate to write down his accumulated knowledge while there was yet time. Hewett declared, "Nothing will be allowed to interfere with the shaping up of my accumulated material to the end that whatever value it has will be assured, and that my obligation to those who managed to do it will be discharged."[4]

As professor emeritus at the University of Southern California and University of New Mexico, Hewett had access to the facilities of both institutions. He continued to keep up his contacts in each, but it became more difficult as national and international scientific sessions were cancelled by wartime needs. Students and associates joined the Armed Forces in increasing numbers. In Washington, only war-related activities were important. In San Diego, blackouts and hysterial rumors of invasion swept the city that had become a naval base and staging area. In Santa Fe, the Museum and the School adapted to war work. The Managing Board of the School could not muster a quorum of its far-flung members; meetings were postponed and business had to be transacted by mail. Efforts of the staff were diverted from research to the keeping of war records. The east end of the Palace became headquarters for the local chapter of the American Red Cross, which handled emergencies for servicemen and their families throughout Santa Fe County and served the mysterious military installation that had ousted Los Alamos Ranch School from Hewett's beloved Pajarito Plateau and thereby ended his dream of turning it into a wilderness preserve. There were whisperings about the nature of the activities on "The Hill," and Hewett held conferences with some old friends who came incognito for consultation with the military, but patriotic citizens did not inquire too deeply or discuss openly what they knew.

Hewett continued to meet his responsiblities to the institutions for which he was still director, busy as always. In addition to preparing his handbooks for the printer, he accepted the sober duty of preparing for *El Palacio* his last tribute to old friends as they came to the end of the trail.

Of Ales Hrdlicka he wrote in appreciation:

> One likes to think of the boy of far Bohemia, who found himself drawn by "insatiable yearning to travel, see, smell, hear, feel with his own senses, and endeavor to find, gather and penetrate. With longing to know this mother earth as intimately as possible. Not to loaf or for adventure; not to range aimlessly or hunt for pleasure, excitement or to slay anything, but just to go and learn and get ever nearer the essentials, the vast secret of it all" . . .

"Most of all," Hewett wrote, "One loves to remember the rugged warm-souled Hrdlicka, lover as well as student of humanity."[5]

Many of the old animosities had quietly faded through the years, but of one contemporary scientist who had often caused Hewett trouble and who died about the same time as Hrdlicka, *El Palacio* carries no tribute beyond a brief paragraph of obituary: "Dr. Franz Boas, 84, internationally known German-born Columbia University anthropologist whose books were burned by the Nazis in 1933, and who for many years has been one of the greatest influences in American anthropology, died in New York on December 21 [1943]."[6]

The following year brought other losses. Sheldon Parsons, one of the first members of the Santa Fe-Taos art colony to establish a permanent residence in the capital city, died in September 1944. His studio home on Palace Avenue where the road turns up Cerro Gordo had become a landmark. Parsons loved the landscape — the softly molded adobe houses, the gently curving streets, and most characteristic of all in his paintings — the gorgeous golden foliage of New Mexico autumns. In the early days of the Art Museum he had served briefly as curator. Some said Hewett appointed him to appease criticism that the Director himself was no artist. Parsons soon found that the museum detail interfered with his own working time, and the stipend hardly justified the sacrifice. His resignation was an amicable one, and he later donated some of his finest work to the Museum. He was one more old friend who would be missed.

Dr. James Fulton Zimmerman, president of the University of New Mexico since 1927 and an enthusiastic collaborator in Hewett's development of his department and his schemes for historic preservation, died suddenly October 20, 1944. Of him Hewett wrote: "Some of us have been privileged to witness the building of the University from the nondescript plant that he took over, into a campus of distinction among the universities of the United States. It was a distinguished achievement for any man, yet he claimed no credit for it."[7]

Zimmerman's death marked the end of the university's devotion to the Hewett concept of the Science of Man as rooted in a classical tradition. Though it was not to become apparent until several years after World War II, the old verities had given way to a new dynamism. Language was changing rapidly as a new jargon was coined for social concepts. For university students, understanding nuclear fission would become more essential than history or art, ethnology or literary tradition. Sensing this, Hewett rejected it. He was too old to change the philosophy he had spent a lifetime developing, and he could only believe that the quest for truth about mankind was still the most important objective in a man's life.

He kept up correspondence with old friends. From San Diego George W. Marston, now ninety-four, wrote a sprightly letter telling him of the changes there. There was constant correspondence with Sylvanus Morley, who maintained a beautiful home in Maya country near his beloved excavations at Chichen Itzá where he welcomed the visitors Hewett sent him.

C. T. Currelly, director of the Royal Ontario Museum of Archaeology, wrote Hewett from Toronto, "When I first visited you there were six hundred whites in Santa Fe and it is largely your doing that there are 30,000 people there now."[8] Hewett must have smiled over the Canadian's implication that only the Anglos in Santa Fe were white; he wanted no credit for the recent growth of Santa Fe. He knew it was the changes brought by the war rather than his efforts that had caused the rapid growth in northern New Mexico. He had wanted only to guide the *way* it grew, and recent events had been too strong for him.

Although he welcomed news from old friends and extended help to former students when he could, Hewett had lost his zest for acquiring new friends. Genevieve Schenk, a young Santa Fe matron, was sometimes asked to help him. As she tells the story, "My father went to school to Dr. Hewett in Greeley. In the last years of Hewett's life he was often bored by visitors who absorbed so much of his time. One day he called me and asked me to take a man from India on a tour of Santa Fe and nearby pueblos. Since I thought Dr. Hewett stood next to God, I was glad to do anything for him. I found that his caller was Dr. Desai, physician to Mahatma Ghandi, and I enjoyed taking him about, as indeed Hewett would have done at my age."[9]

In spite of suffering from arthritis and rheumatism, Hewett remained active and keenly alive to his daily problems through most of his eighty-first year. The end of the shooting war brought relief and a sense of renewed purpose. He hoped that social scientists could get on once more with the world's really important business of advancing civilization, too long delayed by the pressures of national survival. When the managing boards met he presided at sessions, hosted dinners and led expeditions to nearby excavation sites almost as briskly as ever.

As the autumn of 1946 chilled toward winter, Edgar and Donizetta Hewett moved, according to their recent custom, from the Lincoln Avenue house in Santa Fe to Albuquerque where the season was milder. Suddenly Hewett suffered a stroke. For a few weeks he rallied and was able to be up and about for brief periods. Then came a second, more severe cerebral hemorrhage, and he was rushed to Presbyterian Hospital where Doni sat faithfully beside him. The doctors said he

The Old Man in his study, 1946. Courtesy of the Museum of New Mexico.

also suffered from uremic poisoning. After a relapse they sent for his closest friend and oldest associate, Paul A. F. Walter. On the morning of December 31, 1946, Edgar Lee Hewett's heart stopped beating. He quietly disappeared over the horizon to the long-anticipated new adventure. His eighty-one years had reached from the close of the Civil War to the end of World War II—a period that may turn out to be the peaking of the United States' power and influence throughout the world.

The *Santa Fe New Mexican* published a fine picture of him on the front page. It must have been taken some years earlier, for it shows a face unwrinkled, the clear eyes gazing out direct and steady, with a quizzical half-smile confirming the humor wrinkles around his eyes. He wears a small, close-cropped mustache, and his white hair has receded far back from his high forehead. The jaw is still firmly set, but its thrust is offset by the parentheses of laughter around his mouth. Paul Walter must have had the long obituary article ready, for the details of Hewett's life filled four columns spread over the first and second pages. At last the *Santa Fe New Mexican* was giving Hewett the homage due to a great man.[10]

The banner headline of that day read: *President Proclaims End to Hostilities.* Hewett thus shared the front page with articles on the termination of President Truman's extraordinary wartime powers and all their implications and with the news of activities scheduled for the following day (January 1, 1947) in Santa Fe, when Thomas J. Mabry would be sworn in as governor and the newly inducted state officials would meet the public at an afternoon reception in the Art Museum. The institutions Hewett had directed for almost forty years continued to function, as he would have wished.

After Hewett's death some of his staff searched for unpublished notes, seeking especially the record of secret lore given to him by his Indian friends. There were no notes. The things that Edgar Hewett felt he must tell had already appeared in the books written during the last twenty years of his life.

The staff members should have known. He told them many times in his writings. In the preface to *Campfire and Trail* he wrote: "Here are the notes of a thousand and one campfires, ready for the incinerator. Some of my colleagues think they should all be saved and published. I think a few samples will do."[11]

And in the first chapter on "Mountain Trails" he muses,

> The old comrades have gone to their blankets. The campfire holds me in silence. Today's trail is a lap in one that led out into my world. I am looking back over it, trying to understand its windings. Yes, it is a long trail. Looking forward I see its farther reaches that promise adventure without end. It leads on "beyond the ranges" and beyond the horizons. Ah, we can guess what lies "beyond the ranges" but beyond the horizons — who can say? I know it to be a trail that will have no end.[12]

It seems entirely in keeping with Hewett's character that, once the manuscript of samples had been completed, the remaining notes should be destroyed.

As he wished, Hewett's body was cremated. Memorial services first planned for late January 1947 were postponed until a Sunday afternoon in August following a significant joint meeting of the boards of the School and the Museum. At that meeting several actions of importance took place: the appointment of Sylvanus G. Morley to succeed Hewett as Director of the School and the Museum was confirmed; the merger proposed by the Board of Trustees of the Laboratory of Anthropology with the Museum of New Mexico was accepted in principle; the Board of the School was enlarged from twenty-eight to thirty-six members. Among those added were Hewett's early student, Alfred Vincent Kidder, and a Santa Fe resident, Amelia E. White, whose benefactions were to have a large impact on the School's future.

It seemed ironic that the merger between the Laboratory and the Museum could not have been accomplished in Hewett's lifetime, but he had known it was brewing for some time. Ratification of the merger by the Legislature was required before the action would be complete.

Following the adjournment of the joint meeting, Hewett's friends met in St. Francis Auditorium of the Art Museum to pay tribute to him. Frederick W. Hodge presided as President of the Board of Regents; Daniel T. Kelly, who had once been a student under Hewett at Las Vegas, unveiled the portrait bust by Cartaino Scarpitta. The memorial address was given by Dr. Rufus B. von Kleinsmid, chancellor of the University of Southern California. Then the throng moved to the patio, where the urn holding Hewett's ashes had been placed in a wall niche on the opposite side of the doors from those of Alice Fletcher and covered by a similar bronze plaque. It was symbolic of the healing of old wounds that Kenneth Chapman, Assistant Director of the Laboratory of Anthropology and a member of the Managing Board of the School, unveiled the plaque.

The inscription reads:

Edgar Lee Hewett

1865-1946

Organizer and First Director

of the

School of American Research

and of the

Museum of New Mexico.

Leader and Inspirer of Youth

Wise Counselor

And True Friend of the Indian

Scientist and

Outstanding American.

22

AFTERMATH

Yes, I see that I am the Dawn Man — limitless, ageless, deathless. Science does not tell me that I shall never cease to exist, but my own Life does. There is that which has been in man, in humanity, in me since Life began — unbroken, timeless, changeless — more sure than anything that Science knows — in truth, the only certainty absolute. That is my Faith. — ELH

In his will, made in 1941 when Edgar Hewett knew that his wife was failing mentally, he attempted to provide for Doni and at the same time conserve the estate. After making some small bequests, he placed his assets in trust for the benefit of his wife during her lifetime and directed that after her death the body of the estate would be turned over to the School of American Research in Santa Fe, "which corporation shall become the permanent trustee therefore, and which shall devote the income therefrom in perpetuity for the advancement of its work in Hispanic America under the name of 'The Hewett Foundation.'" A codicil executed two years later gave the trustees discretion to use the income for: *a*. Research in Hispanic American countries. *b*. Publication by the Director and Associates of said School of works recommended by them. *c*. Stipend of associates and fellows of said School.

In short, Hewett wanted his money used for almost any purpose except regular operating expenses. By the time his will was probated it was forty years since a fellowship stipend of six hundred dollars had started him on his scientific career. He knew what the encouragement could do for dedicated men and women; he had made such help possible for dozens of students through the years.

As the only member of his family who had achieved outstanding success, he had quietly sent financial help to his brother and sister through the years as it was needed. In his instructions to the trustees of the estate he provided: "My obligation

223

to the family of my deceased brother, Alvin, is for the protection of his widow, Sarah, and his son Harvey and wife. My trustees are authorized and directed to continue my present allowance of $30.00 per month to the end of those three lives, provided the money is not needed for my wife's care."[1]

In the expanding, volatile society in which he had lived, Hewett always insisted that there was no such thing as security. Self-reliant in a world where the Horatio Alger story was no myth but a reality repeated many times in the rags-to-riches experiences of his friends, he had made himself a successful entrepreneur in a profession where no amount of money is ever enough. He thought, moreover, that he had made prudent provision for Doni and the others whom he considered somewhat dependent on him.

After Hewett's death, however, it became apparent that Doni would need increasing care for a prolonged period. Jennie Avery, the family friend who had handled much of Hewett's real estate business, was a member of the School's Managing Board, and her place of business was less than a city block from the Hewett home on Lincoln Avenue. She undertook the responsibility for seeing that Doni Hewett, who had no close relatives, did not suffer neglect. Ruth Elvin, longtime Hewett housekeeper, did her best, but Doni was accustomed to making her own decisions or being guided by her husband, and she was not easily managed. Her round-the-clock care became more than one woman could manage, though Ruth set up her own bed on the sleeping porch outside Doni's bedroom where she could hear any unusual sound.

Ruth had another problem in that she needed to find more remunerative employment that would provide her with some future security. Her daughter, who had grown up in the shelter of the Hewett household, was ready for college and no longer needed her supervision. After consultation with Jennie Avery, it was agreed that Ruth would take an outside job but continue to live with Mrs. Hewett and be responsible for her at night. Two longtime friends were engaged as morning and afternoon "sitters." Jennie herself came from the office at noon each day to prepare lunch and check that all was running smoothly. This was stopgap care, predicated on the tacit assumption that Doni would not long outlive her husband.

One evening while Ruth was clearing away the dinner dishes, Doni Hewett disappeared. Ruth searched frantically until nearly midnight, when a policeman brought home her missing charge. It seemed that Mrs. Hewett had decided to go to the movie theatre some three blocks from the house. She stayed through all the performances until the ushers, closing up for the night, found her peacefully asleep in the empty theatre. Not realizing her dependence, they started her homeward — the patrolman found her wandering in the plaza. After that Ruth removed Mrs. Hewett's shoes and stockings at dinnertime, knowing that she would be too proud to step out into the street barefooted.

Some time later Doni walked to the corner of Palace and Lincoln avenues, only a few yards from her front door, to watch a parade. A spectator wheeling a baby carriage pushed against her and she fell from the curb, breaking a hip. In the hospital she was completely irrational, so her friends scheduled themselves to supplement the floor nurses to be sure that she didn't try to climb over the protective side rails of the bed. When she was able to go home, a day nurse was employed to look after her.

All this patchwork care was most unsatisfactory. Without Edgar she was lost. Finally, some six years after Hewett's death, the trustees of the estate, Paul Walter and Al Ely, asked Jennie Avery to find a permanent arrangement that would not require operating the Director's residence for the exclusive care of his widow. It took some time for Jennie to find a solution. On a visit to California she discussed the problem with Tsianina Blackstone, the Indian singer who long before had been Hewett's protégé and had kept up a friendship through the years. Tsianina had retired from her singing career and become a Christian Science practitioner. She owned a large home, with room for the widow of the man who had done so much for her people. Doni Hewett was eighty-six when she went to live with Tsianina. Under Tsianina's loving care she lived to be ninety-two.

In the meantime the annuities expired and the trustees were unable to close the estate. For a period they sent only forty dollars a month to Tsianina, supplemented by funds privately donated by Jennie Avery and other friends. Jennie finally persuaded the School's Board of Managers that they owed a substantial obligation to take care of Hewett's widow, and the monthly stipend was increased for the balance of Doni's life.

Many changes came in the quarter century after Hewett disappeared over the horizon. Following the addition of the Laboratory of Anthropology, the Museum complex was further enlarged by the acquisition of the Folk Art Museum. Only the Museum of Navajo Ceremonial Art remained independent in Santa Fe, and it went through a fallow period of little activity. Then, with the appointment of Hewett's former student, Dr. Bertha Dutton, who retired from the staff of the Museum of New Mexico to become Director of the Navajo Museum, it sprang to life and growth once more.

The School took over the Hewett house on Lincoln Avenue as its headquarters, and most of the land in Santa Fe that Hewett and Springer had bought for the School's expansion as a cultural center was sold to private owners to finance the School's survival. The dream of an Indian Center and a community college for adult education with a large amphitheater quietly faded from memory. When the decision was made to separate the School and the Museum, with independent directors and staffing, the difficult job of deciding the ownership of artifacts and records began. On the death of Amelia E. White in 1972 her extensive property on Garcia Street was bequeathed to the School, and her home was adapted to form its spacious and gracious headquarters.

With all his veneration for the old Palace, it probably occurred to Hewett that it would be an interesting site for archaeological excavation. Indeed, he had a section of the old puddled-adobe wall cut and covered with glass so that visitors could see that part of its history for themselves. When the floor repairs were undertaken from time to time, the few artifacts discovered in small areas were duly salvaged. In the 1970s, when some major excavation was undertaken in the west end of the

Palace where old floors had to be replaced, archaeologists were able to piece out new information, especially about the years when the building was occupied by the Indians between 1680 and 1692.

In recent renovation, since Victorian decor once again became fashionable, some of the nineteenth-century woodwork around windows and doors of the building's interior was uncovered and restored. The renovation was justified with an explanation by a recent member of the Museum's historical staff:

> It is almost a historical truism that each generation despises the taste of the preceding generation. This is certainly borne out by the remodeling of the Palace in the 1909-1913 period. The attempt was made to eradicate all the vestiges of the 19th century style. The Palace of the Governors was remade into the "Santa Fe style" of architecture. No attempt was made to preserve the entire range of New Mexico history; in fact, the only history considered worthy of the name was that of the colonial period. The attempt was made to turn back the clock to the 17th or 18th century....
>
> On the basis of the flimsiest of evidence and considerable imagination the building was redone. The present facade is that of the romantic early 20th century rather than the authentic colonial architecture. In fact, the interior stylized windows and doorways are only made possible by modern plaster and metal lath. Walls were removed and Victorian fireplaces "puebloized."
>
> Nor did the removal of the 19th century features stop in 1913; as late as 1954 brick coping on the back buildings was removed or covered with stucco. Unfortunately the major thrust of consideration of the Palace has been as a museum rather than as a historic structure. From the first cutting of a doorway between the two east rooms until recent times the prime structural consideration has been to facilitate its use as a museum. This is not to say that this is the only consideration the building has received.[2]

Had Edgar Hewett been primarily an historian, he probably would have concurred, but he might have reminded the writer that efforts to preserve the building for its historical importance were unavailing until it became a museum. Certainly he would have been a fascinated spectator at the "dig" in the west rooms. L. Bradford and Mary Prince would have been happy with the recently installed exhibit which recreates the reception room in which they entertained so regally, and they might even have been pleased that the east end of the building houses a historical library, maintained to this day, though the archival material was moved at long last to a state archives building.

In the Fine Arts building a retrospective exhibit was hung in 1975 honoring the most famous of the Canyon Road School — *Los Cinco Pintores*. Of the original five only Josef Bakos was present at the opening, though Fremont Ellis, the other surviving member, sent his regrets and his daughter to represent him. Josef Bakos has since died, in 1977. Walter Mruk died in 1942, Willard Nash in 1943, and Will Shuster, world famous for his creation of Zozobra — Old Man Gloom — which is burned in a forty-foot effigy each year at Santa Fe's Fiesta, died in 1969. The paintings on exhibit were loaned by relatives and friends; it was surprising how amateurish much of that early work looked in comparison with the artists' later mastery. The opening reception was a gathering of old-timers who were happy to reminisce together.

Almost any day a group of young musicians can be heard rehearsing for an upcoming concert in St. Francis Auditorium, where the Beauregard-Vierra-Chapman murals still grace the walls. The McNary organ reverberates from the vigas as the organist pumps the pedals. Someone may be sitting in the patio where the plaques of Fletcher and Hewett watch quietly from the first yellow daffodils of spring to the sleet and snow of winter. Tourists move through the rooms where a collection of early Indian paintings may be shown, or pause to wander about the latest nonobjective show. Controversy still rages among artists, with the contemporary group and the traditionalists, the nonobjective school and the representationalists vying for exhibition space. It has been many years since all comers could hang in the museum. All showings are juried or by invitation.

The old Elks' Club across Lincoln Avenue from the Hewett residence has been acquired by the Museum, which has moved some administrative functions into it. Most recently a block of private property on the west side of Lincoln Avenue has been purchased. This included acquisition of the Director's residence by the state, through purchase from the School. Ambitious plans have been made for the future development of the Museum. After a lively controversy as to whether the Hewett house should be restored to its old appearance as an officers' barracks, remodeled with few changes from the Hewett days, or demolished to make way for a plaza, it was decided to preserve the house and incorporate it in the expanded Art Museum.

In the Jemez Mountains, the elite Los Alamos Ranch School (which once helped to block the project for turning the Pajarito Plateau into a national park) was replaced by the Los Alamos Scientific Laboratory and its supporting city during World War II. Most of the high mesa and canyon country of the plateau is now federally controlled in restricted areas, national monuments or as Indian reservation land. The lovely little Rito de los Frijoles that once flowed through wilderness in Bandelier National Monument is now flanked by the picnic tables and rock fireplaces of a public campground administered by the Park Service.

If Bandelier, Lummis or Hewett dropped in on Bandelier National Monument for a casual visit, he could spend a few hours of sightseeing, perhaps listen to the spiel of the guide, or purchase postcards to mail to friends. He would scarcely recognize the site as the place where he dreamed of the past and slept under the stars half a century ago. Some areas of Bandelier National Monument have been inundated by the water backed up by Cochiti Dam, forming an artificial lake for recreation and flood control near Cochiti Pueblo to the south. Salvage archaeologists worked diligently to save what they could of the ancient sites before they vanished forever under the impounded waters of the Rio Grande. Conservationists worry that the new accessibility by boat will bring too many visitors, thus destroying forever the remote, wilderness character of the area.

In San Diego a visitor to the well-kept museums in Balboa Park will find no one who remembers Hewett personally, though his name is recognized as one associated in some vague capacity with the Museum of Man. Many installations acquired during the 1915 Exposition are still exhibited from time to time, and the murals painted by Cassidy and Vierra have not been erased. The Vierra murals showing the ruins of Copán, Uxmal, Quirigua, Palenque, Chichen Itzá, and Tikal as Hewett and his associates knew them form a valuable record of the way they looked before extensive excavation and restoration.

Hewett's old college in San Diego has become California State University, San Diego, with a tremendous expansion of the campus and the student body. The chair of anthropology is held by Arthur J. O. Anderson, who sat under Hewett in his earliest exposure to the science and worked in the field schools in New Mexico. Dr. Anderson remembers his teacher with warm affection.

A 1975 article entitled "Digging in the Past" in the magazine *Newsweek* states, "Archaeology, by its very nature, moves at a slow and deliberate pace, yet it is in the midst of a quiet revolution today. No longer does the study of history and prehistory confine itself to quests for exotic art objects that glorified kings and chieftains in times past. Today, archaeologists are trying to put together a working picture of how ancient societies — particularly the common people in those societies — behaved."[3]

One can imagine Hewett and friends, bivouacked by a dancing campfire some place among the stars — perhaps among the Pleiades — smiling in contentment at the news.

The Hewett garden at the rear of their Lincoln Avenue home in Santa Fe. Courtesy of the Museum of New Mexico.

NOTES

EPIGRAPHS

(By Edgar L. Hewett unless otherwise indicated.)

CHAPTER 1. *Two Score Years* (Albuquerque: University of New Mexico Press, 1946), foreword, unpaginated.

CHAPTER 2. Adolph F. Bandelier, *Indians of the Rio Grande Valley* (Albuquerque: University of New Mexico Press, 1937), p. 115.

CHAPTER 3. *Two Score Years*, foreword, unpaginated.

CHAPTER 4. *From Cave Dwelling to Mount Olympus*, Man in the Pageant of the Ages (Albuquerque: University of New Mexico Press, 1943), p. 2.

CHAPTER 5. *Man and Culture*, Man in the Pageant of the Ages (Albuquerque: University of New Mexico Press, 1944), p. 60.

CHAPTER 6. *Two Score Years*, p. 22.

CHAPTER 7. *Man and Culture*, p. 47.

CHAPTER 8. "A Science of Man and a Science of Education," address to Colorado State College of Education, June 15, 1940, *From Cave Dwelling to Mount Olympus*, p. 99.

CHAPTER 9. *Campfire and Trail* (Albuquerque: University of New Mexico Press, 1945), p. 150.

CHAPTER 10. *Campfire and Trail*, p. 150.

CHAPTER 11. Deuteronomy 6:8, from the Latin Vulgate of St. Jerome, inscribed on the California Building, Balboa Park, San Diego, CA.

CHAPTER 12 *Man and Culture*, p. 70.

CHAPTER 13. *From Cave Dwelling to Mount Olympus*, p. 2.

CHAPTER 14. *Ibid.*, p. 3.

CHAPTER 15. *The Quest for Freedom*, commencement address at Knox College, June 14, 1939 (Santa Fe, 1939).

CHAPTER 16. *Campfire and Trail*, p. 80.

CHAPTER 17. *Man and Culture*, p. 23.

CHAPTER 18. *Man and Culture*, p. 61.

CHAPTER 19. *Ibid.*, p. 123.

CHAPTER 20. *Pajarito Plateau and Its Ancient People* (Albuquerque: University of New Mexico Press, 1938), p. 17.

CHAPTER 21. *Ibid.*, p. 19.

CHAPTER 22. *Campfire and Trail*, pp. 164-65.

CHAPTER 1

1. Edgar L. Hewett, *Two Score Years* (Albuquerque: University of New Mexico Press, 1946), p. 3.
2. Harvey James Hewett to Waterman and Patience Hewett, April 24, 1839, Harvey James Hewett Collection, Museum of New Mexico, Santa Fe, NM.
3. Miriam Hewett to Waterman Hewett, November 3, 1850, Harvey James Hewett Collection.
4. Hewett, *Two Score Years*, p. 22.
5. *Ibid.*, p. 27.
6. *Ibid.*, p. 37.
7. *Ibid.*, p. 10.
8. *Ibid.*, pp. 8-9.
9. *Ibid.*, p. 6.
10. In a tribute to Edgar L. Hewett, Paul A. F. Walter said that the Hewett family went to Chicago in 1873 and returned in 1880 "to farm life in Hopkins, Missouri." "Edgar Lee Hewett, Americanist, 1865-1946," *American Anthropologist* 49, no. 2 (1947): 260.

CHAPTER 2

1. Lewis Henry Morgan, *Houses and Home Life of the American Aborigines,* ed. Paul Bohanan, Classics in Anthropology Series (Chicago: London: University of Chicago Press, 1965), p. v.
2. Adolph F. Bandelier and Lewis Henry Morgan, *The Bandelier-Morgan Letters, 1873-1883,* vol. 1, ed. Leslie A. White (Albuquerque: University of New Mexico Press, 1940), p. 48.
3. Adolph F. Bandelier, *The Southwestern Journals of Adolph F. Bandelier, 1880-1882,* ed. Charles H. Lange and Carroll L. Riley (Albuquerque: University of New Mexico Press and School of American Research, 1966), p. 71.
4. Adolph F. Bandelier, *The Southwestern Journals of Adolph F. Bandelier, 1885-1888,* ed. Charles H. Lange; Carroll L. Riley; and Elizabeth M. Lange (Albuquerque: University of New Mexico Press and School of American Research, 1975), p. 3.
5. Adolph F. Bandelier, *The Delight Makers* (New York: Dodd, Mead & Co., 1890), pp.3-4.

CHAPTER 3

1. Edgar L. Hewett, *Two Score Years* (Albuquerque: University of New Mexico Press, 1946), foreword, unpaginated.
2. *Ibid.*, p. 89.
3. *Ibid.*, p. 98.

CHAPTER 4

1. Agnes Morley Cleaveland, *No Life for a Lady* (Boston: Houghton Mifflin Co., 1941), p. 223.

2. *Ibid.*, p. 224.

3. *Ibid.*, p. 225.

4. Lansing B. Bloom, "Edgar Lee Hewett: His Biography and Writings to Date," *So Live the Works of Men*, ed. Donald D. Brand and Fred E. Harvey (Albuquerque: University of New Mexico Press and School of American Research, 1939), p. 16.

5. Edgar L. Hewett, "Introduction," *Papers of the School of American Research* 44 (1951): 2.

CHAPTER 5

1. Edgar L. Hewett, *Campfire and Trail* (Albuquerque: University of New Mexico Press, 1943), pp. 142-43.

2. *Ibid.*, p. 144.

3. Edgar L. Hewett, *The Call of the Spade*, a leaflet with no identifying data on it, Beatrice Chauvenet Collection.

4. *Campfire and Trail*, p. 150.

5. *Ibid.*, preface, unpaginated.

CHAPTER 6

1. Edgar L. Hewett, *Two Score Years* (Albuquerque: University of New Mexico Press, 1946), p. 120.

2. Edgar L. Hewett to "Little Friend," undated, Edgar L. Hewett Collection 1907, Museum of New Mexico, Santa Fe, NM.

3. Sterling Dow, "Report of the President," *Bulletin of the Archaeological Institute of America* 37 (1946): 3.

4. Edgar L. Hewett to William H. Holmes, June 12, 1906, Edgar L. Hewett Collection 1906.

5. Edgar L. Hewett to George Mills, March 7, 1907, Edgar L. Hewett Collection 1907.

CHAPTER 7

1. "Cliff Dwellings To Be Put in Cañon Close to Manitou," *Colorado Springs Gazette*, May 1, 1906.

2. Edgar L. Hewett to Atherton Noyes, February 15, 1907, Edgar L. Hewett Collection 1907, Museum of New Mexico, Santa Fe, NM.

3. Edgar L. Hewett to Lucy E. Peabody, March 10, 1907, Edgar L. Hewett Collection 1907.

4. This series of letters is in the Edgar L. Hewett Collection 1907.

5. Edgar L. Hewett to Lucy E. Peabody, March 14, 1907, May 17, 1907, Edgar L. Hewett Collection 1907.

6. Lucy E. Peabody to Edgar L. Hewett, August 6, 1907, Edgar L. Hewett Collection 1907.

CHAPTER 8

1. Hubert Howe Bancroft, *Arizona and New Mexico*, The Works of Hubert Howe Bancroft, vol. 17 (San Francisco: The History Company, 1889), p. 640.

2. *Ibid.*, p. 716.

3. Ralph Emerson Twitchell, *Leading Facts of New Mexico History*, vol. 2 (Cedar Rapids, Iowa: The Torch Press, 1912), p. 503, n. 422.

4. Lew Wallace, untitled paper, Lew Wallace Collection, New Mexico Records Center and Archives, Santa Fe, NM.

5. Calvin Horn, *New Mexico's Troubled Years* (Albuquerque: Horn and Wallace, 1963), p. 208. In his footnote the author gives his source as Susan E. Wallace, *The Land of the Pueblos* (Troy, Nims & Knight, 1889), unpaginated.

6. *Ibid.*

7. Nancy A. Melin, "Santa Fe and Governor Prince," *El Palacio* 80, no. 3 (1974) 31.

8. *Ibid.*

9. Bancroft, *Arizona and New Mexico*, p. 790.

CHAPTER 9

1. Lansing B. Bloom, "Edgar Lee Hewett: His Biography and Writings to Date," *So Live the Works of Men*, ed. Donald D. Brand and Fred E. Harvey (Albuquerque: University of New Mexico Press and School of American Research, 1939), p. 20.

2. Edgar L. Hewett to John R. McFie, February 14, 1907, Edgar L. Hewett Collection 1907, Museum of New Mexico, Santa Fe, NM.

3. W.G. Tight to Edgar L. Hewett, February 22, 1907, Edgar L. Hewett Collection 1907.

4. W.G. Tight to Edgar L. Hewett, March 29, 1907, Edgar L. Hewett Collection 1907.

5. Edgar L. Hewett to John R. McFie, February 14, 1907, Edgar L. Hewett Collection 1907.

6. A copy of House Joint Resolution No. 6, labelled by a hand-written note in margin, "Copy for Judge McFie," with a cover letter from John R. McFie to Edgar L. Hewett, March 20, 1907, stating that the resolution was passed by the Legislative Assembly without opposition, Edgar L. Hewett Collection 1907.

7. John R. McFie to Edgar L. Hewett, June 4, 1907, Edgar L. Hewett Collection 1907.

8. Ralph Emerson Twitchell, *Leading Facts of New Mexico History*, vol. 2 (Cedar Rapids: The Torch Press, 1912), pp. 573-74 n. 483.

9. *Ibid.*

10. Ina S. Cassidy to Beatrice Chauvenet, interview, August 1954, Beatrice Chauvenet Collection.

11. Edgar L. Hewett, *Campfire and Trail* (Albuquerque: University of New Mexico Press, 1943), pp. 151-52.

CHAPTER 10

1. Edgar L. Hewett to D.I. Bushnell, November 7, 1911, Edgar L. Hewett Collection 1911, Museum of New Mexico, Santa Fe, NM.

2. This exchange of letters is in the Edgar L. Hewett Collection 1911.

3. Governor William J. Mills, Judge John R. McFie and Nathan Jaffa to Donizetta M. Wood, November 14, 1911, Edgar L. Hewett Collection 1911.

4. Edgar L. Hewett to Frederick W. Hodge, June 19, 1911, Edgar L. Hewett Collection 1911.

5. Franz Boas to Francis W. Kelsey, December 16, 1910, Edgar L. Hewett File of Minutes and Correspondence of the American Institute of Archaeology and the School of American Archaeology 1909-1916, Museum of New Mexico, Santa Fe, NM.

6. Edgar L. Hewett, *Campfire and Trail* (Albuquerque: University of New Mexico Press, 1943), p. 16.

7. Ronald P. Rohner, *Pioneers of American Archaeology* (Seattle: University of Washington Press, 1966), p. 181.

8. Hewett, *Campfire and Trail*, p. 16.

9. Edgar L. Hewett to Franz Boas, May 11, 1911, Edgar L. Hewett Collection 1911. A reprint, without identifying source, of the entire Boas correspondence in the matter is in the 1911 correspondence.

10. R. E. Twitchell to Edgar L. Hewett, February 28, 1911, Edgar L. Hewett Collection 1911.

11. Jesse Nusbaum to Edgar L. Hewett, December 13, 1911, Edgar L. Hewett Collection 1911.

12. *Ibid.*

13. Jesse Nusbaum to Edgar L. Hewett, December 19, 1911, Edgar L. Hewett Collection 1911.

14. Barbara Freire-Marreco to Edgar L. Hewett, September 13, 1911, Edgar L. Hewett Collection 1911. Miss Freire-Marreco was associated with the London School of Economics and was working among the American Indians under a grant from the Somerville College Research Fund.

15. Sumner P. Hunt to Mr. Neusbaum (sic) c/o School of Amer. Archaeology, February 1, 1911, Edgar L. Hewett Collection 1911.

CHAPTER 11

1. Gov. Jack Campbell, "The Decline of the Republican Party 1910-1925," August 20, 1967. Remarks in a lecture series, *Political Happenings in New Mexico Since Statehood*, sponsored by the Santa Fe Historical Society at La Fonda. Copy supplied from his file by Gov. Campbell, Beatrice Chauvenet Collection.

2. Edgar L. Hewett to Members of the Executive Committee, School of American Archaeology, November 7, 1911, Edgar L. Hewett Collection 1911, Museum of New Mexico, Santa Fe, NM.

3. Frederick W. Hodge to Edgar L. Hewett, June 12, 1911, Edgar L. Hewett Collection 1911.

4. Edgar L. Hewett to Minor C. Keith, November 6, 1911, Edgar L. Hewett Collection 1911.

5. Jesse Nusbaum to Edgar L. Hewett, December 19, 1911, Edgar L. Hewett Collection 1911.

6. Florence Christman, *The Romance of Balboa park*, 2nd edition (San Diego: Neyenesch Printers, Inc., 1973), p. 48.

7. D. C. Collier to Edgar L. Hewett, November 11, 1911, Edgar L. Hewett Collection 1911.

8. G. A. Davidson in *Exposition News*, December 1911.

9. *Exposition News*, October 1912.

10. Edgar L. Hewett, "Ancient America at the Panama-California Exposition," reprint from *The Theosophical Path*, February 1915, unpaginated, Edgar L. Hewett Collection 1915.

11. "The Panama-California Exposition, 1915," *The Theosophical Path*, February 1915, Edgar L. Hewett Collection 1915.

CHAPTER 12

1. "Santa Fe Is Declared 'The Oldest City' in the United States," *Santa Fe New Mexican*, September 17, 1913.

2. This and following letters concerning Santa Fe as the oldest city, Edgar L. Hewett Collection 1913, Museum of New Mexico, Santa Fe, NM.

3. Edgar L. Hewett to R.E. Twitchell, July 25, 1913, Edgar L. Hewett Collection 1913.

4. "What Santa Fe Still Needs," *Santa Fe New Mexican*, October 3, 1913.

5. "My Board Takes Orders from E.L. Hewett," *Santa Fe New Mexican*, October 9, 1913.

6. *Ibid.*

7. "Many Offer Quarters to Chamber of Commerce," *Santa Fe New Mexican*, October 9, 1913.

8. "How Four Scientists Regard E.L. Hewett," *Santa Fe New Mexican*, October 27, 1913.

9. "No Danger of Losing the School," *Santa Fe New Mexican*, November 12, 1913.

10. Paul A.F. Walter to Edgar L. Hewett, November 15, 1913, Edgar L. Hewett Collection 1914.

11. H.H. Dorman et al. to Prof. F.W. Shipley, President of the Archaeological Institute of America, December 20, 1913, Edgar L. Hewett Collection 1913-1914.

12. Edgar L. Hewett to John R. McFie, January 3, 1914, Edgar L. Hewett Collection 1914.

13. Edgar L. Hewett to Paul A.F. Walter, February 5, 1917, Edgar L. Hewett Collection 1917.

CHAPTER 13

1. Edgar L. Hewett, *Two Score Years* (Albuquerque: University of New Mexico Press, 1946), p. 28.

2. J.K. Shishkin, *An Early History of the Museum of New Mexico Fine Arts Building*, Museum of New Mexico Press, 1968, unpaginated.

3. José D. Sena, letter to *Santa Fe New Mexican*, April 21, 1915.

4. Paul A.F. Walter to Edgar L. Hewett, November 14, 1916, Edgar L. Hewett Collection 1915, Museum of New Mexico, Santa Fe, NM.

5. Edgar L. Hewett to D.C. Collier, September 1, 1917, Edgar L. Hewett Collection 1917.

6. Edgar L. Hewett's speech, "On Opening the New Museum," 9-13; Frank Springer's address, "Dedicatory Words," 5-7; Francis W. Kelsey's address, "The New Humanism," 4-29; and Natalie Burlin's article, "The Indian's Part," 31-32, were published in *Art and Archaeology* 7, nos. 1 and 2 (1918), a double number edited by Hewett and W.H. Holmes which was devoted almost exclusively to the opening of the Santa Fe Art Museum.

7. Edgar L. Hewett to Mrs. Cabot Ward, February 6, 1918, Edgar L. Hewett Collection 1918.

CHAPTER 14

1. Edgar L. Hewett To W. H. Holmes, August 23, 1917, Edgar L. Hewett Collection 1917, Museum of New Mexico, Santa Fe, NM.

2. Edgar L. Hewett to Alice Klauber, December 19, 1918, Edgar L. Hewett Collection 1918.

3. Information regarding beginnings of Taos art colony was provided by Helen Blumenschein, daughter of Ernest L. Blumenschein, in several interviews with Beatrice Chauvenet and letter of October 27, 1980, Beatrice Chauvenet Collection.

4. "Cassidy Exhibit of Paintings at Old Palace," *Santa Fe New Mexican*, January 15, 1916, in Oliver LaFarge, *Santa Fe. The Autobiography of a Southwestern Town* (Norman: University of Oklahoma Press, 1959), p. 222.

5. "Work of William Penhallow Henderson Ranks Very High," *Santa Fe New Mexican*, April 1, 1916, in LaFarge, *Santa Fe*, p. 224.

6. Mary Austin to Edgar L. Hewett, October 10, 1918, Edgar L. Hewett Collection 1918.

7. Mary Austin to Paul A. F. Walter, March 20 (1919 or 1920?), Edgar L. Hewett Collection 1919.

8. "Real Bolshevists," *Santa Fe New Mexican*, September 29, 1920.

9. Alice C. Henderson to the *Santa Fe New Mexican* (draft), October 11, 1920, Edgar L. Hewett Collection 1920.

10. *Ibid.*, unsigned marginal note written in longhand on last page of draft. Could have been written by Bronson Cutting or E. Dana Johnson, editor of the *Santa Fe New Mexican*.

11. Bronson Cutting to Natalie Burlin, October 29, 1920 (copy), Edgar L. Hewett Collection 1920.

12. *Ibid.*

13. *Ibid.*

14. Robert Henri to Edgar L. Hewett, December 20, 1920, Edgar L. Hewett Collection 1920.

15. Edgar L. Hewett, "Art Policy of Museum and School," *El Palacio* 10, no. 5 (1921): 2-216.

CHAPTER 15

1. Edgar L. Hewett, "The Conquest of War," *Man and Culture*, Man in the Pageant of the Ages (Albuquerque: University of New Mexico Press, 1944), p. 105.

2. Ruth Seligman to Beatrice Chauvenet, interview, August 21, 1963, Beatrice Chauvenet Collection.

3. "Plaza Fiesta Will Be Great," *Santa Fe New Mexican*, July 4, 1912, in Oliver LaFarge, *Santa Fe. The Autobiography of a Southwestern Town* (Norman: University of Oklahoma Press, 1959), p. 209.

4. "Pueblos Gather in Barbaric Splendor to Participate in the 'Indian Day,' Opening Santa Fe Fiesta in Blaze of Glory," *Santa Fe New Mexican*, September 6, 1921.

5. *Ibid.*

6. "'Buenos Noches' of Old Santa Fe Delightfully Shown at Fiesta," *Santa Fe New Mexican*, September 7, 1921.

7. *Ibid.*

8. "Zuni Runners in Race Round the Circle Drive," *Santa Fe New Mexican*, September 8, 1921.

9. "A Marvelous People," *Santa Fe New Mexican*, September 6, 1922, in LaFarge, *Santa Fe*, p. 273.

10. "The 1924 Santa Fe Fiesta," *El Palacio* 17, nos. 6-7 (1924): 132.

11. *Ibid.*, 137.

12. Tsianina Blackstone, *Where Trails Have Led Me* (Santa Fe: Vergara Printing Co., 1970), p. 35.

13. *Ibid.*, p. 37.

14. *Ibid.*, p. 77.

15. *Ibid.*, p. 39.

16. *Ibid.*, p. 112.

17. Edgar L. Hewett, "Alice C. Fletcher Memorial Meeting," *El Palacio* 15, no. 5 (1923): 85.

18. Charles F. Lummis, "In Memoriam," *El Palacio* 15, no. 6 (1923): 94.

CHAPTER 16

1. Edgar L. Hewett to Grant Wallace, June 19, 1919, Edgar L. Hewett Collection 1919, Museum of New Mexico, Santa Fe, NM.

2. Lewis B. Paton to Edgar L. Hewett, May 22, 1923, Edgar L. Hewett Collection 1923.

3. Edgar L. Hewett, *Campfire and Trail* (Albuquerque: University of New Mexico Press, 1943), p. 96.

4. *Ibid.*, p. 98.

5. Edgar L. Hewett to Albert T. Clay, February 25, 1924, Edgar L. Hewett Collection 1924.

6. R. V. D. Magoffin to Edgar L. Hewett, June 27, 1924, Edgar L. Hewett Collection 1924.

CHAPTER 17

1. A copy of the reporter's letter, dated December 5, 1926, with the names of the reporter and recipient omitted, Edgar L. Hewett Collection 1926, Museum of New Mexico, Santa Fe, NM.

2. *Ibid.*

3. Kyle S. Crichton, "Philistine and Artist Clash in Battle of Santa Fe," *New York World*, June 27, 1926. Copy in files of Old Santa Fe Association, Santa Fe, NM.

4. *Ibid.*

5. *Ibid.*

6. *Ibid.*

7. *Ibid.*

8. *Ibid.*

9. Reporter's letter, December 5, 1926, Edgar L. Hewett Collection 1926.

10. Copy of reply to *ibid.*, dated "Friday," Edgar L. Hewett Collection 1926.

11. The Old Santa Fe Association, "An Open Letter to the Federated Club Women of Texas," undated, Edgar L. Hewett Collection 1926.

12. *Ibid.*

13. Paul A. F. Walter to Mrs. N. B. Laughlin, January 7, 1927, Edgar L. Hewett Collection 1927.

14. Texas Federation of Women's Clubs to Mrs. Francis C. Wilson and Mrs. Ashley Pond, November 10, 1926. A copy is attached to a letter on the letterhead of the Texas Federation of Women's Clubs from Mrs. W.C. Martin, chairman, Culture Center, to Paul A.F. Walter, December 24, 1926, Edgar L. Hewett Collection 1926.

15. Paul A.F. Walter to Milburn Hobson, November 27, 1926, Edgar L. Hewett Collection 1926.

16. Edgar L. Hewett to Hartley Burr Alexander, May 24, 1926; Edgar L. Hewett to Percy Jackson, May 22, 1926; Edgar L. Hewett to Mrs. H.K. Estabrook, June 7, 1926, Edgar L. Hewett Collection 1926.

17. Oliver LaFarge, *Santa Fe. The Autobiography of a Southwestern Town* (Norman: University of Oklahoma Press, 1959), p. 294.

CHAPTER 18

1. C.J. Crandall to Edgar L. Hewett, July 23, 1925, Edgar L. Hewett Collection 1925, Museum of New Mexico, Santa Fe, NM.

2. R.V.D. Magoffin to Edgar L. Hewett, August 18, 1926, Edgar L. Hewett Collection 1926.

CHAPTER 19

1. George W. Marston to Edgar L. Hewett, September 1, 1926, Edgar L. Hewett Collection 1927, Museum of New Mexico, Santa Fe, NM.

2. Edgar L. Hewett to Santa Fe Chamber of Commerce, June 26, 1927, Edgar L. Hewett Collection 1927.

3. Lansing B. Bloom, "Edgar Lee Hewett: His Biography and Writings to Date," *So Live the Works of Men*, ed. Donald D. Brand and Fred E. Harvey (Albuquerque: University of New Mexico Press, 1939), p. 22.

4. Edgar L. Hewett to D.C. Collier, October 2, 1929, Edgar L. Hewett Collection 1929.

5. Edgar L. Hewett to Percy Jackson, May 22, 1926, Edgar L. Hewett Collection 1926.

6. H.K. Raymenton, *San Diego's Exposition* (San Diego, 1963), unpaginated. Copy in file of San Diego Historical Society, Serra Museum, San Diego, CA.

CHAPTER 20

1. Arthur Stanley Riggs to Edgar L. Hewett, June 30, 1930, Edgar L. Hewett Collection 1930, Museum of New Mexico, Santa Fe, NM.

2. Edgar L. Hewett to Arthur Stanley Riggs, June 10, 1930, Edgar L. Hewett Collection 1930.

3. Edgar L. Hewett, *Campfire and Trail* (Albuquerque: University of New Mexico Press, 1943), p. 160.

4. Edgar L. Hewett, *Pajarito Plateau and Its Ancient People* (Albuquerque: University of New Mexico Press, 1938), p. 13.

5. Edgar L. Hewett and Adolph Bandelier, *Indians of the Rio Grande Valley* (Albuquerque: University of New Mexico Press, 1937), p. 20.

CHAPTER 21

1. Edgar L. Hewett to Mr. and Mrs. Miller, May 11, 1938, Edgar L. Hewett Collection 1938, Museum of New Mexico, Santa Fe, NM.

2. Edgar L. Hewett, *Man and Culture*, Man in the Pageant of the Ages (Albuquerque: University of New Mexico Press, 1944), p. 105.

3. *Ibid.*, p. 117.

4. Edgar L. Hewett to John Harrington, April 16, 1942, Edgar L. Hewett Collection 1942.

5. Edgar L. Hewett, "Ales Hrdlicka: An Appreciation," *El Palacio* 50, no. 10 (1943): 246-49.

6. "Dr. Franz Boas Dies," *El Palacio* 50, no. 1 (1943): 24.

7. Edgar L. Hewett, "James Fulton Zimmerman," *El Palacio* 51, no. 11 (1944): 205.

8. C. T. Currelly to Edgar L. Hewett, February 28, 1945, Edgar L. Hewett Collection 1945.

9. Genevieve Shenk to Beatrice Chauvenet, interview, about 1975 (exact date not recorded), Beatrice Chauvenet Collection.

10. "Dr. Edgar L. Hewett Dies in Albuquerque," *Santa Fe New Mexican*, December 31, 1946.

11. Edgar L. Hewett, *Campfire and Trail* (Albuquerque: University of New Mexico Press, 1943), preface, unpaginated.

12. Edgar L. Hewett, *Campfire and Trail*, p. 4.

CHAPTER 22

1. Edgar L. Hewett, Codicil to Will, File Number 2103, Probate Court Records, Santa Fe County, NM.

2. Michael F. Weber, "The Problems of Preservation," *El Palacio* 80, no. 3 (1974): 39.

3. "Digging in the Past," *Newsweek* (August 25, 1975): 44.

WORKS CITED

The principal source of information for this book is the Edgar L. Hewett Collection in the History Library of the Museum of New Mexico, Santa Fe, New Mexico, a document collection of Hewett's personal and business papers written between 1905 and 1946. The collection is arranged as nearly as possible as Hewett had it, chronologically, with some topics set apart from the chronology.

Hewett's published writings illustrate how he used and reused material, drawing on lectures and reports for articles in periodicals and for his books, which were issued between 1930 and 1946. The reader is referred to *The Bibliography of Edgar L. Hewett, 1893-1944,* compiled by Leslie V. Murphey, Librarian, School of American Research, Santa Fe, New Mexico, 1944, supplemented with additional titles for 1945 and 1946, for a listing of Hewett's published works.

UNPUBLISHED MATERIALS

Beatrice Chauvenet Collection
Kenneth Chapman File, School of American Research, Santa Fe, New Mexico
Edgar L. Hewett Collection, History Library, Museum of New Mexico, Santa Fe, New Mexico
Harvey James Hewett Collection, History Library, Museum of New Mexico, Santa Fe, New Mexico
Estate of Edgar Lee Hewett, Santa Fe County Probate Court Records, Santa Fe, New Mexico

PUBLISHED MATERIALS
Works by Edgar L. Hewett

"Ales Hrdlicka: An Appreciation." *El Palacio* 50, no. 10 (1943): 246-49.
"Alice C. Fletcher Memorial Meeting." *El Palacio* 15, no. 5 (1923): 83-88.
"Ancient America at the Panama-California Exposition," reprint from *The Theosophical Path,* February 1915.
Ancient Andean Life. Indianapolis: Bobbs-Merrill Co., Inc., 1939.
Ancient Life in Mexico and Central America. Indianapolis: Bobbs-Merrill Co., Inc., 1936.

Ancient Life in the American Southwest. Indianapolis: Bobbs-Merrill Co., Inc., 1930.

Archaeology. Report of the Governor of New Mexico on the Archaeology of the Territory, to the Secretary of the Interior. Washington, D.C.: Government Printing Office, 1903.

"Art Policy of Museum and School." *El Palacio* 10, no. 5 (1921): 2-3.

Baccalaureate Addresses (1899-1903). San Diego: Arts and Crafts Press, 1903.

The Call of the Spade. N.p., n.d.

Campfire and Trail. Albuquerque: University of New Mexico Press, 1943.

The Chaco Canyon and Its Monuments. Albuquerque: University of New Mexico Press, 1936.

From Cave Dwelling to Mount Olympus. Man in the Pageant of the Ages. Albuquerque: University of New Mexico Press, 1943.

"James Fulton Zimmerman." *El Palacio* 51, no. 11 (1944): 205-6.

Man and Culture. Man in the Pageant of the Ages. Albuquerque: University of New Mexico Press, 1944.

Man and the State. Man in the Pageant of the Ages. Albuquerque: University of New Mexico Press, 1944.

Pajarito Plateau and Its Ancient People. Albuquerque: University of New Mexico Press, 1938.

"The Proposed National Park of the Cliff Cities." *El Palacio* 3, no. 3 (1916): 50-56. *The Quest for Freedom.* Commencement address at Knox College, June 14, 1939, Santa Fe, 1939.

The Student's Goal. Baccalaureate address to graduating class, Normal University, Las Vegas, New Mexico, 1919. Santa Fe: Santa Fe New Mexican Press, 1919.

Two Score Years. Albuquerque: University of New Mexico Press, 1946.

With Adolph Bandelier. *Indians of the Rio Grande Valley.* Albuquerque: University of New Mexico Press, 1937.

With Bertha Dutton. *The Pueblo Indian World.* Albuquerque: University of New Mexico Press, 1945.

With Reginald F. Fisher. *Mission Monuments of New Mexico.* Albuquerque: University of New Mexico Press, 1943.

With Wayne L. Mauzy. *Landmarks of New Mexico.* Albuquerque: University of New Mexico Press, 1940.

Works by Other Writers

America 1870-1900, The Fabulous Century. New York: Time-Life Books, 1970.

Bancroft, Hubert Howe. *Arizona and New Mexico.* The Works of Hubert Howe Bancroft, vol. 17. San Francisco: The History Company, 1889.

Bandelier, Adolph F. *The Delight Makers.* New York: Dodd, Mead & Co., 1890.

———. *The Southwestern Journals of Adolph F. Bandelier 1880-1882.* Edited by Charles H. Lange and Carroll L. Riley. Albuquerque: University of New Mexico Press and School of American Research, 1966.

———. *The Southwestern Journals of Adolph F. Bandelier 1883-1884.* Edited by Charles H. Lange; Carroll L. Riley; and Elizabeth M. Lange. Albuquerque: University of New Mexico Press and School of American Research, 1970.

———. *The Southwestern Journals of Adolph Bandelier 1885-1888.* Edited by Charles H. Lange; Carroll L. Riley; and Elizabeth M. Lange. Albuquerque: University of New Mexico Press and School of American Research, 1975.

With Lewis Henry Morgan. *The Bandelier-Morgan Letters, 1873-1883,* vol. 1. Edited by Leslie A. White. Albuquerque: University of New Mexico Press, 1940.

Blackstone, Tsianina. *Where Trails Have Led Me.* Santa Fe: Vergara Printing Co., 1970.

Brand, Donald D., and Fred E. Harvey, eds. *So Live the Works of Men.* Albuquerque: University of New Mexico Press and School of American Research, 1939.

"'Buenos Noches' of Old Santa Fe Delightfully Shown at Fiesta." *Santa Fe New Mexican,* September 7, 1921.

Cable, Mary, and the editors of *American Heritage. American Manners and Morals. A Picture History of How We Behave and Misbehave.* New York: American Heritage Publishing Co., 1969.

Carson, Ruth. "Indians Call Her 'The Measuring Woman.'" *American West* 12, no. 4 (1975): 12.

Ceram, C. W. *The First American. A Story of North American Archaeology.* New York: Harcourt, Brace, Jovanovich, Inc., 1971.

Chauvenet, Beatrice. "Adventurer Among the Delight Makers." *New Mexico Magazine* 25, no. 11 (1947): 11, 46-47.

Chávez, Fray Angelico. *La Conquistadora. The Autobiography of an Ancient Statue.* Paterson, New Jersey: St. Anthony Guild Press, 1954.

———. *Our Lady of the Conquest.* Santa Fe: The Historical Society of New Mexico, 1948.

Christman, Florence. *The Romance of Balboa Park.* 2nd Edition. San Diego: Neyenesch Printers, Inc., 1973.

Cleaveland, Agnes Morley. *No Life for a Lady.* Boston: Houghton Mifflin Co., 1941.

"Cliff Dwellings Represent Early Indian Culture." *Colorado Springs Gazette-Telegraph,* May 20, 1973.

"Cliff Dwellings to be Put in Cañon Close to Manitou." *Colorado Springs Gazette-Telegraph,* May 1, 1906.

"Cliff Ruins Are Ready." *Colorado Springs Gazette-Telegraph,* May 31, 1907.

Crichton, Kyle S. "Philistine and Artist Clash in Battle of Santa Fe." *New York World,* June 27, 1926.

Curtis, John B. "The First 125 Years of The New Mexican." *The New Mexican,* November 17, 1974.

Department of Archaeology and Anthropology, University of New Mexico. *Annual Report.* Albuquerque, 1931.

"Digging in the Past." *Newsweek* (August 25, 1975): 44.

Dow, Sterling. "Report of the President." *Bulletin of the Archaeological Institute of America* 37 (1946): 5.

"Dr. Edgar L. Hewett Dies in Albuquerque." *Santa Fe New Mexican,* December 31, 1946.

"Dr. Franz Boas Dies." *El Palacio* 50, no. 1 (1943): 24.

Helm, June, ed. *Pioneers of American Anthropology.* Seattle, London: University of Washington Press, 1966.

Historical Facts of the Ancient Cliff Dwellers and a Glimpse of the Ruins and Cañon at Manitou (Colorado). Manitou Cliff Dwellers Ruins Co., ca. 1907.

Horn, Calvin. *New Mexico's Troubled Years.* Albuquerque: Horn and Wallace, 1963.

"How Four Scientists Regard E. L. Hewett." *Santa Fe New Mexican,* October 27, 1913.

Kidder, Alfred V. "Sylvanus Griswold Morley, 1883-1948." *El Palacio* 55, no. 9 (1948): 267-74.

LaFarge, Oliver. *Santa Fe. The Autobiography of a Southwestern Town.* Norman: University of Oklahoma Press, 1959.

Lord, Clifford L., ed. *Keepers of the Past.* Chapel Hill: University of North Carolina Press, 1965.

Lummis, Charles F. "In Memoriam." *El Palacio* 15, no. 6 (1923): 93-95.

Makers of the San Diego Panama Pacific Exposition and Southern California. Special Edition Deluxe Booklet #133 presented to Edgar Lee Hewett. San Diego, 1915.

"Manitou Cliff Dwellers' Ruins." *Colorado Springs Gazette-Telegraph,* Annual Edition, 1907.

"Many Offer Quarters to Chamber of Commerce," *Santa Fe New Mexican,* October 9, 1913.

Masters, Edgar Lee. *The Tale of Chicago.* New York: G. P. Putnam's Sons, 1933.

McDonald, Craig. "A Few Men Worked Miracles for San Diego." *San Diego Union,* February 17, 1974.

McGregor, John C. *Southwestern Archaeology.* 2nd ed. Urbana: University of Illinois, 1965.

Melin, Nancy A. "Santa Fe and Governor Prince." *El Palacio* 80, no.3 (1974): 29-36.

"Mesa Verde. America's Ghostliest Town." *Friends. A Publication of Chevrolet Motor Division.* November, 1973.

Morgan, Lewis Henry. *Houses and Home Life of the American Aborigines.* Edited by Paul Bohanan. Classics in Anthropology Series. Chicago, London: University of Chicago Press, 1965.

Murphey, Leslie V. *Bibliography of the Writings of Edgar Lee Hewett.* Supplemented with additional titles for 1945 and 1946. Santa Fe: School of American Research, 1944.

"My Board Takes Orders from E. L. Hewett." *Santa Fe New Mexican,* October 9, 1913.

"New Mexico Needs a Hall of Records." *El Palacio* 50, no. 8 (1943): 178-82.

"The 1924 Santa Fe Fiesta." *El Palacio* 17, nos. 6-7 (1924): 127-81.

"No Danger of Losing the School." *Santa Fe New Mexican,* November 12, 1913.

Papers of the School of American Research 44 (1951).

Powell, J. W. *Bureau of American Ethnology, 23rd Annual Report.* Washington, D. C.: Government Printing Office, 1904.

"Pueblos Gather in Barbaric Splendor to Participate in the 'Indian Day,' Opening Santa Fe Fiesta in Blaze of Glory." *Santa Fe New Mexican,* September 6, 1921.

Raymenton, H. K. *Forty-Seven Years. San Diego Museum of Man.* San Diego, n.d.

Raymenton, H. K. *San Diego's Exposition.* San Diego, 1963.

"Real Bolshevists." *Santa Fe New Mexican,* September 29, 1920.

Rohner, Ronald P. *Pioneers of American Archaeology.* Seattle: University of Washington Press, 1966.

Santa Fe Fiesta. Official program, 1921.

"Santa Fe Is Declared 'The Oldest City' in the United States." *Santa Fe New Mexican,* September 17, 1913.

Saunders, Lyle. *A Guide to Materials Bearing on Cultural Relations in New Mexico.* Albuquerque: University of New Mexico Press, 1944.

School of American Research. *Annual Report.* Santa Fe, 1931, 1934, 1936.

Sena, José D. Letter. *Santa Fe New Mexican,* April 21, 1915.

Shishkin, J. K. *An Early History of the Museum of New Mexico Fine Arts Building.* Santa Fe: Museum of New Mexico Press, 1968.

Twitchell, Ralph Emerson. *Leading Facts of New Mexico History,* vol. 2. Cedar Rapids, Iowa: The Torch Press, 1912.

Visitors Handbook, San Diego Museum of Man. San Diego, January-June, 1974.

Walter, Paul A. F. "Edgar Lee Hewett, Americanist, 1865-1946." *American Anthropologist* 49, no 2 (1947): 260-71.

Weber, Michael F. "The Problems of Preservation." *El Palacio* 80, no. 3 (1974): 37-45.

"What Santa Fe Still Needs." *Santa Fe New Mexican,* October 3, 1913.

"Zuni Runners in Race Round the Circle Drive." *Santa Fe New Mexican,* September 8, 1921.

INDEX

References to photographs are printed in boldface type.

A

Agassiz, Louis, 54
Alexander, Hartley Burr, 203
American Academy for the Advancement of Science. *See* American Association for the Advancement of Science
American Anthropological Society, 54
American Anthropologist, 46, 58
American Antiquities Act, 42, 56, 57, 58, 133
American Association for the Advancement of Science (AAAS), 14, 16, 45, 46, 52, 53, 89
American Folklore Society, 54
American Institute of Archaeology. *See* Archaeological Institute of America
American Journal of Anthropology, 136, 137
American Museum of Natural History, 71, 87, 97, 118
Anderson (farm hand), 8, 11
Anderson, J.O., 195, 202, 228
Anderson, W.B., 16, 17
Applegate, Frank, 140, 200
Archaeological Institute of America, 16, 46, 85, 99, 115, 124, 161, 193; Bandelier supported by, 17-18, 37, 55, 72; Hewett fellowship in, 55-58, 71, 160; Hewett supported by, 118-20, 127; organization of, 53-54, 166, 171, 205-06; publications of, 89, 136, 137; School of American Archaeology sponsored by, 72-78, 80, 131, 132
Archaeological Society of New Mexico, 40, 115, 116
Armijo, Manuel (Governor), 65
Arnold, Charlotte (Mrs. Lee Daves), 196, 203
Art and Archaeology, 133, 135-37, 139, 161, 206
Art Museum of New Mexico. *See* Museum of Fine Arts
Austin, Mary, 140, 177, 178-80, **179**, 181, 182, 183, 186, 200, 211
Avery, Jennie, 124, 224, 225

B

Baca, Roman L., 76, 119, 177
Bakos, Josef, 140, 226
Balboa Park, 100, 101, 104, 128, 148, 185, 228
Bandelier, Adolph, 12, 13, 16-21, **19**, 27, 37, 40-41, 47, 54, 72, 95, 111, 114, 121-22, 210, 227
Bandelier, Fanny (Adolph's second wife), 121-22, 210
Bandelier, Josephine Huegy (Adolph's first wife), 16, 18
Bandelier National Monument, 227
Barrott, A.F., 84

Baumann, Gustave, 122, 196
Beauregard, Donald, 129, 227
Bellows, George, 122
Bishop, Carl A., 155
Black Hawk, 6, 9
Blackstone, Tsianina. *See* Tsianina
Blood, Jeremiah Perkins, 26
Bloom, Lansing B., 72, 122, 166, 195, 197, 203, 210
Bloom, Maude McFie (Mrs. Lansing), 130, 155
Blumenschein, Ernest L., 138
Board of Managers. *See* School of American Archaeology; School of American Research
Board of Regents. *See* Museum of New Mexico
Boas, Franz, 56, 71, 92-94, 100, 111, 114, 118, 217
Bobbs-Merrill Company, 206, 208, 211
Bowden, A.O., 201, 203
Bowditch, Charles, 55, 57
Bowman, George D., 23-24, **25**, 214
Bradfield, Wesley, 106, 166, 193, 195, 196, 198
Brand, Donald B., 210
Brown, Bush, 160
Bureau of Ethnology, 18, 46, 56, 71-72, 89, 90, 136, 205, 209, 210
Burlin, H. Paul, 122, 142
Burlin, Natalie Curtis (Mrs. H. Paul), 137, 142, 144-45
Bushnell, David, 98, 99
Bynner, Witter, 139, 155, 180, 183, 185, 196

C

Cadman, Charles Wakefield, 130, 131, 132, 157-60, 196
California Building (Panama-California Exposition), 102, 104, 122
Carroll, Mitchell, 136-37, 206
Carson, Kit, 9, 154
Casas Grandes (Chihuahua), 57, 164
Cassidy, Gerald, 79-80, 104-06, 128, 139, 149, 228
Cassidy, Ina Sizer (Mrs. Gerald), 79-80, 104, 149
Chamber of Commerce. *See* Santa Fe Chamber of Commerce
Chapman, Kenneth, 38, 83-84, 89, 102, **103**, 109, 118, 122, 129, 166, 193-94, 195, 199-200, 202, 208, 221, 227
Chautauqua, 152-53, 155, 177, 178, 180, 181, 185
Cheney, D.L., 12, 23, 214
Chichen Itzá, 9, 104, 218, 228
Clarkson, R. Hunter, 187
Clay, Albert T., 166-70
Clay, Mrs. (Albert T.), 166, 168
Cleaveland, Agnes Morley, 34-35
Collier, D.C., 98, 100-02, 107, 108, 128, 197

Collier, John C., 164, 192
Colorado Archaeological Society, 57, 60, 61
Colorado Federation of Women's Clubs, 57, 60
Colorado Springs Gazette, 59
Colorado State Normal School (Greeley), 30, 33, 35
Committee on American Archaeology (Archaeological Institute of America), 55, 71
Connelly, Henry (Governor), 66
Cooper, James Fenimore, 13
Copán, 9, 104, 228
Corwin, R.C., 171, 193
Crandall, C.J., 192
Crichton, Kyle S., 180-82, 188
Crucible, The, 33
Culture Colony of the Southwest, 178, 180-81, 185, 188, 194
Currelly, C.T., 218
Curtin, Leonora S., 210
Cushing, Frank H., 37, 72
Cutting, Bronson M., 97-98, 111, 112, 114, 120, 132, 141, 144-45, 152, 177, 204, 209

D

Davey, Mrs. Randall, 155
Davidson, G. Aubrey, 100, 101
DeHuff, Elizabeth Willis, 155
Delight Makers, The (Adolph Bandelier), 21, 35, 37, 41
Densmore, Frances, 131
De Vargas, Diego (General), 65, 67, 111, 148, 150-51, 153
Die Koshare. See The Delight Makers
Dixon, Roland B., 72, 100, 114, 118
Dodds, Dr., 26
Doll, Charles E., 180
Dorman, Harry, 110, 111, 113-14, 118-20, 141
Dorman, Helen, 203
Dorsey (George A.), 115
Dutton, Bertha, 202, 211, 225

E

Ellis, Florence Hawley (Mrs. Bruce T.), 203
Ellis, Fremont, 140, 226
Ellison, Samuel, 18, 67
El Palacio, 89-90, 133, 136, 138, 146, 152, 154, 155-56, 163, 170, 200, 217
El Palacio Real. *See* Palace of the Governors
El Rito de los Frijoles, 20-21, 36, 72, 92, 97, 122, 160, 165, 193, 227
Elvin, Ruth, 215, 224
Ely, Albert, 203, 205
Espinosa, Gertrude, 156

F

Fairclough, H.R., 206, 210
Federation of Women's Clubs of the Southwest, 173, 175-86; New Mexico Federation, 175, 180, 182; Texas Federation, 175-76, 184-85. *See also* Colorado Federation of Women's Clubs
Ferdon, Edwin N., 202
Fergusson, Erna, 187, 190
Fewkes, H. Walter, 56, 71, 72, 208
Fiesta. *See* Santa Fe Fiesta
Fine Arts Building. *See* Museum of Fine Arts
Fisher, Reginald, 203, 211
Fletcher, Alice Cunningham, 42-43, 44, 45-46, 54, 56, 71, 72, 98, 100, 127, 131, 158, 160-61, 171, 208, 214, 221, 227
Fletcher, John Gould, 80, 82, 139
Folk Art Museum, 225
Fred Harvey Company, 187, 189-90
Friere-Marreco, Barbara, 94, 95, 99

G

Goddard, P.E., 118
Gonzales, Juan (Aguaono), 93
Gordon, G.B., 115
Greeley Teachers' College. *See* Colorado State Normal School
Greeley Tribune, 33
Guatemala, 85-86, 92, 102

H

Halseth, Odd, 189
Harrington, John P., 90, 92, 98, 99, 106, 118, 210, 216
Harvey Company. *See* Fred Harvey Company
Harvey, Fred E., 210
Harwood (Bert), 122
Hawley, Florence. *See* Ellis, Florence Hawley
Henderson, Alice Corbin (Mrs. William Penhallow), 138, 142-45, 149
Henderson, William Penhallow, 122, 138, 149
Henri, Robert, 122, 135, 137-38, 139, 146
Hewett, Alvin (Edgar's brother), 5, 7-8, 9, 52, 224
Hewett, Cassie (Edgar's sister), 7, 52
Hewett, Cora Whitford (Mrs. Edgar Lee, Edgar's first wife), 26, 28-30, 29, 39, 40, 47, 48, 50, 51, 52-53, 56, 58, 89, 208
Hewett, Donizetta Jones Wood (Mrs. Edgar Lee, Edgar's second wife), 87-89, 88, 92, 102, 148, 165, 166-70, 207, 215, 216, 218, 223-35
Hewett, Edgar Lee, articles by: "Anthropology and Education," 46; "Archaeology of New Mexico," 42; "The Conquest of War," 147; "Ethnic Factors in Education," 52; "A General View of the Archaeology of the Pueblo Region,"

53; "Man and Destiny," 42; "Man and God," 42; "Man and Man," 42; "Man and Nature," 42; "Man and Self," 42; Master Motives," 33; "The Study of Anthropology," 33; "A Zuni Creation Myth," 42; books by: *Ancient Andean Life*, 211; *Ancient Life in the American Southwest*, 206; *Ancient Life in Mexico and Central America*, 208; *Call of the Spade*, 49; *Campfire and Trail*, 48, 80, 168, 170, 209, 215, 220; *Chaco Canyon and Its Ancient Monuments*, 210; *From Cave Dwelling to Mount Olympus*, 215; *Indians of the Rio Grande Valley* (coauthor with Adolph Bandelier), 210, 211; *Landmarks of New Mexico* (coauthor with Wayne Mauzy), 211; *Man and Culture*, 211, 215; *Man and the State*, 215; *Mission Monuments of New Mexico* (coauthor with Reginald Fisher), 211; *Pajarito Plateau and Its Ancient People*, 210-11; *The Pueblo Indian World* (coauthor with Bertha Dutton), 211; *Two Score Years*, 26, 215; poems by: "Dream Clouds," 33; "Mist Wings," 33; photographs of: 24, 27, 36, 81, 112, 165, 172, 201, 207, 219
Hewett Foundation, 223
Hewett garden, **228**
Hewett, Harvey Hanson (Edgar's father), 4, 6, 7, 7, 9, 10-11, 52
Hewett, Harvey J. (Edgar's grandfather), 5-6, 8
Hewett, Lawrence (Edgar's brother), 7-8, 9-11, 52
Hewett, Miriam (Mrs. Harvey J., Edgar's grandmother), 5-6, 8
Hewett, Nora (Edgar's sister), 7
Hewett, Noy (Edgar's brother), 7-8, 9-11, 52
Hewett, Tabitha Stice (Mrs. Harvey Hanson, Edgar's mother), 4, 6-7, 7, 8, 12, 121
Highlands University. *See* Normal University of Las Vegas
Historical Society of New Mexico, 41, 68, 70, 74-76, 79-80, 109, 113, 119
Hodge, Frederick W., 37, **88**, 90, 98-99, 111, 114, 137, 210, 221
Hollenbach, Marion, 203
Holmes, William H., 42, 43, 46, 56, 71, 94, 135, 136-37, 170, 209, 214
Horses, Hewett family's: Charley, 10; Don and Dot, 29, 48; Kit, 10; Lion, 9-10; Pompey, 11-12; Spider and Snoozer, 48-49; Francis Schlatter's: Butte, 34-35, 57-58
Hough (Walter), 94
Hrdlicka, Ales, 71, 94, 102, 210, 217
Huddleson, Sam, 152
Huegy, Josephine. *See* Bandelier, Josephine Huegy
Huegy, Maurice, 37
Humboldt, Alexander von, 17

I

Indian Arts Fund, 193, 200, 208
Indian Detours, 187-88, **188**, 190, 192, 194, 196

J

Jackson, Percy, 193, 209
James, James, 39
Janowitz, Janie, 196
Jaramillo, Cleofas, 124-25
Jaramillo, Venceslao, 124-25
Johnson, E. Dana, 141, 144-45, 151, 177, 180, 184, 196, 204
Jones, Hester, 203
Judd, Neil M., 86-87, 94, 118

K

Kaune, H.S., 119
Kearney, Stephen Watts (General), 65, 164
Kelly, Daniel T., 221
Kelsey, Francis W., 56, 71, 92, 119, 129, 132, 137
Kidder, Alfred Vincent, 80, 82, 98, 99, 118, 133, 210, 221
King, Willard, 193, 210
Klauber, Alice, 137
Kleinsmid, Rufus B. von, 133, 221
Kluckhohn, Clyde, 203
Kroeber, A.L., 72
Kurty, Alice M., 92

L

Laboratory of Anthropology, 199-200, 203, 208, 221, 225
Lacey, J.F. (Congressman), 42, 56, 58, 72, 100
Lacey Law. *See* American Antiquities Act
Lackey, Mary McFie, 130
La Farge, Oliver, 186
La Fleche, Bright Eyes (Mrs. Thomas Henry Tibbles), 45
La Fleche, Francis, 45
Lambert, Marjorie Ferguson (Mrs. E.V. Jack Lambert), 202
Las Vegas Normal. *See* Normal University of Las Vegas
Laughlin, Mrs. N.B., 160
Laughlin, Napoleon Bonaparte, 113, 117
La Villa Real de Santa Fe de Asis, 64, 111
Lewis, Dan, 25
Los Alamos Ranch School, 165, 177, 216, 227
Los Cinco Pintores, 140, 226
Lotave, Carl, 87, 97, 122
Lucero, Antonio, 119, 132
Lujan, Anthony (Tony), 192

Lummis, Charles F., 40, 41, 56, 57, 71, 111, 114, 115-16, 117, 161, 170, 210, 227
Lummis, Quimu. *See* Quimu

M

McClurg, Mrs., 61
McDonald, William C. (Governor), 115, 119, 120
McFie, John R., 40, 41, 72, 74, 75-76, 89, 113, 119, 122, 125, 130, 160, 177
Magoffin, R.V.D., 166, 171, 193, 205, 210
Manitou Cliff Dwellings, 59-62
Marston, George W., 195, 218
Martinez, Julian, 91, 189, **189**
Martinez, Maria, 152, 189, **189**
Massie, James A., 119, 177, 184
Mauzy, Wayne L., 202, 203, 211
Meem, John Gaw, 200
Mera, Frank, 176-77, 202
Mera, Harry, 200
Mesa Verde National Park, 54, 55, 56-57,   60, 61, 87, 190, 200
Miller, Mr. and Mrs., 215
Mills, George, 56, 57
Mills, W.J. (Governor), 78, 83
Morgan, Lewis Henry, 12, 13-17, 15, 21, 27,   46, 54
Morley, Ada McPherson, 34-35, 37
Morley, Sylvanus Griswold, 80-82, 81, 83,   86, 92, 99, 110, 118, 133, 210, 218
Morley, William Raymond, 34
Morris, Earl, 83, 86, 99, 118, 148
Mruk, Walter, 140, 226
Museum of Fine Arts, 104, 130, 136, 148, 160, 194, 199, 200, 208; art in, 141-46, 152; building of, 122-25; Hewett's ashes in patio of, 221; Los Cinco Pintores retrospective in, 226-27; opening of, 127-33, 137, 138, 158; Sheldon Parsons as director of, 217. *See also* Saint Francis Auditorium
Museum of Man, 102, 108, 128, 136, 158, 195, 228
Museum of Natural History. *See* American Museum of Natural History
Museum of Navajo Ceremonial Art, 203, 225
Museum of New Mexico, 82, 95, 97, 118, 120, 124, 131, 164, 175, 193, 196-97, 208, 227; Board of Regents of, 100, 113-15, 199, 221; Chamber of Commerce headquarters in, 110, 113, 124; collections of, 87, 89, 140, 210, 217; founding of, 76-79, 83; staff of, 99, 123, 127, 155, 166, 199, 200, 202, 216, 225, 226; war work in, 127, 163. *See also* Laboratory of Anthropology; Museum of Fine Arts; Palace of the Governors

N

Naranjo, Santiago (Oyegepi), 93, 95, 191
Nash, Willard, 140, 226
National Art Gallery, 135
National Museum, 52, 94, 102, 135, 200
Naville, Edouard, 51, 214
New Mexican. See Santa Fe New Mexican
New Mexico Building (Panama-California Exposition), 105
New Mexico Historical Society, 41, 66, 67, 76, 109, 120, 122, 178
Normal University of Las Vegas, 38-39, 41-42, 46, 47, 70, 83, 112, 118, 133, 209
Norton, Charles Eliot, 18, 20, 46, 53-54
Noyes, Professor, 60
Nusbaum, Jesse, 79-80, **86**, 94, 100, 102, 106, 118, 123, 124, 148, 150, 153, 190, 200

O

Old Santa Fe Association, 177-78, 182-86, 194
Olsen, Clara, 115
Oskenonton, 156, 196
Otero, Miguel Antonio (Governor), 46, 112, 119, 141

P

Palace of the Governors, 83, 97, 112, 123, 182, 198, 216; artists' studios in, 122, 135, 139; Chamber of Commerce in, 110, 113-15, 124; early history of, 64-69, 74-80, **78**, **79**, 87, 89, 109, 110; Fiesta activities in, 153-54; renovation of, 225-26. *See also* Museum of New Mexico
Palenque, 9, 104, 228
Panama-California Exposition, 105, 109, 111, 122, 124, 127, 128, 138, 151, 152, 190-91, 197, 204, 205, 228; opening of, 106-08; preparing for, 98, 100-06; Tsianina and Cadman at, 157-58
Parker, Mrs. Frank W., 178
Parkman, Francis, 18
Parsons, Sheldon, 122, 139, 142, 149, 217
Pate, William E., 195
Paton, Lewis Bayles, 166-67
Peabody, Lucy, 61, 62
Peabody Museum, 45, 47, 55, 122
Peña, Antonio Domingo (Weyima), 93, 94
Peña, Tonita, 152
Phillips, Bert, 138
Pile, William A. (Governor), 66
Pitaval, J.B. (Archbishop), 119
Postlethwaite, W.W., 210
Powell, John Wesley, 18, 42, 71, 72, 214
Prince, L. Bradford, 41, 67, 68-70, 74, 75-77, 79-80, 94, 109, 110, 112, 119, 122, 226

Prince, Mary C. (née Beardsley, Mrs. L. Bradford), 69, 79-80, 109, 122, 226
Pritchard, George W., 119
Pritchard, Mrs. George W., 178
Pueblo Pottery Fund. See Indian Arts Fund
Pueblos, abandoned: Abo, 39; Gran Quivira, 39; Mesa Verde (later Mesa Verde National Park), 54, 55, 56-57, 60-61, 87, 200; Otowi, 37; Pecos, 18, 20, 39, 82, 97, 188, 190; Puyé, 37, 49, 97, 122, 133, 189; Sankowi'i, 37, 49; Tsirege, 37, 49; Tyuonyi, 20-21, 91, 92, 97, 122; inhabited: Acoma, 129; Cochiti, 92, 153, 156, 192, 227; Isleta, 190; Jemez, 39, 153; San Ildefonso, 153, 189; Santa Clara, 94, 95, 99, 153, 189, 192; Santo Domingo, 190; Taos, 138, 192; Tesuque, 153; Zuni, 37, 72, 153, 154
Putnam, Frederick W., 18, 42, 45-46, 54-56, 71, 80, 122

Q

Quimu (Lummis), 86
Quirigua (Guatemala), 9, 83, 85-86, 92, 98, 99, 104, 200, 228

R

Rambo, Ruth, 203
Randolph, H.M. (Major), 61-62
Rapp, I.H., 104, 123, 150
Rapp, W.M., 123
Read, Benjamin M., 111, 114
Reiter, Paul, 203
Riggs, Arthur Stanley, 137, 206, 210
Robinson, David M., 136-37
Rockefeller grant, 203
Rockefeller, John D., Jr., 171, 192-93, 199, 208
Rockefeller, Mrs. John D., Jr., 199
Rollins, Warrren E., 122
Roybal, Diegito (Potsunutsee), 93

S

Saint Francis Auditorium, 126, 129, 130, 155, 160, 185, 221, 227. See also Museum of Fine Arts
Saint Louis Archaeological Society, 83, 85, 98, 99
Sandburg, Carl, 139
San Diego Archaeological Society, 108, 114, 148, 171
San Diego Exposition. See Panama-California Exposition
San Diego Museum, 108, 124, 148, 163-64, 170, 193, 195-96, 197, 200, 228

San Diego State College (later California State University, San Diego), 148, 170-71, 195, 197, 200, 228
Santa Fe Chamber of Commerce, 110-11, 113-15, 118, 120, 124, 153, 156, 175, 180-85, 196
Santa Fe Fiesta, 148-58, 160, 191, 196-97
Santa Fe New Mexican, 69, 123, 132, 186, 194; art publicized by, 138-39; "Bolshevist" art attacked in, 141-46; controversy over "The Oldest City" in, 110-12; culture colony opposed by, 177-78, 181, 188; E. Dana Johnson as editor of, 140-41, 177, 196, 204; Fiesta publicized in, 151, 153-54; Hewett attacked by, 113-16; Hewett obituary in, 220
Santa Fe Women's Club, 114
Scarpitta, Cartaino, 221
Schenk, Genevieve, 218
Schlatter, Francis, 34-35, 57-58, 164
School of American Archaeology (later School of American Research), 71-72, 73, 74-80, 82-87, 90, 92-94, 98-100, 114-20, 121, 124, 127-28
School of American Research, 126, 127-28, 131, 141, 163, 184-85, 198, 223, 227; managing board of, 135, 160, 171, 185, 193, 197, 199, 204, 208, 209-10, 216, 221, 224, 225; papers of, 210, 216; participation of, in Santa Fe Fiesta, 151, 152, 155, 173, 191, 197; summer schools of, 148, 175, 200, 202
School of Oriental Research, 164, 166, 167, 170
Sciences of Man, 102, 104, 106, 107, 118, 198, 217. See also Museum of Man
Scott, Earl W., 155
Scott, Marian Gallager (Mrs. Earl W.), 155
Seligman, James L., 113, 123, 148, 150-51
Seligman, Ruth (Mrs. James L.), 148, 150-51, 153
Sena, José D., 119, 123, 139, 153, 156, 196
Seymour, Thomas Day, 55
Sharp, I.H., 138
Shijo, Velino, 152
Shipley (Professor), 119, 136
Shuster, Will, 140, 151, 226-27
Simms, Ruth Hanna McCormick, 210
Sloan, John, 139, 180
Sloan, Mrs. John (Dolly), 155
Smithsonian Institution, 46, 53, 90, 102, 104, 106, 135, 136, 205, 209. See also Bureau of Ethnology; National Museum
Southwest Indian Fair, 154-56
Southwest Museum, 210
Spencer, Frank C., 210
Spinden (Herbert J.), 100
Springer, Charles, 41, 204
Springer, Eva, 126
Springer, Frank, 40, 41, 83, 112, 125, 137, 160, 209; Hewett backed by, 37-38, 47, 58, 74, 177, 209, 225; Museum of Fine Arts sponsored by, 122-31

Stauffer, Charles, 152
Stauffer, John K., 152
Sterne, Mabel Evans (Mabel Dodge Evans Sterne Lujan), 140
Stevens, Thomas Wood, 196
Stevenson, James, 72
Stevenson, Matilda Coxe (Mrs. James), 72
Stice, Charles (Edgar's grandfather), 6
Stice, Martha (Mrs. Charles, Edgar's grandmother), 6

T

Tanquist, Mamie R., 203
Tarkio College, 26
Tibbles, Thomas Henry, 45
Tight, W.G., 75, 198
Tikal, 228
Tozzer (Alfred M.), 100, 114
Trowbridge, Lydia, 209
True, Clara, 94-95, 192-93
Tsianina (Blackstone), 130, 131, 132, 153, 156, 157-60, 159, 196, 225
Twitchell, Ralph Emerson, 66, 67, 69, 94, 104, 106, 110-11, 112-13, 139, 151, 153, 154, 157

U

Ufer, Walter, 139
United Fruit Company, 83, 85, 99
United States Geological Survey, 42
University of California, 114, 118, 122
University of Geneva, 50-51, 214
University of New Mexico, 75, 197, 198, 200, 202, 208, 210, 214, 216, 217
University of New Mexico Press, 210, 211
University of Southern California, 200, 201-02, 203, 214, 216, 221
Uxmal, 9, 84, 228

V

Van Stone, G.G., 119

Van Stone, Mary R. (Mrs. George H.), 203
Vierra, Carlos, 104, 105, 106, 122, 126, 129, 139, 227, 228

W

Wallace, Charles, 23, 25, 30-31, 33, 35, 47, 51, 209
Wallace, Henry, 67-68
Wallace, Hulda (Mrs. Charles), 31, 47, 209
Wallace, Lewis (Governor), 18, 41, 66, 67-68
Wallace, Susan (Mrs. Lewis), 68
Walter, Dorothy, 203
Walter, Paul A.F., 40, 74, 103, 116, 124-25, 160, 177, 184, 185, 209, 210, 220, 225; banking career of, 142, 152, 157, 178, 200; editorial work of, 41, 89, 136, 151-52, 166, 200; Fiestas directed by, 151-53; Hewett correspondence with, 118, 120, 123, 170; Museum duties of, 102, 109, 127, 129, 132-33, 140, 152, 195
Warfield, Carlotta. *See* Arnold, Charlotte
Washington Society (of the Archaeological Institute of America), 205-06
Wheelwright, Mary Cabot, 203
Wheelwright Museum. *See* Museum of Navajo Ceremonial Art
White, Amelia E., 221, 225
Whitford, Cora. *See* Hewett, Cora Whitford
Williams, Hugh H., 119
Wilson, Francis C., 119, 164
Wissler, Clark, 87, 118
Women's Board (of the Museum), 132, 160
Wood, Donizetta Jones. *See* Hewett, Donizetta
Wreck (in Arabian Desert waddy), 169
Wuarin, Lewis, 51, 214

Y

Yale Babylonian Expedition, 166

Z

Zimmerman, James F., 197, 198-99, 210, 217
Zuni Creation Myth, 42